BRIDGES TO THE WORLD

Henry Noble MacCracken.

BRIDGES TO THE WORLD

Henry Noble MacCracken
and Vassar College

ELIZABETH A. DANIELS

COLLEGE AVENUE PRESS
Clinton Corners, New York

COLLEGE AVENUE PRESS
is an imprint of
The Attic Studio Press
P.O. Box 75
Clinton Corners, NY 12514

SAN: 298-2838
Phone: 914-266-4902

PRINTED IN THE UNITED STATES OF AMERICA

ISBN 1-883551-02-1
Library of Congress Catalog Card Number 94-31965

94 95 96 97 98 99 00   5 4 3 2 1

Library of Congress Cataloging-in-Publication Data
Daniels, Elizabeth A. (Elizabeth Adams)
    Bridges to the world : Henry Noble MacCracken and Vassar College / Elizabeth A. Daniels
        p.   cm.
    Includes bibliographical references and index.
    ISBN 1-883551-02-1 (pbk.) : $18.50
    1. MacCracken, H. N. (Henry Noble), b. 1880. 2. Vassar College—Presidents—Biography. 3. Vassar College—History.   I. Title.
LD7182.7.M33D36   1994
378.747'33—dc20   94-31965

The following letter is cited with permission: *James Monroe Taylor to John D. Rockefeller, 26 December 1888, folder 342, box 45, series III.1.CO, record group 1.2, Rockefeller Family Archives, Rockefeller Archive Center, North Tarrytown, N.Y.*

The typescript *Conversation between Miss Constance Warren, President of Sarah Lawrence College 1929-1945, and Dr. Henry Noble MacCracken, Chairman of Sarah Lawrence College Board of Trustees 1926-1936, taped in Poughkeepsie, New York, October 13, 1961* is quoted with permission from Esther Raushenbush Library, Sarah Lawrence College, Bronxville, New York, as are Constance Warren's notes on MacCracken, April 15, 1946; the recollections of Dudley Lawrence, July 1958; and the letter from MacCracken to Marion Coats, November 30, 1925.

Photographs are courtesy of Special Collections, Vassar College Library, except for photograph on page 191, courtesy of Esther Raushenbush Library, Sarah Lawrence College.

COVER ILLUSTRATION:
Photograph of Henry Noble MacCracken at Vassar College, Founder's Day, 1946.

For John L. Daniels,
*who has encouraged my scholarship
year in and year out over the last 52 years.*

CONTENTS

ILLUSTRATIONS

SOURCES
AND ACKNOWLEDGEMENTS

T HE one hundred and forty or so boxes of MacCracken papers in
the Vassar College Library constituted the main source for my
research on Henry Noble MacCracken. Through Maisry MacCracken,
the MacCracken family has very kindly given me permission to quote
liberally from MacCracken's personal papers contained in the collection, and Special Collections, Vassar College Library, has given me
permission to quote from Vassar's institutional files, including the
material in the MacCracken papers. Maisry MacCracken also allowed
me to see and quote from the daybook of her mother Marjorie Dodd
MacCracken, for which I am grateful. There are other papers in the
Vassar College collection which were important to my study, including
the Lucy Maynard Salmon papers, from which I have quoted excerpts
from the correspondence between MacCracken and Salmon; the autograph collection of Franklin D. Roosevelt, who was a Vassar trustee
between 1923 and 1945; the papers of Helen Morris Hadley, Class of
1883; Helen Drusilla Lockwood, 1912; and James Monroe Taylor,
Vassar's fourth president. The Vassar library has biographical files on
faculty members, trustees, and important alumnae, which have been
extremely instructive. Then, too, there is a running collection of
chronological files, photo files, files on buildings such as the Blodgett
Hall of Euthenics and the Alumnae House, and subject files for many
particular aspects of Vassar history of the MacCracken period, such as
Euthenics, the American Junior Red Cross, and activities during the
world wars. The photographs in the book are separately listed and are
reproduced courtesy of Special Collections of the Vassar College
Library.

When I started this project in 1980 under the auspices of a summer stipend from the National Endowment of the Humanities, which I
acknowledge here with gratitude, I consulted the archives of Radcliffe

College, the Arthur and Elizabeth Schlesinger Library on the History of Women in America, Wellesley College, Mt. Holyoke College, and Bryn Mawr College. I am grateful to Marjorie Sly, archivist, for her help over the years at the Smith College Library. Some records of the early years of Barnard College were examined in the Columbia University Library. I also consulted the papers of Chancellor Henry Mitchell MacCracken in the archives of New York University at Washington Square College. I searched the archival collection at the Sterling Library of Yale University for traces of MacCracken at Yale. In part, the information connecting Franklin and Eleanor Roosevelt with MacCracken came from material at the Franklin D. Roosevelt Library in Hyde Park, New York: the President's Personal Files, the Eleanor Roosevelt papers, and the C. Mildred Thompson folders. I am indebted to the Roosevelt library staff for assistance, especially Frances Seeber, Assistant Director. Some of the material in chapter 16 appeared in "FDR, ER, and VC," *Vassar Quarterly*, 88, no. 2, pp. 22-28. James Mazza, Vassar 1991, was my research assistant ferreting out Roosevelt material from the Vassar library collections, the Roosevelt collections, and the press. His systematic analysis of materials was a credit to his training in the Vassar history department. Jane Plimpton Plakias, 1942, very kindly shared her knowledge of relations between the Roosevelts and the Vassar community with James Mazza and me. Orlando Segura, Vassar undergraduate Ford intern, assisted me one summer with research at the Rockefeller Family Archives on connections between James Monroe Taylor and John D. Rockefeller, an early trustee of Vassar. I wish also to thank Susan Gleason, archivist of the Esther Raushenbush Library at Sarah Lawrence College, for all her generous help.

I began this project alone, but was joined by a former student, Roberta Cashwell, 1976, who consented to help me research and write parts of the book. Every aspect of the book was discussed with her during different long working sessions for several years. She did the primary research for chapters 14 and 15 and drafted the first version of those chapters. I regret that we were unable to continue the project together through publication, but she is responsible for the sharpening of the book in many ways. With Professor Barbara Page, a colleague in the English department, I collaborated on a paper entitled "Suffrage As A Lever For Change at Vassar," for the Berkshire Conference of Women Historians' meeting held at Vassar in 1982, and subsequently we published the paper in *Vassar Quarterly*, 79, no. 4, pp. 32-36.

Professor Page provided much of the background context of the suffrage movement and, in particular, the information about Inez Milholland. Some of that material has been incorporated into this book in chapter 3.

Early in my research I decided to interview a sampling of Vassar alumnae and faculty members who knew either MacCracken or Taylor, or both. To that end, one spring on leave from my duties in the Vassar English department I toured south by car from Poughkeepsie and interviewed approximately thirty alumnae who were students in college between 1905 and 1920. At various times, both in Poughkeepsie and in other places around the country, I continued my interviews.

The following alumnae, trustees, faculty members, former employees of the college, Poughkeepsie residents, and others, many of them now deceased, gave me permission to make use of their oral histories, and in some cases, letters, and to deposit them subsequently in Special Collections, Vassar College Library, for use by other scholars in the future: Julia C. Coburn Antolini '18; Julia G. Bacon '23; Christine S. Spofford Beadle '18; Louise H. Seaman Bechtel '15 (interview conducted with Professor Joyce Bickerstaff and Professor Nancy Willard); Elizabeth R. Brownell '23 (correspondence); Mrs. Roland Carreker; Harry Chapman; Ralph Connor; Professor Marjorie Crawford; Winifred W. Curtis '17; Margaret L. Weyerhaeuser Driscoll '23; Elizabeth P. Moffatt Drouilhet '30; David Dutton; Shirley Empleton; Louise Forbes Erskine '11; Gabrielle Forbush '12; Leah Cadbury Furtmuller; Dorothy Hand Geer '17; Margaret M. Gerrity '13; Mae Gessner; Josephine M. Gleason '14; Harmon Goldstone; Mary Nettleton Haight '25; Hilda Tait Hall '07; Sylvia Woodruff Heath '16; Irma Waterhouse Hewlett '14; Rhoda Hinkley; Anne Bowen Hilton '18; Gladys E. Hull Hopkins '14; Catharine W. Hoppin '18; Louise Stuerm Infanger '19; Alice Mary Irmisch '29; Marion Jeudevine '28; Lucile Johnston '28; Ellen Jones '14; Hester Jones '17; Grace Strobel Kern '09; Elizabeth C. Langhorne '31; Edward Linner; Margaret Lovell '15 and Lucy Lovell '12 (joint interview conducted with Professor Barbara Page); Mary McCarthy '33; Caroline Mercer '29 (letter); Winifred Castle Millikin '32; Ruth Mills; Sarah Morris '06; Laura Hadley Moseley '20; William Murphy; Margaret Myers; Marie Stankovich Novakova '22; Frances W. Olmsted '25; Janet Richards Peterson '40; Frances Atwater Pleus '16 ; Dorothy Plum '22; E.W. Poucher '18; Lucy Dunlop Smith '17; Lydia Babbott Stokes '17;

Barbara Swain '20; Christine Vassar Tall '47; Margaret Taylor '23; Vera B. Thomson; Edna Jeffrey Van Buskirk '06; Ruth Dillard Venable '25; Vernon Venable; Mary St. John Villard '34; Josephine T. Voorhees '17; Hulda Bradbury Walsh '32 (conversation); Caroline F. Ware '20; A. Scott Warthin Jr.; Charlotte P. Wierum '16; John Wilkie; Florence Clothier Wislocki '26.

In preparation for the 50th reunion of the Vassar Class of 1935, between 1980 and 1985 I collaborated with Anne Bassage, 1935, and Professor Marque Miringoff of the Vassar Sociology Department in conducting life-cycle interviews with approximately 60 members of the class of 1935. This was a project conceived and carried out by a committee consisting of Anne Bassage, Cornelia Baker Mendenhall, and Katherine Gesell Walden, all members of the Class of 1935, and Professors Miringoff, Anne Constantinople of the Psychology Department, and myself, at the time Professor of English. These interviews are now available for consultation in Special Collections in the Vassar College Library, thanks to a gift of the Class of 1935. They were used as basic sources in a cooperative course that I taught in 1985 with Professors Constantinople and Miringoff, entitled "The Vassar Class of 1935." All of these interviews and the material created by the twenty-two members of the interdisciplinary class have had an impact directly or indirectly on this book. From those sources I learned of subtle differences between the administrations of Taylor and Mac-Cracken. Some of the oral history materials were used in an article called "The MacCracken Tapes" that I published in the *Vassar Quarterly,* 57, no. 4, pp. 12-17. Three times in recent years I taught an interdisciplinary course called "Testimony of the Past" of which Vassar history was the subject; and almost every semester I supervise or assist students writing papers or theses on Vassar history. In all of these ways I have had an opportunity to learn more about women's education at Vassar College.

I am grateful to the following friends and advisers, some of them Vassar-affiliated, for their help to me in innumerable ways: Margaret Harrison Case; the late William Ciolko; Professor Evalyn A. Clark; Joy M. Dawson; Virginia Dearborn; Charles Henry; Judith Ogden Henry; the late Edward Linner; Calvin MacCracken; Maisry MacCracken; Charles Morrissey; Jane Plimpton Plakias; Caroline Rittenhouse; Professor Mary Shanley; and Georgette Weir. Two editors have assisted me with the book: Judith Posner with the first draft, and Carol Scarvalone Kushner, with the final draft and preparation for publication. Trip Sinnott, my publisher, was also extremely helpful in bringing this book into being.

The rich resources of Vassar College Special Collections and the Vassar College Library as a whole, which MacCracken so loved and fostered, have enabled me to become very familiar with Vassar College history and to concentrate on the life and times of MacCracken. I could not have completed this book without the help and cooperation of Nancy MacKechnie, Curator of Rare Books and Manuscripts, and her assistants, Melissa O'Donnell and Elaine Pike. It is appropriate here to recognize also the enormous help to the future of Vassar's archives from my student assistants in recent years, especially: Laura N. Stoland '91, Patrisha Woolard '93, Carnella Stephens '93, Ufasaha Matthews '94, Elizabeth K. Marshall '96. They did the inventory of uncollected materials and the preparation of early student records for microfilming. The microfilming project was funded by grants from the Mary Ridder Hartmann Fund. My wish for the future can only be that the archives will flourish.

The publication of this book was generously assisted in part by grants from the president of Vassar College, Dr. Frances D. Fergusson; from the Vassar College Library, courtesy of Charles Henry, Director of the Library; and from Calvin D. MacCracken. I am very grateful for their support.

The title of the book was suggested by a phrase used by the Rev. Duane Smith, pastor of the First Congregational Church of Poughkeepsie, New York, during remarks made at MacCracken's memorial service, May 1970.

PREFACE

F ELLOW SCHOLARS at New York University, Harvard, or Yale might have predicted that their colleague, Henry Noble MacCracken, would someday be one of the country's leading specialists on Lydgate, Chaucer, or Shakespeare, but they could hardly have foreseen that he would become an innovator in women's education. In 1912 President Arthur Hadley's annual report to the Yale trustees indicated that MacCracken was a most promising young scholar; his recent publications took up half a page of the report. Letters written from MacCracken in Oxford to his wife Marjorie outside London during a post-doctoral year abroad in 1908 tell of grueling hours in the library comparing sentence-structure in variant Chaucerian manuscripts, an activity broken only by a subsequent hour of punting on the river. It seemed as if this twenty-eight year old scholar with a prodigious energy for intellectual work was destined for a chair of Elizabethan drama at a major university. But something happened along the way: he got interested in women's education and became president of Vassar College, where in 1915 he officially succeeded James Monroe Taylor.

Even when he was chosen Vassar's fifth president, it might have looked to most people that he would settle into accustomed routines. Certainly that was what the trustees who chose him thought. MacCracken observed in his book *The Hickory Limb* that the trustees did not seem interested in his general educational philosophy, which by 1915 was becoming as important to him as his scholarship and personal teaching.

When he died in May 1970, *The New York Times* emphasized in his obituary that he pioneered in "the fight to abolish academic formalism." His colleagues at Vassar wrote in a memorial minute that his "overarching achievement here was to foster an academic community...offering freedom, and governed increasingly by its citizens."

Nowhere are the differences in educational philosophy between Henry Noble MacCracken, Vassar College's fifth president, and his predecessor James Monroe Taylor more clearly pinpointed than in their attitudes towards the role of the college in the community. Towards the end of his book *Vassar*, written after he retired and shortly before he died in 1916, Taylor confronted what he considered a menacing new question: what should be the attitude of the college towards the community and the "great public causes" beyond it? His answer was pure, simple, old-fashioned, and conservative: the college should hold itself apart and deal with the present from a distance. "It is not the chief mission of an undergraduate to deal with the untried," he said. The college should "enlighten, broaden, train to careful weighing of evidence, to a scholarly knowledge of facts and the experiences of history, to the testing of theories of what has already been tried, and all as the basis of individual independence in thought and life." Taylor's sense of the mission of a woman's college was that it should provide space and time for women to be set apart from the world's affairs, to learn and theorize about life from a safe distance. He viewed the new causes and concepts, such as suffrage and the networking for particular purposes in emergent groups of like-minded women, as irrelevant to classical education and a threat to the status quo.

MacCracken regarded education for women quite differently. His lighthearted book *The Hickory Limb*, which addressed life at the college during his time and earlier, pinpoints his stand. The title refers, of course, to the nineteenth century jingle: "Mother, may I go out to swim? Yes, my darling daughter. Hang your clothes on a hickory limb: but don't go near the water." He believed that by 1915 college women, and Vassar women in particular, were ready to plunge, but that their clothes were still hanging on a by-then bent hickory limb.

The book I have written, which has been ten years in the making, is not the same book I originally conceived. It follows MacCracken's unique quest to establish new ground rules for educating women, and indeed, adult students of both sexes. That quest took him far beyond the college campus into the affairs of a post-war world in flux. When I started the book, I intended to contrast what went on in MacCracken's Vassar (1915-1946) with similar periods at the other "sister" colleges: Smith, Mt. Holyoke, Wellesley, Barnard, Bryn Mawr, and Radcliffe. While moving from one "sister college" archives to another during my period of research, I learned that each college was renewed in both predictable and unpredictable ways between 1915 and 1925, a decade of significant changes. But as I continued my work, and it drew me out to follow MacCracken into the global sphere that he inhabited, I realized that a book such as I had conceived would no longer do. What interested me more were both MacCracken's sense that a college should be part of the larger community—not just a place apart—and the impact that he and his philosophy had on Vassar and women's education in general. Many of the changes which he promoted as Vassar's leader had to do with his vision of global outreach and his desire to educate American women to become better citizens of their democracy and improve the quality of life in their communities and in the nation. Singly or cooperatively, he created institutions to implement that outreach. Not only did he modernize and transform Vassar itself, but he changed the way Vassar as an institution related to the larger issues of the post-World War I society, and he championed a new role for students, faculty, and alumnae alike as citizens of the world.

No one remembered more sharply than MacCracken Matthew Vassar's words at the June 24, 1864 trustees' meeting in the days before the college opened:

> *Things made by human hands are generally without life; but educational institutions should be living entities, and rise in strength and grandeur by an inherent power. Inanimate things may be made complete by the ingenuity of man, but decay begins immediately when his work is finished. So does a tree grow through the same process, absorbing the elements contiguous for its development and life; and when these elements receive their right direction, they repair its waste, and bring out, at last, its strength and beautiful symmetry in magnificent proportions. A College should rise in power by a similar process. ... So much may be done to plant and prune, and aid a college to absorb in itself the forces of society; but it will never become what we desire till those forces have produced their results. The old limbs will die and new ones will shoot up in their places, and perhaps give it a better form than anticipated. You cannot make a plantation today as it will appear half a century hence. So of colleges ... it is a necessary condition of success to have a large margin for changes.*

Clearly MacCracken had his mandate for a new Vassar from Matthew Vassar himself.

The book I have written examines both "the large margin for changes" at Vassar early in the twentieth century, and what Mac-Cracken, with his unstemmed driving energy, accomplished for both Vassar and the education of students in general, especially women, as he drew Vassar into a larger world. Since many of the changes were profound, where there were not instruments at hand to understand and deal with change, MacCracken helped to create those instruments. Addressing a complexity of contemporary issues to offer new educational opportunities, MacCracken's Vassar created new contexts for learning both inside the classroom and outside, among and between the alumnae and students, between "town and gown." With a governance in place, MacCracken sought to create a college community organic in nature.

MacCracken's years as president were not without fights and disagreements. His role was difficult, especially at first. He was a very political man who needed to keep all the balls in the air all the time. Often, just going from day to day was not that easy, even with the most compatible of his associates. He was perceived by people as not radical enough or as too radical. Many of the trustees found that he threatened a way of life—a status-quo—that had seemed perfectly practical and satisfactory. Some of the alumnae found him too stodgy. A good number of the faculty were already in the mood to respond to the quick initial moves of his first days and months at the helm. But later individuals and groups, disagreeing with him for various reasons, became more contentious. Student leaders preferred handshakes, often followed by petitions for open changes. Some students found him less comfortable to deal with than the "Prexy" who reminded them of their grandfathers. MacCracken was so accessible at both intellectual and social levels that he was puzzling to them. He did not seem to believe that the president should be an authority figure or a paternal force. Not being a minister, he did not see himself as presiding over a congregation of students and faculty members all worshipping at the same altar of learning. Rather, he regarded himself as an implementer of a complex and changing organization seeking a variety of new ways to improve the education of women in a time of shifting sights and mobility. He was a modern leader and faced many of the problems confronted by CEOs of companies today. The ministerial aspect of the presidency disappeared with Taylor's departure and was replaced by the social and ethical vision of a young leader with high hopes for human progress and the will and energy to transform and improve society through education. Over time, he established a model decentralized collegiate system to implement the educational mission of the college while allowing for change.

The contradictory voices from the past make the tumult of Mac-Cracken's Vassar come alive. They give us differing perspectives that link up with the broad sweep of order in his accomplishments. This book would not have been of much interest without these voices. Listening to them, we unexpectedly perceive familiar themes as his world bridges into ours, and we discover the modern college.

CHAPTER ONE

A DOUBLE ARMISTICE, NOVEMBER 1918

I N THE FALL OF 1918, as more than a million U.S. troops were engaged in the Meuse-Argonne campaign in Europe, a less global conflict, but one with deep implications for the future of higher education in America, ruptured on the Vassar campus. The conservative guard of Vassar trustees trumped up a reason connected with war service to use as an excuse for firing the thirty-seven year old president they had hired three years earlier. Assured of support, the progressive president decided to stand his ground and have a public showdown. The forces on his side—faculty members, students, and a handful of women trustees—egged him on to do battle. By evening of the day after Armistice Day, back on campus after a prolonged leave during which the battle had been developed and won, Henry Noble MacCracken gave a triumphal speech. As reported on November 13 in *The Poughkeepsie Eagle News,* he endorsed President Wilson's thoughts on the implications of victory for the victor and indicated that he, too, would use them as his mandate. Covered with the mantle of victory, Wilson had said, the victor must proceed immediately to the task ahead of setting things right. MacCracken now believed he was empowered to set things right on the Vassar campus.

The differences leading to the showdown between the conservative trustees, and the president and his largely progressive faculty, had developed gradually over the preceding years. But they surfaced after the United States entered the war and as the wartime emergency put a strain on the college's economy. In February 1918 the trustees had consented to MacCracken's request for a part-time leave from the college to engage in war-work for the spring term and had raised no objections to his being away. Actually, some of them were probably happy to see him go off and hoping he wouldn't come back.

His problem with the trustees lay in what he had already displayed about his attitude towards the status quo: he was impatient with it and in a hurry to change it. Those trustees who had been on the board quite a while, working with his conservative predecessor Taylor, who retired in 1914, were uncomfortable with his new ideas and attitudes and his lack of respect for the established way of doing things. Those trustees preferred to let continue undisturbed the ivory-tower Vassar that held itself aloof from the community and the outside world. Many of them didn't approve of suffrage and so were more or less out of sympathy with the times, both on campus and off. Perhaps more important, the trustees were accustomed to having their own way, uninterfered with, on the campus. Internally, the college had never really had an overall plan of operation. It had had no budget. (Nor was this unusual: neither did other colleges.) Bills came in and bills were paid, first served. There was very little coordination between the business side of the college and the educational side. Somehow the college had scraped along in this fashion without an overall plan until 1915.

The college had been without a president from February 1914 to January 1915, and the trustees, after their customary fashion, had taken care of all financial matters during that period. After Mac-Cracken assumed office in January, trustee George Dimock, who had been chairman of the executive committee—the group of power brokers that was the inner circle of the trustees—approached him to say that the board did not wish him to be burdened with the financial affairs of the college. He should instead be free to devote his energies to work on the educational side, and leave the business and finances of the college to the trustee businessmen. Dimock said a motion would be introduced at the June 1915 meeting rescinding the resolution (which Taylor had insisted upon at the beginning of his presidency in 1886) that the president should be *ex officio* chairman of the executive committee.

At the time, MacCracken did not object to being excluded from the executive committee, because, as he later observed, it was consistent with what had previously been told him (although that was very little), and because it coincided with his own wish to be allowed to give his chief effort to the educational administration of the college. But he said that he "understood perfectly the nature and significance of this action. It meant that the authority in the executive control of the business of the College, upon which Dr. Taylor had insisted by securing the action making him *ex officio* chairman of the executive committee, had been removed from the office of the President..." Furthermore, it meant that "the responsibility of the Treasurer to the President of the College as *ex officio* chairman of the Executive Committee had lapsed."

Even though MacCracken thought he understood the nature of the action of the board and agreed to it without objection, he could not have realized its full significance. It was a crippling arrangement. New on the scene and new to administration, he perhaps could not in 1915 have anticipated the consequences of relinquishing the right that Taylor had judiciously kept. He was not yet in a position to understand how he would be hamstrung from doing long-range educational planning for the college, or even conducting the day-to-day business of the president's office, without being adequately tied to the pursestrings and the planning of how the college's money would be spent.

Between 1915 and 1918, however, he had discovered all too clearly his error. Mr. H.V. Pelton, who was the trustee treasurer of the college, spent the college's money according to the direction of the executive committee, and what went on in that committee was not always communicated to MacCracken. That meant that MacCracken did not necessarily know what sums had been committed by the treasurer and the executive committee, and was sometimes caught short. Occasionally he was not even asked for an opinion about an expenditure of college funds by the treasurer until it was too late. Such was the case with expenditures of $25,000 for a new heating plant with new boilers in the summer of 1918.

The president's report to the trustees in June 1918 indicated that the college's financial affairs were in critical condition. Largely owing to an increase in the cost of living, but also to emergencies, the college's annual expenses had increased over $100,000 a year since the beginning of MacCracken's tenure. The situation in the spring of 1918 was complicated by the fact that a fire had occurred the previous February in the largest Vassar building, which housed many of the students, and that the loss was not fully covered by insurance. An emergency fund had to be raised for rebuilding. Separated from the college's immediate budgetary concerns, the associate alumnae in 1915, at the time of the Fiftieth Anniversary celebration of the college (an event connected with MacCracken's inauguration), had undertaken to raise a fund designated for endowment. Between 1915 and February 1918, in this first fund drive of their organization, they had raised the better part of a million dollars. But it was not for running expenses of the college.

In 1918, in the wartime economy, John Adriance, a "local trustee," was trying to get a new heating plant installed in the college. Owing to the government's need for metal, new boilers could not be obtained, and so second-hand boilers were substituted. Costs soared and although the executive committee authorized the treasurer to spend $25,000 for the heating system, the bill had already run up to over $200,000. The money had to be found some place. The local trustees apparently suggested to some of those in the inner circle that it was MacCracken's fault because he was not keeping his eye on the campus. It seemed a good chance to get rid of the thorn in their side.

*   *   *

ON SATURDAY, SEPTEMBER 7, 1918, MacCracken was sick in bed in his residence on campus with a septic sore throat and a fever of 104 degrees. As a consequence, his secretary decided to wait until the following Monday, when he undoubtedly would feel better, before showing him a letter requesting a conference. The letter, short and non-committal, asked for an interview the following Tuesday morning. It came from Frank Chambers, a Vassar trustee, who was a business man in Manhattan, but it did not offer any hints about what was on Chambers's mind. Although still confined to his bed, MacCracken was feeling better on Tuesday, and he agreed to see Chambers in the afternoon.

Chambers was ushered into MacCracken's bedroom at about four o'clock and first expressed polite concern about MacCracken's health. MacCracken, who assumed Chambers could only have come to see him about fiscal matters, turned the conversation without hesitation towards his formulations of a new plan to develop a budget system for the college. Chambers, however, interrupted him to say that he had not come to discuss college finances, but for a reason quite different.

He then explained that he had expected to be joined in making this visit by two other trustees, Florence Cushing and George Dimock. Since MacCracken hadn't communicated with him until that morning, however, the others, who lived further away, didn't have time to get there. These three trustees, it turned out, had been delegated by a larger group, but not the full board, to "wait on" MacCracken and deliver a message, which was really an ultimatum. Polite, but indirect, the message stated that since MacCracken's interest in the college seemed not to be as great as his desire to do war work away from the college, he should leave. The trustees had decided they would like to free him for full-time war service. Decoded, MacCracken knew the statement meant that he had too many radical ideas and was not long for Vassar if the trustees had their way.

This unfriendly ultimatum was unacceptable to MacCracken, whose capacity for work was enormous, and who believed he had not neglected his Vassar duties while at the same time imaginatively serving his country. He had been working hard in Washington, D.C., to develop the policies of the American Junior Red Cross, the organization that he had just founded the previous fall and which already had several million American school-children as members. But, even so, he had spent more time in Poughkeepsie than he had imagined he would be able to manage. He was on top of affairs in the president's office, and actively pressing for many different reforms in the way the college was run. Now in the fall, as previously agreed, he had returned to Vassar full time. He was, however, just then both physically and mentally exhausted from everything he had been doing, and in need of rest.

When MacCracken tried to explore with Chambers the grounds of the trustees' dissatisfaction with him, Chambers hedged, and it seemed in spite of his initial remarks that the problem was not so much MacCracken's war service as the way he was running the college's finances on the home front. MacCracken then pointed out emphatically that any criticism of him with respect to finances was completely unjustified since the control of expenses of the college rested with the executive committee of the board, of which he was not even a member.

The executive committee in the summer of 1918 consisted of George Dimock, an officer of the Standard Oil Company, chairman; John Adriance, a wealthy Poughkeepsie plow-manufacturer; Helen Hadley, the brilliant Vassar alumna wife of Arthur Twining Hadley, president of Yale, who was the sister-in-law of Charles Pratt, chairman of the board of trustees, also an officer of Standard Oil; Florence Cushing, an early Vassar graduate from New England, who had been a trustee since 1887, when, after twenty-six years, women first fought

their way onto the board; and Daniel Smiley, the Quaker owner of
Lake Mohonk Mountain House in the Shawungunk Mountains across
the Hudson River from Poughkeepsie, to which the Vassar students
were always invited for an annual outing. Since three of the members
of the executive committee lived at considerable distance from the
college—in New York City, Connecticut, and Massachusetts—most of
the actual financial business of the college was transacted by the so-
called "local members," Adriance and Smiley, in consultation with
Pelton.

Now in his bedroom, completely surprised by the unexpected
criticism of the trustees, which he certainly felt he did not deserve,
MacCracken asked if the committee would be willing to give him
another chance. Chambers returned an emphatic "no," saying, furthermore, that the rest of the board, other than the members of the un-
named "group of seven," whose emissary he was, didn't know anything
about this episode at all, and he assured MacCracken that the matter
would be kept confidential within the conclave of those individuals.
MacCracken, horrified, responded that he would refuse to leave Vassar
College in any such way, and that it seemed to him that a proposal
that a college president should resign, "based primarily upon his
patriotic services in time of war," would not bear scrutiny. He went on
to say that he would make a public statement in self-defense.
Chambers, accustomed, as were all the old-guard trustees, to carrying
out plans in private, warned against such a move, saying it would
injure MacCracken's reputation.

Immediately after Chambers withdrew from his bedroom, Mac-
Cracken sent for his wife to tell her what had happened. They agreed
that he should at once consult Professor Herbert Mills, chairman of
the economics department, a senior member of the faculty, who had
been its interim acting chairman after MacCracken's predecessor left
the college in February 1914. Mills would surely be able to give good
advice, as he not only knew the faculty and its moods very well and
had his ear to the local ground, but he also had a long acquaintance
with the ways of the trustees, having been on the faculty in the college
community since 1890. During the summer just past, Mills had been
the dean of a special wartime emergency summer school of nurses, and
he was now mopping up details after its conclusion. It had brought
approximately 450 college women from around the United States to
learn basic nursing skills and prepare themselves for wartime service.
So it happened that although college was not yet in academic session,

Mills was in his campus office, where MacCracken sent for him, and within twenty minutes after Chambers's departure, he arrived in MacCracken's bedroom.

Mills seemed stunned when he heard the president's news and said that he would have to think over his advice "but that his first feeling was that if he were in [MacCracken's] place he [should] consider it futile to remain [at Vassar] against so important a group of trustees." His remarks made a profound impression on the young president, who then decided he should be in touch as soon as possible with George Dimock, the chairman of the trustee executive committee, to make sure that the trustee decision was as final as it had been made to seem. He was assuming that an answer from him would be expected before the beginning of the scheduled meeting of the committee, which was to be held the following day, Wednesday, September 11.

When MacCracken contacted Dimock on campus on Wednesday (it is not clear by what means, as MacCracken was still confined to his room), Dimock, who had been the chairman of the search committee that invited MacCracken to become president, was brutally frank and direct, much more so than Chambers had been. The business men on the board were agreed, he said, that they could not in the future go along with his radical policies. It was as simple as that. The college was not in a position to expand in the next few years and consequently would not be able to offer him an opportunity for the employment of his "constructive and administrative faculties."

Hearing that, MacCracken replied that if the trustees were so determined to part company with him, as described, he was willing to give in to the suggestion that he should resign. When he asked Dimock what kind of terms he was thinking about, Dimock refused to give any specifics, and MacCracken said that in that case he would have to set his own terms. He would ask to be given four months' terminal salary and to have the announcement of his resignation postponed until after October first. Dimock only then backed off and conceded that the charge that absence for war work was hurtful to the college's stability and to MacCracken's administration "was not unanimous among the trustees." The fact of the matter, unknown at the time to MacCracken, was that quite a few of the twenty-eight trustees didn't even know what was going on. There were no rules compelling mandatory communication among various trustee groups, and a handful of trustees in the know had more or less run the show for many years.

Immediately after MacCracken's interview with Dimock on Wednesday, he again consulted Mills, who, having thought about it overnight, still felt that MacCracken should resign. When Mac-Cracken mentioned Chambers's and Dimock's entailment of secrecy, however, Mills was outraged and thought such a condition would be impossible to carry out. At this point, MacCracken realized that he had made a mistake in not mentioning to Dimock that he would not keep the matter of his dismissal a secret. He sent him a message, which arrived just as Dimock was beginning to preside over the committee meeting in the trustee room in the college's Main Building, that he wished to "retain the liberty of announcing his own resignation" with whatever statement he himself thought best and according to his own timing.

That same day, immediately after the adjournment of the executive committee's meeting, Dimock and Florence Cushing called at the president's house to see MacCracken. Marjorie MacCracken, who greeted them, said he was still too ill to see them. Dimock then gave her, to pass along to her husband, the resolution voted by the committee in their meeting, which granted him a leave of absence retroactively from September 1, 1918, to September 1, 1919, with full salary.

In an attempt to mollify the situation, Dimock said that the president's house was available to the MacCracken family for the year. (The MacCracken family at this time consisted of two daughters—Maisry and Joy—and an aunt of Mrs. MacCracken's, Miss Sarah Dodd, who lived with them.) Cushing, whose trustee responsibilities involved overseeing the appointments of the president's house, joined in to underline that offer. Marjorie, however, responded quickly that—to the contrary—she and the president were planning to leave before the students returned to the campus from their summer break a few days hence on Monday, September 16.

Both Cushing and Dimock expressed dismay at that revelation, saying that the MacCrackens should reconsider because such a move would involve the college in scandal. Then Dimock, unable to cope and putting the matter in Cushing's hands, left the gathering. Cushing told Marjorie that "no one was to know about the meeting of the group of Trustees in New York or about the discussion at the interviews of September 10 and 11, not even the other Trustees. Everything was to be kept secret." The idea was that the president was to leave immediately and the family would stay in the house "as if he was to return." He should look for a position, and when he found one, he would return to the college and make an announcement "that the call of patriotic service had been pre-eminent and that he must therefore resign."

Marjorie MacCracken, perhaps feeling a special responsibility because she was taking the place of her feverish husband, was aghast at this ultimatum. She and her husband would not "live a lie," she said with pique, nor would she be willing, as Cushing suggested, to stay in the president's house with her children while her husband went out to find another job. They definitely would not be willing to "hold their tongues" until the new job was found and then announce their departure. They would not play the trustees' game of charades.

MacCracken, "weak," as he described himself, and "in a highly nervous condition," subsequently wrote Dimock on Friday, September 13 that he would defer further response to the committee for some days. A trustee meeting was set for September 20. Presumably Dimock and the other members of the conspiring group had wanted the matter cleared up before then, but MacCracken apparently had no intention of meeting the trustee deadline and needed time to consider the situation. He also needed the time to maneuver, as it turned out.

The action of the executive committee granting MacCracken the leave of absence was confirmed on September 20 by the full board of trustees, with the alumnae trustees, however, voting in the negative, "which proved to be very telling and made a good effect," as one of them later put it. MacCracken must have telegraphed Pratt an acceptance of the proffered leave of absence, as Pratt later wrote, "On September 22nd you telegraphed to me acceptance of the leave of absence voted by the Trustees. This acceptance did not modify in any way the leave of absence as granted by the Trustees but did state that poor health required its acceptance."

During the nine days between the executive committee meeting on September 11 and the full board meeting on September 20, MacCracken had conferred with many concerned members of the Vassar faculty. The trustee move against him was now an open secret which had spread like wildfire, a development which was an unpredicted embarrassment to the conspiring trustees. Most of the persons MacCracken heard from completely disagreed with Mills's insistence that he should leave Vassar quietly and, instead, encouraged him to stand his ground, openly fight, and under no circumstances resign. Thirty-two members of the faculty met on Thursday the 12th and adopted a statement protesting MacCracken's firing. Mills (apparently now won over), J. Leverett Moore, professor of classics, and Margaret Washburn, professor of psychology—all senior professors—sent the faculty resolution to the sympathetic alumnae trustee Helen Hadley. They protested the summary way the action of the trustees against MacCracken was handled, without calling a meeting of the whole board and without giving him a chance to reply to the reasons advanced for the request. MacCracken claimed at the time that he did not know that this communication was being drawn up.

Meanwhile, the college opened on schedule although the country was in the midst of a serious epidemic of influenza. Dean Ella Mc-Caleb took the place of the president at the annual student convocation, announcing, "It is a matter of very great regret that President MacCracken is unable to be with us this morning to preside at this convocation and to give you a personal greeting, but he is unavoidably detained." During these opening days the MacCrackens kept to their house until the president was well enough to travel. They then went to Old Point Comfort, Virginia, to bide their time and think things over during the president's further recuperation, leaving their children with Miss Dodd. Many on the Vassar faculty during this period were angry about the trustee ultimatum.

✳   ✳   ✳

IN THE THREE YEARS that MacCracken had been on campus, he had listened to the faculty, taken their suggestions seriously, and encouraged them to think that the time had come for them to take the educational policy of the college into their own hands under his leadership. He had plans to free the institution from its conservative ways of the past, under which the faculty had very little power, and to turn the educational policy-making of the college over to the faculty. The ringleader of the faculty revolt, which had already been well under way when MacCracken arrived at Vassar, was the maverick Lucy Maynard Salmon, a distinguished historian and one of the leading spokespersons of the faculty. Completely unbeknownst to Mac-Cracken, who had not met her prior to his arrival at Vassar, her sentiments about reorganizing college governance had been placed before the national reading public in September 1913 when *The Popular Science Monthly* had published an article entitled "The Next College President." Although it was attributed to a "Near Professor," and published anonymously, the article was definitely written by Vassar's Lucy Salmon, who was no "Near Professor," but a most unconventional "Full" one, who had been at Vassar since 1887.

Her article cleverly analyzed the pitfalls of the college presidency in the early twentieth century and dealt with all the vested interests which had to be overcome, avoided, and managed before a president could shape his own policy. She examined the power of boards of regents or trustees, parents, and alumnae who, for the most part, always liked the existing institution and didn't want it to change. "Does someone suggest dropping the Latin salutatory and the valedictory from the commencement exercises, the parent 'likes the present plan' and therefore the Latin salutatory and the valedictory are retained." Of college benefactors, she noted: "The benefactor is a member of the board of trustees and as such wields great authority. . . . If the benefactor is interested in science and wishes to give the college a physical laboratory, the college accepts it without question although its greatest need may be a new library building." Continuing her analysis of various categories, she found that "[t]he force of tradition is strong and tradition makes the student, at least in theory, passive and receptive rather than active and creative." However, there is a "thin entering wedge of alumni representation on boards of college trustees" which, given time, would influence plans in the future. And the faculties everywhere, as the article was being written, were beginning to work in new ways to gain legislative power over educational policy. The article, in short, constituted an indictment of the archaic, authoritarian system that prevailed in colleges and universities just before World War I and colorfully expressed a belief that a more organic system could take its place, under forward-looking presidents of the future.

Salmon, although she was writing anonymously, addressed some of the issues that the Vassar faculty itself had been mulling over in 1913 when they had delivered the trustees an ultimatum. They were concerned about the increasingly conservative educational policies of James Monroe Taylor, who seemed to them to be failing to respond to perceived needs for change in student and faculty life and in the curriculum, especially in reference to faculty suffrage, and faculty freedom of speech and action. After Taylor's resignation under pressure in 1913, which took effect in February 1914, and while the search that identified MacCracken as the winning candidate for the presidency was taking place, the faculty had quietly accrued new power as they stepped together into the vacuum created by Taylor's departure. Uniting in group action for purposes of their own empowerment was in itself a novelty.

In May 1914, the trustees had put out a call through the Alumnae Council for suggestions for Taylor's replacement. No doubt the five alumnae trustees on the board forced this call. At least one faculty member—Salmon—took advantage of the invitation, but instead of just mentioning possible candidates that she had in mind—MacCracken not among them—Salmon wrote the committee at once a reasoned analysis of the principles that should affect the choice of president. It corresponded with her published article.

Now, especially Salmon, but others too, foresaw that this showdown between MacCracken, himself a faculty member as well as president, and the trustees, was a unique opportunity to open the larger subject of academic governance. The issues were clear-cut and well-defined. The questions to be resolved, not Vassar's alone, were vital to every college in the country. A newly-formed national American Association of University Professors had just drawn up its charter and laid some basic groundwork concerning professional ranks and employment. Other colleges were in revolt; reform was in the air. It seemed a perfect time for action.

Salmon, a superb goader, exhorted MacCracken twice by letter—once on September 23, 1918, and again on October 1—the day after the faculty passed a rousing endorsement of MacCracken's progressivism—not to resign.

> *This is the beginning,* **not the end. Do not resign.**
>
> *The fight will be on with president, faculty, and alumnae ranged against an antiquated system of academic organization. Some of us have long protested against the control of a body holding office for life, self-perpetuating, meeting but once a year, committing its work to a small executive committee, publishing no records of its meetings, and admitting no one to its discussions.*
>
> *The opportunity is ours to lead the way in the open discussion of the whole question of academic control. The issue is clear-cut and well-defined. I know of no institution that has had the opportunity that is ours and that one day may be realized in practical form if you stay with us . . . [The question is] vital to every college in the country . . . I wish we might make a permanent contribution to educational theory and practice in the form of a*

plan of academic government that would truly represent all the elements included in a college.

Events had conspired to produce exactly the right circumstances for a progressive turnabout in college governance at Vassar. As history professor Louise Fargo Brown told MacCracken in a supportive letter, the faculty had the "wrecking crew"—the 1918 nucleus of conservative trustees—on the run. MacCracken had a perfect opportunity to go on the offensive and change the system of governance across the board at Vassar. If he would lead the way, there were plenty, even on the board of trustees, who would follow. The arcane, involuted ways of the male-dominated board would be subjected to self-examination and presumably found wanting, changed by the new breed of trustees, many of them alumnae, who would in the future be attracted to the board by MacCracken.

The members of the outer circle of trustees were now trying to clarify the situation in which they found themselves. There were uncommon confusion and dissension. One of them, Henry Cobb, minister of the West End Collegiate Church in New York City (who had been a member of the search committee that nominated Mac-Cracken), claimed that he didn't attend the trustee meeting at which the MacCracken affair was discussed because he wasn't given proper notice. Had he been informed, he said, he certainly would have attended the meeting to hear MacCracken's side of the case. Having heard a version of the trustee charges that had been levelled, he found them "entirely unreasonable." Cobb asserted that control of the board had fallen into a "small clique."

Mrs. Hadley wrote Pelton on October 5 saying that it was not clear to her that the executive committee (of which she was a member) had the authority to act unilaterally. If it did, it did not require a meeting of the board to ratify its action, and, "[i]f it didn't have the power to act, it should have called a meeting of the Board before, instead of after, making any communication to the President." She went on to say that the "nature of the relationship between the trustee executive sub-committees and the trustees were matters of simple fact that every trustee ought to know, but no one seemed to!" She wondered, "who chooses the Executive Committee and what is their power to act?" So unsure was she of the answer to any of these questions that she observed that "The president could probably fight the matter if he wished, but it would undoubtedly do more harm than good to his reputation. Everyone would accept a resignation to go into war work as a patriotic action on his part." Hadley also wrote Pratt on October 15 saying that even though the "president shifted ground rather rapidly and unsteadily—to say the least—alumnae and most people feel that [he] should be allowed to finish out the year and to take his own time about resigning." He must, she felt, be allowed to come back unconditionally for the year.

Within the circle of alumnae trustees and the alumnae organization, other aspects of the same question were being thrashed out, too. Elizabeth Kemper Adams, Class of 1893, noted in a communication to George Perkins, fellow trustee, that a number of the male trustees were as ignorant as were the alumnae trustees of the whole matter, and she expressed concern over the fact that "when you have a board of twenty-eight members divided into ten committees and three of those committees have absolute control, then you are involved with an obsolete machinery, especially since these committees are largely made up of people representing one business and family group." (She was referring to the Pratt and Dimock families and the Standard Oil Company.) Adams felt that the educational welfare of Vassar was at stake, and she personally urged MacCracken to persist in his cause, but thought he was in no shape right then to do that, either "physically or nervously." She said she was not afraid of the bad publicity the college would incur; she wanted to protect the principles of trustee organization which she believed were at stake and had been violated by the self-appointed group of seven. She privately admitted to Perkins, though, that MacCracken "does act on impulse" and "has certain defects of judgment."

Helen Kenyon, 1904, was the incumbent chairperson of the Alumnae Association during these months. She wrote Hadley on September 12 that she couldn't understand why the trustees were trying to fire MacCracken, especially as this was the time for the college to be raising an emergency fund. The college had a debt of $400,000, which had accumulated because of the high cost of living in recent years, and because lack of foresight meant that tuition fees had not been raised sufficiently to cover costs. It was also necessary to finance the rebuilding of Main, the campus's largest building, after a fire that destroyed its back wing on February 12, 1918, with damage estimated at $165,000.

Kenyon canvassed the situation between the president and the trustees for several days early in the controversy, interrogating various members of the community in an endeavor to ferret out the facts. Later, in a report to alumnae on the board of trustees and alumnae in the alumnae organization, she summed up what she had heard from various people and what she had done about it. Her report stated that on Thursday, September 12 she had had a short interview with the president in the company of professors Salmon and C. Mildred Thompson, on which occasion the president gave a narrative of the past days from his point of view; on September 13 she conducted a second interview with the president, with Professor Washburn present. She heard from Miss Cushing on September 16 that the action of the executive committee in giving the leave was at the president's request and from Mrs. Sarah Armstrong, 1877, a trustee, and trustees Hadley and Adams, that they had all been unaware of the existence of the committee of seven. John Adriance told her in advance that a trustee meeting was being called for September 20, without agenda, and with insufficient notice. She saw the president a third time and wired alumnae trustees asking for a conference, at the same time wiring the directors of the alumnae association asking them to protest the ignoring of alumnae trustees in this whole action. On the evening of September 18 Kenyon had an interview with Pelton, and the next day received by wire the protests she had solicited from thirty-two alumnae. Later, on October 2, she wrote MacCracken, asking for a written statement of his educational policies, thus opening the way for a formal response to the alumnae.

Kenyon reported factually to the alumnae on her conversations with trustees. Adriance, she said, thought the resignation had to be; Smiley alleged that the group of seven was a group "in existence to consider matters of importance." When Kenyon asked him how the group thought the matter could be kept quiet, Smiley replied that they hadn't thought the president would go to the faculty and alumnae as he did. "Any sane man," he said, "would act in one of two ways—for his own interests or for those of the college." (Presumably he thought that the refusal of MacCracken to leave was not in his own interest.) Kenyon asked him what would have been in his interest. He said, "to get out quietly." Kenyon then said, "To his own best interest when the college had a deficit of $400,000?" And Smiley observed that "it was better to go quietly than to be kicked out."

Miss Cushing told Kenyon that a leave of absence was the "kindest way to do it." Kenyon inquired why the interview didn't take place in June—what was the reason that the group of seven delayed their action until just before the opening of college? Cushing responded that they had the interview with him before September 12 (Draft Day), thus avoiding answering the question that had been asked. Kenyon wondered why they hadn't waited for him to be tapped on Draft Day, knowing that he would not claim exemption from the draft, but Cushing responded that that was the very thing they were not sure of. Frank Chambers said that temperamentally MacCracken was *not* the right man for the place. A business man, he said, knows when a person in his employ is *not* the right person, and such was Chambers's opinion of MacCracken.

All told, from what she had heard from her collective sources, Kenyon concluded that there was nothing to prevent MacCracken from coming back, that the trustees thought he would come back, and that the September 20 meeting of the board had been illegal, since notice was too short and the business of the meeting was not stated in the call.

VOICES:

Mary Morris Pratt, sister of Helen Morris Hadley and wife of Charles Pratt, was very upset and wrote to a correspondent on October 18 predicting a revolt:

> *[If] he goes he may take the radical half of the faculty and students with him, but maybe Vassar would be better off if he did. This is mob rule. . . . The faculty and students and alumnae are not playing their defined roles in siding with MacCracken. . . . [She foresaw that there would be what she called a] long and unseemly quarrel—a constant taking of sides, perhaps by Trustees as well as by faculty, alumnae, and students [and possibly even] the resignation of those of the faculty who cannot go hot-foot with him and the more radical members. [She predicted that he would return] in triumph [and his] unwise adherents of whom there seem to be a deplorably large number— would stop at nothing for his complete vindication. . . . His are the faults of youth—give him a chance to become a man . . . that is all right, he should have every chance, only not at Vassar. Vassar is not an institution for training presidents. He is a round peg in a square hole; he didn't have the wisdom to welcome the protection of silence. . . . His temperament is so*

impulsive, so headlong in its rashness. ... The unhealthy enthusiasm of Faculty, Alumnae, and Students for their assumed rather than their assigned jobs is in striking contrast to the habits of discipline, subordination and exact obedience under which their brothers and lovers are living [in the men's colleges].

Professor Woodbridge Riley of the philosophy department wrote the absent MacCracken in Virginia, expressing the common consensus of the "liberal" faculty. He said that Vassar College had badly needed a progressive leader to replace Taylor, who had admitted to (and written to justify), his conservatism a few years before his retirement. It had needed a "freer" curriculum, "greater liberty of action by the faculty," and "a general atmosphere of energy." All these things had come to pass when a young president was installed. Just as with Arthur Twining Hadley at Yale, a change from a clerical head "to expert educational guidance also met the advancement of learning." Riley believed the faculty in every department at Vassar were now energized. Vassar and the other women's colleges had the chance of their lives to keep up the humanities during this wartime period when men's colleges were necessarily militarized, but Vassar would certainly lose its chance under a "policy of repression, secrecy, and arbitrary action."

Professor Frederick Saunders of the physics department in a letter to trustee Florence Cushing wrote:

... not wishing to criticize the Vassar of Dr. Taylor which was held together by his wonderful personality. ... For myself I regard Dr. MacCracken as the most valuable person connected with Vassar College. ... His imagination, energy, enthusiasm and fairmindedness have given us a new sense of vitality.

While he has introduced a host of new ideas, he has not forced them upon us but always has favored a thoroughly democratic method, and has secured thereby the hearty support of his colleagues. ... If the trustees desired to bring about the cessation of intellectual growth in the college, to hamper the efficiency and lower the enthusiasm and fidelity of the faculty, they could do it no more successfully than by removing Dr. MacCracken. ... It seems unfair to judge his record according to peace-time standards, just as it seems unfair to judge his personality by a one-sided view of him at a time when the strain has worn even his vigorous health nearly to the breaking point. This aspect of the

recent action of some of the trustees seems to me so obvious that I
wonder how the inhuman cruelty of it escaped notice.

C. Mildred Thompson, head of MacCracken's new Committee on
Admission and before long to become dean of the college, in a letter to
a colleague summed up MacCracken's chief characteristics:

> *(1) His mind works in a positive constructive mode. . . . He
> has genius in seeing a situation in the large and organizing a
> scheme to make an idea effective, instead of futilely wasting energy
> in imposing objections and finding obstacles. (2) He is a scholar
> and values scholarship. He has made it possible for research to be
> done. (3) He has a totally new spirit of neighborliness. He has
> disarmed hostility to the college on the part of neighbors. The
> college has become more cosmopolitan. He has respect for women
> and faith in their capacities.*

After a lapse in communication of a few weeks, MacCracken wrote
Pratt and the trustees a persuasive and masterful thirty-nine page
letter, outlining the progress he had already made as fundraiser and
budget balancer for the college in spite of the fact that he hadn't been
given fiscal responsibility.

In part he said:

> *. . . While authority in these financial matters was not vested
> in the President, the financial situation of Vassar has always
> been a matter of deep concern to me, and I think I can say that I
> have never declined to perform any part assigned to me in that
> connection. Early in my term I suggested the raising of a Fiftieth
> Anniversary Fund, and on April 2nd, 1915, Mr. Pratt wrote
> me in that connection as follows:*
>
> > *"Vassar College does need an increased educational
> > endowment. It has been on my mind for a long time
> > but had not come home to me as needing attention now
> > until your letter came . . . The burden of such an effort
> > as you propose naturally falls upon you to initiate and
> > follow. I am in full accord with your own judgment and
> > that of Mr. Dimock and his associates regarding the
> > plan and purpose of this proposed effort."*
>
> *I assumed the responsibility thus placed upon me and I shall
> never forget the hearty co-operation of the various class committees*

of the alumnae and the other good friends of Vassar who so ef-
fectively served and so generously gave, that not only was the
million dollar fund completed on the scheduled date, October
13th, 1916, but an additional $50,000 had been added to
it.

In his letter MacCracken convincingly pointed out also that his war service had been initially undertaken with the enthusiastic approval of the trustees. He reminded the trustees that his war work had really begun not in Washington in 1918, but rather in Albany in May 1917, when he was appointed by New York State Governor Charles Whitman as "Chief of the Division of Instruction of the New York State Council of Defense" and had ended up in the mobilization of eight million school children in a totally new division of the American Red Cross, which involved a transfer of his administrative efforts to Washington. He reminded them also that the American Academy of Political and Social Sciences had voted him their Gold Medal for the year 1918 to honor his war service. Meanwhile, he pointed out:

> *It seems scarcely to be an accident that the advanced reg-*
> *istration of entering students during the summer of 1918 was*
> *larger by fifty percent than the advanced registration for the*
> *summer of 1917, although our registration has already reached*
> *the extraordinary date limit of closing of over three years and six*
> *months in advance, and this notwithstanding the trebling for*
> *this year the amount of the recently established maintenance fee.*

After a chaotic month of scrimmaging and lobbying, the trustees, with MacCracken's long letter in their hands, met in New York and voted to allow MacCracken to return full time to his duties as president. Now eager to resume his work of modernization, MacCracken quickly set the stage scenery for his return and bathed himself in the limelight. With the same exquisite sense of dramatic timing which he was so frequently to exercise in the future, both on and off the Vassar stage, he took a train from Manhattan and entered the campus gate in a kind of regal processional the evening of the day after Armistice Day. Taking full advantage of the heightened emotions of joy and relief on campus and off, he managed to stretch the ceremonies attached to the national armistice celebration to encompass his personal victory over the trustees.

The Poughkeepsie Eagle News reported a day later:

Vassar College was riotously happy Tuesday night at the sudden return of President Henry N. MacCracken to his post of duty, following an indefinite leave of absence because of health. The leave was extended to him in September by the trustees of the college and during that time Dr. MacCracken has been at Old Point Comfort and in New York recuperating from a severe attack of septic sore throat. His return followed a meeting of the board of trustees of the college in New York on Tuesday.

During chapel service Tuesday evening word came to the campus that Dr. MacCracken was returning to the college on a train due in Poughkeepsie at eight o'clock and would resume his duties at the college.

In no time at all the enthusiastic girls had arranged a grand reception with torches, songs, and cheers. All the faculty members within available distance were notified and hurried to the campus, and the entire community around the campus joined in the throng which eagerly awaited the return of President MacCracken at Taylor Gate.

. . . No sooner had he arrived than the girls crowded around him and began to sing and cheer for him. The reception was a great surprise and pleasure to the returning chief executive. The whole procession swept along to the residence of Dr. MacCracken on the campus, where more songs and cheers were the order of the day.

Called Upon for Speech

Of course, he had to make a speech, and although it was short, it was heartfelt. Dr. MacCracken said substantially that he noticed they seemed to be glad about something, and if they were glad for the same reason he was glad, he knew they were not half so glad as he was. . . . He also referred to the armistice as a cause for greater rejoicing. . . . He then spoke of the need for taking this whole matter of victory in the right spirit. Victory had fallen like a mantle on the nations of the world. He thought the finest words in President Wilson's address referred to the task immediately ahead of the United States and Allied Nations, that of going into the central nations of Europe and getting things right.

*After the dispersal of the mass meeting the faculty and friends
joined him in an informal reception in his home.*

MacCracken was now on center stage and in a pivotal position for
"getting things right" on the homefront. In fact, the next day the
executive committee met with him and made plans to wipe out the
deficit, which were successfully executed within the next six weeks.
Two years later when he was offered the chancellorship of the University of Buffalo at a larger salary, he stayed at Vassar, and the trustees
agreed to the reorganization of the college and the board of trustees on
his terms.

There was to be no turning back, thereafter, either on the college
campus or in the world at large from the cultural, technological, political, and social levers for change set in place during the world war.
They would continue to affect and redirect life at every level.
Certainly they affected women's roles and women's expectations.
MacCracken in the years ahead addressed the changes and new needs
in the post-war world in the field of education. Together with his
colleagues, and with the active cooperation of the students, and a
largely new board of trustees, he consciously, step by step, made over
a conservative and stodgy Victorian institution (one, however, which
the founder, Matthew Vassar, had intended to be responsive to
change) into a thriving modern one.

CHAPTER TWO

MacCRACKEN BEFORE VASSAR

E DUCATION was in the MacCracken blood. An unprecedented piece of news in the world of higher education was announced in *The New York Herald* of December 20, 1914. Each of two colleges that week named a different son of Chancellor Henry Mitchell Mac-Cracken of New York University as its new president. John N. MacCracken, the older of the two at age thirty-nine, was appointed president of Lafayette College, in Easton, Pennsylvania, and his brother Henry Noble MacCracken, aged thirty-four, was named president of Vassar College.

John MacCracken had already completed a four-year term as president of the Presbyterian Westminster College in Missouri, a position he was awarded in 1899 at age twenty-three, making him at that time the youngest college president in American history. He had also been syndic, as well as philosophy professor, at New York University, taking the temporary administrative post in 1910 upon the retirement at age seventy of his father from the position of chancellor.

Noble, as he was always called by his family, had briefly been a professor of English and drama at Smith College when he was nominated to Vassar's presidency. But the year before his move to Smith, he had straddled a double assignment as professor of English at the Sheffield Scientific School at Yale University in New Haven and professor of dramatic literature at Smith.

A more curious aspect of these two ambitious presidential appointments lay in the fact that both of these men in their thirties had been nominated as candidates for the Vassar position. In fact, John was recommended by Noble himself in a letter to the Vassar search committee in the spring of 1914.

The Reverend Henry Mitchell MacCracken, the father of these academic men, came from a distinguished academic family in Ohio. His father, the Reverend John Steele MacCracken, was one of the leading educators in Ohio of the late nineteenth century. His mother, Eliza Hawkins MacCracken, had established a school for women in Oxford, Ohio, which prepared the way for Oxford Female Seminary and the Western College for Women. Henry himself had studied as a young man at the Universities of Tübingen and Berlin in Germany. Later, he founded Green Spring Academy, near Toledo, Ohio, a nineteenth century feeder-school for Western Reserve College. After that, he was named president of Western University of Pennsylvania in Pittsburgh, which subsequently became the University of Pittsburgh. A modernizer and innovator, he moved that university to a different location in Allegheny, where he gave it "a new lease on life," raising an endowment for it and restructuring it. (It later removed to Pittsburgh.)

In 1884 the senior MacCracken was hired by New York University to be a professor of philosophy. Once there he almost immediately became vice-chancellor and then chancellor of the university, at a time when the institution (situated in Washington Square in Manhattan) consisted of one hundred students, a law school, and a medical school. Eventually he presided over the removal of part of the university to Washington Heights. He retired in 1910 four years before the *annus mirabilis* of the younger MacCrackens.

In the heady academic environment in Washington Square, Noble MacCracken had grown up with unusual academic advantages and encouragement. The family lived on Gramercy Park, where Edwin Booth and Cyrus Field were their neighbors and, according to Noble, played marbles with them. If one is to believe what he says in his somewhat embroidered *The Family on Gramercy Park*, Noble roamed the streets as a boy. He recounts being a member of a gang from his side of the tracks which was constantly at war with other gangs, such as the "Micks" from lower Broadway or the choirboys of Calvary Church. His father and mother provided him with an interesting home life, where family conversation and discussion constantly kept him on his toes. Because his mother, Catherine Hubbard MacCracken, hailed from Vermont, Noble remembered a never-ending discussion in the small talk of his household about the virtues of Ohio as compared with Vermont.

Noble's first schooling was at a schoolmaster's called M.W. Lyons where, according to *The Family on Gramercy Park*, he enrolled at age six. Lyons was a drillmaster of the old school, but he took a fancy to Noble, who was his prize student, the only one to enroll in Lyons's Greek class the year Noble took the subject up. An account in *The New York Herald* indicated that Noble was reading Caesar in Latin when he was nine years old, and so interested was he in the study that:

> . . . he made an army of toy Roman legionaries and even a remarkable bridge in miniature which has given much pause to the students of the classics. . . . "I can make these soldiers march and build bridges and cross them," he said one day to his mother, "but I wish that Caesar had been beaten once so that I would know how to make them retreat." . . . He was well up in Greek and Latin when hardly more than a child, for his father, who had much to do with his preparation, believed [like James Mill before him] that these languages could often be mastered better by a boy of ten than by a man of forty.

After attending Lyons's school, Noble transferred to the Berkeley School uptown in New York.

In his spare time, Noble went to parties, entertainments, and political rallies with his Republican father. But his favorite pastime was going with a friend of his, whose father managed theaters, to sit in free seats in the balconies of playhouses. His own father took him to see Booth as Shylock and as Hamlet, and Barrett as Bassanio. The first play he ever saw at night was when he went with his friend to see *The Black Crook*, an extravaganza. He and his father had a serious discussion about what MacCracken saw the next morning after that performance and why he was so fascinated with it. His father, instead of dressing him down for roaming the streets until midnight, gave him a latchkey and told him he trusted him to be "reasonable." Mac-Cracken's future career teaching drama and his lifelong enjoyment of acting perhaps took seed in these Fourteenth Street theaters.

When he had graduated from school, Noble went on to New York University, where his brother John had preceded him. There he studied "Greek and Latin, Spanish, Hebrew, one term of Arabic, Comparative Philology, Ethics, Psychology, the History of England, [general] History, Physics, Chemistry, Biology, Solid Geometry, and Trigonometry, and some electives." After he graduated with a bachelor's degree at age nineteen in 1900, he had the wanderlust and "wanted nothing more than to be an explorer."

> *The gold rush was in progress in Alaska and I tried to get a job in the Klondike, but they told me I wasn't built for that kind of work—too thin and too young. So I tried to get a job on a steamship. The last thing I wanted to do was to teach, but finally it was all that was left.*

He ended up taking a position offered him at the Syrian Protestant College at Beirut (in its modern transformation, the American University of Beirut), where he eagerly began teaching English to the Middle Eastern student population. This he found to be a great challenge as there were difficulties in teaching a class which had students who spoke as many as eleven different languages, with none in common. He began to work on the problem and spent the summers of 1902 and 1903, between Syrian terms, in Europe developing his linguistic skills. In the winter of 1903 he began to write the text of a book called *First Year in English*, which was published that spring, and subsequently went through several editions, being used in fifty colleges and academies in the Middle East.

MacCracken's letters to his parents and family during these three years abroad detail interesting travels with some of his Syrian colleagues and students to remote places over holidays. Officials of the college were impressed with MacCracken and offered him a position as dean after he had been there a few months, but he turned them down.

An attack of illness, probably scarlet fever, gave him a high fever and nearly ended his life. He returned to New York in 1903 and got a master's degree in English from New York University in 1904. Following that he went to Harvard for a second master's degree in the same field, which he received in 1905. Between 1905 and 1907 he enrolled in and completed work for a Ph.D. at Harvard, producing as his thesis a study of Lydgate, the fifteenth century poet, and simultaneously serving as an instructor and assistant professor in the English department at Harvard. He was a glutton for work, so he also took on an additional job at Simmons College teaching English literature and composition to women who were planning to become teachers. There he developed a healthy respect for the aptitude of women for studies, which he had previously not thought about one way or the other. He found that these particular women, already launched on their teaching careers, knew what they wanted and went after it.

Before the next academic year, which he spent as a postgraduate John Harvard Fellow in Oxford and London, England, he and Marjorie Dodd of New York were married in New York on June 12, 1907. Marjorie and Noble got to know each other through her brother Lee Dodd, who was MacCracken's talented, artistic classmate at the Berkeley School in New York, from which they both had graduated. Like Noble, Marjorie and Lee had grown up in a well-to-do, but not wealthy, family. While the MacCrackens lived downtown in Gramercy Park housing provided by the university, the Dodds lived uptown in a brownstone house near the corner of Madison Avenue and 64th Street.

Marjorie's father, S.C.T. Dodd, a prominent New York lawyer, was the solicitor for John D. Rockefeller, and as such, drew up the contract for the Standard Oil Trust. The story was handed down that when the trust partnership agreement took place in Dodd's office in Franklin, Pennsylvania, Dodd turned down the chance to become a Standard Oil shareholder. After the signing, according to a descendant of Luke McKinney, one of the members of the trust, Rockefeller said they were short on money and would like to pay Dodd's fee in shares, to which Dodd replied, "No indeed, I expect my usual fee of $100 cash." A different view, however, was expressed by Marjorie Mac-Cracken in a passage in a notebook of recollections of her family:

> *Because Father was Solicitor for the Standard Oil Co. he knew all its millionaires well. In refusing to own any of its stock because he wanted to be fair in his judgments concerning the company, even though John D. Rockefeller urged his help, Father never became rich. And he did not want his children to grow up among the very wealthy. Fortunately, we did not want to. But we saw them, called on them, heard of their characteristics, and were polite. Mother entertained them very formally since she had social talent, doing her duty and keeping them at a distance. They respected both my parents and when they heard that burglars had broken in our house and stolen all Mother's and Father's silver, just as the 25th anniversary of their wedding was approaching, the millionaires arranged a surprise party on that day and showered them with marvelous silver pieces of all shapes and sizes.*

MacCracken was fond of his father-in-law and thought him a very upright man, the most radical progressive in the New York of his time with respect to civil liberties and civil rights.

Talented as a painter, Marjorie had graduated from the Spence School, a fashionable private school for girls in the city, and after making her debut, was pursuing her interest in painting at the Art Students' League, where she studied for several years with Robert Henri. Marjorie later continued her profession as artist at Vassar, but probably not with the intensity she would have enjoyed had she not been the wife of a college president. A studio was built for her in the attic of the president's house. She took painting lessons from Clarence Chatterton, Professor of Art at Vassar and a former colleague of Henri at the Art Students' League. Her portrait of Laura Wylie, a Vassar English professor, hangs today in the college's parlors.

A shy, family woman of quiet, firm conviction, yet one who developed several causes of her own, Marjorie was to help her much more tempestuous husband keep on course during the highs and lows of his times at Vassar. Letters and clippings in the MacCracken files attest to her genius in sustaining Poughkeepsie's only settlement house, Lincoln Center, which she founded with her husband in 1918, keeping it going for many years during the Depression. Franklin Roosevelt, as governor, appointed her as a visitor to the Hudson River State Hospital in Poughkeepsie. For much of her life, she was interested in the Moral Rearmament movement, started in Oxford after the first world war, and she shared her husband's pacifism.

In England, the newly-married couple spent the summer of 1907 in Oxford and later rented a house at Lauderdale Mansions in Maida Vale outside London. MacCracken's primary purpose in being abroad was to continue various scholarly projects for publication that he already had under way from his graduate school days and to initiate and finish others. He became deeply involved in establishing the canon of certain works of Lydgate and Chaucer and was soon invited by Sir Israel Gollancz, the head of the Early English Text Society, to work on editions to be published in the series of replications of texts the society was then introducing. The Text Society was attempting to get accurate and authoritative texts into print of pre-Renaissance literary works. His work on this project involved MacCracken in many trips to university libraries, where he examined and compared manuscripts. He went frequently to Cheltenham and Cambridge and spent many hours at Oxford as well. No matter how long or how briefly he was gone, he wrote affectionate and newsy letters back to Marjorie, telling her of his daily adventures, whom he had talked with and what the conversation had been about. When in Oxford or Cambridge, he almost always ended eight or ten hours work, poring over manuscripts, with two hours of strenuous exercise, punting on the rivers. And he took walks around the cities, observing the flora and fauna in detail.

June 20 [1908] Cambridge Friday night
I cleared up 76 of the 110 folios of the big R.33, a very interesting text [of Chaucer] which gives one reading, and probably more, that are of great interest.

July 18 [1908] 1 p.m. [Cambridge]
As usual a most interesting manuscript with readings in the Reve's Tale much better than Skeat's.

At the British Museum in London he cultivated a scholarly relationship with Dr. Frank Furnival. Furnival and a group of continental and American followers—a "little coterie of scholars"—met daily in the museum's manuscript room and after their hours of research, or over lunch, they exchanged views and got to know each other. Among the young scholars that MacCracken met was a Pole named Roman Dyboski. Dyboski, who was subsequently both shipped to Siberia and tortured by the Nazis, fascinated MacCracken with his studies of popular speech in Shakespeare's time. He was busy working on an early manuscript which MacCracken described as "long and narrow," and which had fitted into the pocket of a fifteenth century itinerant grocer who had written down on it songs, ballads, and carols that he heard sung in the market place. Dyboski's fascination with speech and the oral traditions of literature sold MacCracken on dramatics as a mode of communication and the field of literature in which he was to remain most interested because it was closest to human feeling and thought.

The couple's first son, Noble Jr., was born in England the spring of 1908, and Marjorie and Noble were enveloped in the pleasures and problems of preparation for first time parenthood in a less than completely familiar culture. That spring, too, Chancellor MacCracken was invited to give a series of talks in Denmark. His wife came to England and stayed with Marjorie while Noble accompanied his father abroad. The two men had an audience with Haakon II, King of

Denmark, and travelled around Denmark while the chancellor gave his speeches at the chief universities on various subjects. Noble thoroughly enjoyed basking in his father's light and getting to meet scholars of the university world as well as men in Danish government circles. He wrote to Marjorie and his mother about his father's astonishing energy, almost universal approval, and their excursions through the Danish countryside. He managed by himself to make a side expedition to Elsinore to visit Hamlet country.

Back in London that spring, suffragist demonstrations came to a climax and caught MacCracken's attention. He wrote in *The Hickory Limb:*

> *I was deeply interested at the time in the woman's movement for economic equality and for suffrage. With my wife Marjorie Dodd MacCracken, I had stood in Hyde Park, London, for an entire afternoon, watching Mrs. Pankhurst and her inspired daughter Christabel, as they fought for a hearing. An instinct for fair play drove me to listen to them. Their eloquence won my assent. From that day I was for women's votes.*

Before the MacCrackens returned from their time in England, Noble had either published or readied for publication ten scholarly volumes, emanating mostly from his graduate study. There were two volumes of the works of Lydgate and two volumes of poems in the manner of Lydgate, edited for the Early English Text Society. There followed one volume of selections from Lydgate and an edition of Lydgate's *Serpent of Division*. A volume of scholarly essays, an "Answer of Adam," another edition of his *First Year in English*, a one volume edition of the works of Chaucer, and a book of fifteenth century ballades rounded out the number of volumes to ten. He also wrote and published five scholarly journal and magazine articles, achieved mention as a prominent young scholar in the *Cambridge History of English Literature*, and won a coveted contract with the Clarendon Press in Oxford for his book on Lydgate—all within twelve months. All told, it was to be the only period of his professional life when he could devote his intellectual energies, as reflected in research and publications, so intensely and exclusively to the scholarly domain.

After this period, most of his thousands of publications, talks, and speeches were to be in different voices, different veins, not "scholarly" but popular. He would vividly bring all this intellectualized material to life at the lay person's level and relate it in meaningful ways to the interests of his audiences. As college president he would later reap rich, double-value returns from these English days devoted mostly to scholarship. Not only did he do his share to interpret and preserve the English past with his meticulous scholarly publications, he also ingested what the kings and the pardoners and the peasant workers were saying about their lives, and he hoarded their words and expressions and ideas for future reference. He would startle his commencement audiences in Poughkeepsie and high school principals in St. Louis and around the country with his learned but pertinent references.

During the summer of 1908 the young MacCracken family and Marjorie's aunt returned from England and soon MacCracken settled on a position at Yale, where the lively senior teachers were Henry Seidel Canby and Wilbur Cross. Before he had returned to the United States, he had tried to negotiate through his father a position at New York University, which he would have preferred to the one at Yale. He had been the top English student as an undergraduate at N.Y.U., and he felt that with a position in the university English department, he would be in line to help out his administrator brother John and to get ahead himself. "No one worries about nepotism in England," he said, trying to convince his father that his plan was a good idea. "Archbishop Benson's three sons all live by incomes from their college or Church and people are proud of 'em. I don't see why New York should not welcome two sons to carry on business at the old stand." Marjorie also apparently very much wanted to live in New York City again. But no offer came through from New York University, and, as Yale seemed to want him, he took the job he was offered at the Sheffield Scientific School although he didn't think very highly of the institution or of the calibre of its students. Still, he was, he knew, in a very healthy career position, as his accomplishments "occupied half a page in the president's report" at Yale at the end of his first year, as he wrote his mother.

He and Marjorie immersed themselves in civic work in New Haven. He became a member of the governing board of the university settlement house which provided recreational resources for New Haven poor children, and Marjorie was on the mills committee of the Consumers' League. But they were both horrified by some of the things that they saw. "The more we get into civic life here," Noble wrote his parents in 1911, "the more we see how corrupt and inefficient our municipalities are, and how every man's motto is 'a public

office is a private privilege.' ... Two blocks from Yale [was] a district of
saloons, dance-halls, and loose-livers [where arrests were] continuous
for rows and drunkenness." MacCracken's settlement house committee proposed that policewomen be hired to check "the worst
features of the matter [i.e. prostitution]" and "a howl of derision went
up from the respectable folks. I was told to let it alone." Undaunted
and still ready to take a controversial position, MacCracken then
joined with some others to create a public committee, the Connecticut
Society for Social Hygiene, to try to bring what he considered to be
the seamy side of Yale male sexual irresponsibility under control. This
organization undertook to work out "better techniques in the field."
On the Yale campus itself students were unruly and continuously in
trouble with the law. "Last week," he wrote in 1911, "students at Yale,
Princeton, and Cornell were fined for rioting, while a wheelbarrow full
of signs was trundled out of Guild Hall. Respect for the law [was]
noted by the lack of it only."

He was not very happy with the academic achievement of his
Sheffield students either. Many of them did not seem to be motivated
for liberal study as far as he could tell—only interested in trying to
make the right connections and preparing themselves to find the right
job. Meanwhile, they were determined to have fun before they settled
down. This lack of interest and misplaced motivation were disappointing by comparison to the seriousness of the women students that
he had taught at Simmons College when he was a graduate student at
Harvard. He had found those women excited and ambitious about
their work. In New Haven, he also taught women teachers "as part of
[his] job. The university was offering extension courses to teachers at
Bridgeport and New Britain trying to stave off a movement for a state
university by going out to the people." He commuted to offer courses
to these older women who were trying to earn credits towards advanced degrees. Those women "seemed genuinely to enjoy their own
minds, to be infected with the fever of intellectual curiosity, to seek
the connection between art and life." MacCracken was beginning to
believe that women were more open to a liberal arts education than
were men.

As he thought about the contrasts posed between the Yale men
and the Bridgeport and New Britain women, he began to raise questions to himself about men and women and the ways in which they
were educated. What were "the patterns of education for women?"
Why did women have so little space in their lives for education

designed for self-improvement when they desired it so much, and why did male students—judging by those in his classes in New Haven— occupy male space in New Haven with so little interest in self-improvement? Was it not up to the teacher in the classroom to call the student to civic responsibility? Was it not just as important for students to learn to become ethically responsible as to pursue their own more private purposes? Wasn't college really the time to prepare for citizenship? According to his account of himself at this time in *The Hickory Limb*, MacCracken was mulling over these questions in connection with motivations in his own career:

> *Might not a man design a pattern of education for women, if a design were needed, and still respect himself as a man? . . . Was teaching always to be celibate and monastic? . . . a mind was a mind, whether it was a man's or a woman's. As a profession, I theorized, teaching took no account of sex.* (pp. 1-3)

MacCracken admitted that it was very hard to hang on to that attitude in New Haven, a town of football heroes and macho activities.

Even though MacCracken was somewhat in a turmoil about making a career out of teaching unreceptive Yale students, other aspects of life were quite agreeable for him and Marjorie in New Haven, and their young family of Noble Jr. and a new sister, Maisry, born in 1910. Marjorie's inheritance from her parents, who had died, provided them with the means to have a nurse for the children and a cook (who became an integral member of the family and lived with them for many years until she declared her independence and opened her own boarding house in Poughkeepsie later in her life). The prosperity of the newcomer MacCrackens was noted with some degree of scepticism and astonishment by other members of the Yale community who had to live more penuriously on their teaching stipends alone.

They chaperoned parties at the New Haven Lawn Club. They involved themselves in community affairs. As a promising and well connected member of the department, MacCracken associated with its leading lights. He participated in meetings of the Graduates' Club, "listening to Uncle Toby, as my chief Wilbur Cross was known to us all, and to Thomas Lounsbury, his famous predecessor. . . . Lounsbury sympathized with my feelings on what he called the 'infinite capacity of the undergraduate mind to resist the intrusion of knowledge.'" They joked over the entrance exams that they read together in July 1909. MacCracken wrote Marjorie, who was summering at Lake Sunapee in New Hampshire, that he had read 700 exams that day (July 3) of students seeking admission: "The papers are rotten! They make you ashamed of the American school system." Together with Cross, Lounsbury, a colleague named Corwin, and another named George Nettleton, MacCracken learned a great deal about his new profession that July, talking about entrance requirements, how to write effective exam questions, how to teach languages, and engaging in other shop talk.

But he was restless and ready to move on almost from the moment he got to New Haven. The ambience there was not right. In addition, in 1913 the MacCrackens suffered a painful loss when their five-year-old-son died from erysipelas. This death was followed later on in the year by that of Noble's brother, George, to whom he was very close, who died in a boating accident. These adversities, combined with his misgivings about Yale and his future there, worked together to make him ready for a change. He was aware of the fact that Harvard Ph.D.s at that time automatically had a strike against them when it came to advancement in the Yale department. Even though his relations with the department seemed to be promising on the surface, he sensed that he would have difficulty in getting ahead. At this point came an offer from President Marion Burton of Smith College, presenting Mac-Cracken a welcome opportunity to try out his ideas and theories about women's education in the Smith English department, which was badly in need of a man with fresh views. On paper MacCracken seemed to be just the man Burton was looking for.

THE ANGEL'S VISIT: MacCRACKEN'S
BRIEF STAY AT SMITH COLLEGE, 1913-1914

The college is fairly weeping—we feel so badly. We all have been so enthusiastic about his course and to think we won't have him the second semester.

— Letter home from Agnes Betts,
Smith 1916, to her parents,
December 17, 1914.

In his brief stay at Smith College, he has secured unprece-
dented influence and interest among the undergraduates. They
insist they have entertained an angel, but not unawares.

> — Mary Jordan, "The President
> Elect of Vassar and His
> Problems," *Vassar Miscellany,*
> February 26, 1915.

In 1883 the Smith College English department had been staffed by two people—Heloise E. Hersey (Vassar 1876), who taught English language and Anglo-Saxon, and Lawrence Seelye, the president of the college, who taught rhetoric and composition. Immediately after he had become president of Smith in 1875, Seelye (like Milo P. Jewett before him at Vassar College in 1863) had visited universities in Europe and England to observe how women were being educated. He also studied what had been going on at the pioneering Vassar College, which had been working on its curriculum for the ten years it had been in existence. He concluded that strong attention should be paid at Smith, as at Vassar, to the study of the English language and literature and to the writing of original essays. Seelye was not satisfied with the practices in teaching languages which existed in men's colleges, the prototypes for much that went on in the new women's colleges. He wanted Smith to have an innovative system of teaching in which the teachers of ancient and modern languages would combine to supply important connections rather than compete with each other. However, much as Seelye hoped to the contrary, divisions apparently developed between the branches of the English department as it grew larger in the 1880s. During that period one of its members, Mrs. Julia Ray, who previously had taught at Vassar, suggested that President Seelye would do well to go over to visit Vassar and entice highly qualified Mary Augusta Jordan, then acting as "critic" in the English department at Vassar, to come to Smith.

As it happened, Miss Jordan at that time was feeling unhappy about her future at Vassar. She had attempted without success to persuade Samuel T. Caldwell, president of the college from 1878 to 1885, to promote her from "teacher" to more senior professorial status when Truman Backus, head of the Vassar English department, left the college in 1883. After considerable maneuvering in which she tried again to get a commitment from Caldwell, she accepted an offer from Seelye to move to Smith as an associate professor. Even after Jordan arrived at Smith, however, internal departmental relations in the English department did not improve and the language teachers remained divided from those who taught literature. In 1902 two more English teachers were promoted to the associate professorial rank. One was Mary Augusta Scott, who had graduated from Vassar in Jordan's class, a teacher of language and linguistics, rather than literature. Scott, according to Jordan's departmental history, "remained permanently in opposition to new lines of union of the English Department."

Attempts to buttress those lines were officially renewed when Marion Leroy Burton, also an English scholar, became the second president of Smith in 1910. He went immediately about the business of revising the standards, curriculum, and management of the department. The discussion was prolonged for two years during which two plans for unification were proposed, while department members continued to be uneasy and disgruntled. President Burton finally offered a plan of his own. The resignation owing to ill health of Adelaide Crapsey, a 1900 Vassar graduate teaching in the Smith department in 1910, afforded Burton the opportunity to appoint someone new who was more likely to see things his way and help him accomplish his objectives. The person he hired in 1913 was MacCracken.

Such was the situation between Burton, the president, and Jordan, the head of the department, that only after Burton had hired MacCracken was he presented to Jordan. Half Jordan's age, he was hired as a full professor at a salary of $3000 (although he was so flustered he forgot to ask the salary during the interview) and told that he would be in charge of the teaching of drama and criticism in the department.

MacCracken seemed to assume that he would be able to work out an arrangement with Yale so that he could continue teaching there full time while also teaching full time at Smith. Marjorie didn't want to move from New Haven at that point since she was pregnant again, and they had a comfortable house in which to await their expected child (Joy). So the first year he arranged to teach full time at both places—on alternate days—a total of twenty-six lecture hours and many more conference hours. He could commute by train, a trip of two hours each way, and he would have time for reading themes as he came and went. The situation was promising. By the next fall however, MacCracken had decided to pull up stakes in New Haven and move to

Northampton. Cross was not very happy with MacCracken's departure, and in the Yale department there was a general air of consternation and betrayal that anyone would want to leave Yale for Smith.

Life in the Smith English department certainly was quite different from that at Yale. With the exception of a professor nicknamed "Bunny" Abbott, who had been there for quite a few years, MacCracken was the only male. The department was dominated by the two Vassar alumnae—Mary Augusta Jordan and Mary Augusta Scott—who cordially disliked each other and whose notions of a coherent department were deeply at variance with each other's. To make matters worse, Jordan was outspokenly against women's suffrage, and Scott was outspokenly for it. Jordan taught literature, Scott taught language and rhetoric. Both had large egos. MacCracken lightheartedly laughed the situation off in *The Hickory Limb:* "Since both Miss Scott and Miss Jordan were Mary Augusta, the talk at department meetings consisted chiefly of: 'Mary Augusta, you are mistaken.'"

Smith was going through rather sweeping changes in 1913 under Burton. It was a good place for a young ambitious man, interested in women's education, to take stock of what the issues were in a college for women. This MacCracken proceeded to do, although at the time he did not have the idea of becoming a college president. President Burton had become concerned about the proliferation of housing for the students, who were scattered all around Northampton, and he wanted to bring them back on campus. But there was no room. Soon after MacCracken arrived, the state insane asylum property bordering the campus became available, and Burton wanted to persuade the trustees to purchase it so that the college could expand and become a university—Sophia Smith University. This never came to pass because just at the juncture when the sale might have taken place, Burton accepted a position as president of the University of Minnesota, and his push to change the character of Smith was over. The next president, William Allan Neilson, and the trustees did not agree with Burton that enlarging Smith into a university was a worthy goal, so the size of the college continued as it was.

An issue that occupied a great deal of the administration's time was that of relationships with high schools. Now that there were more colleges for women and more applicants for college around the country in general, it behooved colleges and high schools to find a way to smooth the transition for students. The situation for college-bound students had been chaotic in the beginning years of the women's colleges, not just at Smith but in the other leading sister colleges as well. Where previously in the nineteenth century, certificates and testimonials had served as credentials, examinations and standardized tests were now—in 1913—beginning to be used in admission, just as in the men's colleges. At Yale, for example, they were being tried out. The newly founded College Entrance Examination Board's system of testing was in its infancy. But from college to college, admissions were handled differently and, as it often seemed to the students, perhaps somewhat arbitrarily. From the students' point of view, the prospect of dealing with different procedures in different institutions was an increasingly confusing one. Furthermore, with the spread of college education for women, secondary education had continuously been upgraded. By 1910, according to Thomas Mendenhall, a later Smith president, "two years of what had once been included in a college program had shifted down to the secondary school," and the college was trying to redefine its curriculum to correspond with these changes.

In what was to prove to be his very brief time at Smith, Mac-Cracken was introduced to these and other problems connected with college administration. The governance of the college was changing, women were just beginning to be elected to the board of trustees, and the alumnae were playing a stronger role in the college's affairs. Further, there was considerable agitation for suffrage on campus, with both students and faculty beginning to make themselves heard on political issues.

MacCracken later recalled that he first learned of the vacancy of the Vassar presidency in the Smith English department office in the spring of 1914 after he had been at Smith one year. One day, Mary Augusta Jordan let drop that Vassar was looking for a president since the incumbent, James Monroe Taylor, who had been at Vassar since 1886, had resigned. She asked MacCracken if he had any suggestions for the trustee search committee, of which her brother-in-law, George Dimock, was the chairman. MacCracken immediately thought of his brother John and went home that evening and wrote a letter "outlining first the kind of president a women's college ought to have, pointing out the great opportunity such a post held at the time, and arguing [his] brother's fitness for the job." Unfortunately, that is all we know about the letter, as it and all the other papers pertaining to the search for the Vassar president were shrouded in the secrecy that pertained to all Vassar trustee business at the time, and have not come to light since.

Nothing happened for a while except that MacCracken received a formal acknowledgement of his suggestion. However, one day in the middle of the summer, guests arrived unannounced and unexpected at the door of the house the MacCrackens were then renting in Amherst, Massachusetts. (Believing they were at Smith permanently, they had decided to build a large architect-designed house on the banks of the Connecticut River near Northampton and had begun construction, but had moved into temporary quarters until the house was ready.) Their unexpected guests were Charles M. Pratt, chair of the Vassar board (although MacCracken did not know this at the time of the visit), and his wife, Mary Morris Pratt, a Vassar alumna who was the sister of Helen Morris Hadley, a Vassar alumna trustee and the wife of the president of Yale. The Yale connection was used as the excuse for the visit, as the Standard Oil connection might well have been also. MacCracken was annoyed to have to break into his work schedule that day since he was collaborating that summer with Tucker Brooke of Yale and John Cunliffe of the Columbia School of Journalism on an edition of twenty of Shakespeare's plays, and he was rushing against time on his deadline. The subject of the Vassar presidency did not come up, and the Pratts withdrew after the visit and went on about their business. This was the first in a series of guarded meetings in a masquerade that took place over the next few months. Not once was MacCracken told that he was under consideration as a candidate, or that his brother was not.

After a while, MacCracken wrote to Dimock again, urging more eloquently that his brother be considered. As a result of that communication, the two MacCracken brothers were invited to Glen Cove, Long Island, to meet the power-wielding brothers-in-law, Pratt and Dimock, at the home of Emily and Henry Folger (later benefactors of the Folger Library in Washington). Mrs. Folger, the hostess, had been president of the Vassar Class of 1879 and had earned an M.A. in English from Vassar *in absentia* in 1896. She was the sister of Mary Augusta Jordan, Vassar B.A. 1876, M.A. 1878; and Elizabeth Jordan Dimock, Vassar 1879, the search committee chairperson's wife, who was also present. It was a gathering of very important Vassar people, both trustees and graduates, looking over the two young men.

According to MacCracken's account, after he and his brother consumed the elegant Folger lunch, John was taken off to a private room to talk with Pratt (about Noble), and Dimock and Folger cornered Noble in conversation. Even then the two hosts did not bring up subjects related to the presidency, and did not tell Noble they were considering him. A strange kind of candidate's interview it must have been! After the talks, the MacCrackens returned to John's house in Mamaroneck, New York, and on the way John, no doubt with a sinking heart, pointed out to Noble what he had not perceived for himself—that he, not John, was the candidate. Noble was incredulous, but decided to let the matter rest and not make the next move.

Without further interruption, the summer of 1914 gave way to fall, the Smith term started again, and MacCracken settled into a schedule of scholarly work and teaching that he quite liked. He finished his part of the Shakespeare book and started on the next project, this time a grammar. His faculty duties were fairly light, especially now that he didn't have a two-way commute to New Haven every other day, and that was the way he liked it.

As he recorded in *The Hickory Limb,* he was amused and relieved by a mild joke played on the Smith faculty at their first meeting in the fall of 1914 by Professor John Stoddard, a chemistry teacher, who proposed that the faculty restrict their meetings to the fourth Wednesday of the month. The faculty agreed, "went home and consulted their calendars" and "found the following schedule:"

4th Wed. of Oct. Mountain Day, a holiday
"   "   " *Nov. afternoon a holiday, Thanksgiving.*
"   "   " *Dec. Christmas vacation.*
"   "   " *Jan. Between 1st and 2nd semesters, a holiday.*
"   "   " *Feb. Washington's Birthday, holiday*
"   "   " *Mar. Spring vacation.*

Meanwhile the large new house on the Connecticut River—to be called the "Tryst"—was completed, and the MacCrackens moved in. It was a house that appealed to Noble's and Marjorie's imaginations. Noble reported after he had sold the house that there were two rooms he never did discover. (The house was to be purchased several years later by Calvin Coolidge as a retirement home and renamed the "Beeches.")

❋   ❋   ❋

WHATEVER THE VASSAR TRUSTEES were doing behind the scenes, the wheels of choice revolved slowly. Perhaps they were having a fight. There were five alumnae trustees on the board, and, once the search was under way, those women apparently put out a call through the alumnae association, and also to the Vassar faculty, for suggested candidates. There were hints here and there along the way that some well-placed people might have an idea of what was going on. In the fall, for example, Wilbur Cross wrote to MacCracken from the Yale English Department that the job at Vassar was still open. Then weeks later, MacCracken was invited to meet at dinner Florence Cushing, the powerful Vassar alumna trustee from the Boston area, who, he later discovered, was on the search committee. Still, not a direct word was said about MacCracken's appointment. Following that meeting, however, there was a dinner in Brooklyn at Pratt's house, with the whole Vassar board of trustees present. But whereas MacCracken had prepared himself to forward his opinion that "the students were the college and the rest of us, trustees, teachers, and staff, were their servants, not parental substitutes," the opportunity to express his views never came. The trustees didn't seem to want to know his views on anything, and he left rather disappointed and frustrated.

MacCracken observed in *The Hickory Limb*:

> *Not long after, Mr. Pratt himself made the trip to North-ampton, and sent for me to call upon him in his bedroom at the Plymouth Inn. It was a most painful experience. He had wrought himself to a high tension of nerves, and felt that the occasion demanded something of the sublime, which, however, he was unable to supply. Nothing of importance was said, beyond the bare fact of my election to the presidency of Vassar, and yet the whole meeting was heavy with doom and gloom. I accepted with solemnity and a terrible pain in the head.*

Thus as the European war began to take up newspaper headlines, the two-year search for a Vassar president was over. MacCracken was announced in early December 1914 to be the winner. The news hit the New York papers the day after the announcement of brother John's election to the presidency of Lafayette. It was also in the New Haven papers, where Yale was all agog, wondering for the second time why someone with a potential future in the Yale English Department would possibly have traded that for a spot in a women's college. For their part, the Vassar trustees must have been relieved to have the matter finally settled. Whether those who had chosen him had any real inkling of MacCracken's ideas about education is questionable since they had never openly inquired about his views or given him a chance to express them. In any case, the old guard of the trustees expected that the college would continue the same conservative course it had taken under Taylor.

In a few days, announcements had been made with great ceremony on both campuses. The Smith undergraduates were sorry to see MacCracken go so soon, since they had liked him and he was young and had believed in them. They thought his stay at Smith had had the brevity of an "angelic visit" and they bemoaned his leaving. The Vassar students were told about his coming at a campus vesper service. They were glad he was young—only thirty-four. Mary Augusta Jordan, in an effusive introduction in the February issue of *The Vassar Miscellany* praised him to her sister Vassarians, while stopping short of regretting his loss to Smith.

The Christmas holidays came and the MacCrackens paid their first visit to Vassar. They inspected the president's house and met individual members of the faculty, including Herbert Mills, professor of economics, who was the faculty's acting chairman after the departure of former president Taylor. Mills assured MacCracken that there had been no faculty candidates for the presidency, adding gratuitously that he himself preferred teaching. In February the MacCrackens moved in to the president's house on the Vassar campus. In Northampton the Mary Augustas got back to normal; Jordan could congratulate herself on being very supportive of MacCracken all the way through his Smith sojourn and his Vassar initiation. If MacCracken, with his trained eye for subplots, had detected any self-interest beneath the advocacy of his candidacy for Vassar president by Dimock's sister-in-law, the chairperson of the English department at Smith, he did not let on in public.

He did, though, reveal many things about himself and his attitudes in public, in statements to the newspaper press. He was frequently interviewed by newspaper reporters in the days and weeks following his being named president. Some of his remarks were strictly off-hand; some addressed his first experiences with Vassar students in the spring. Much of what he said may have surprised trustees, alumnae, faculty, and most of all the students.

MEETING THE PRESS: 1914 STYLE

MACCRACKEN:

NEW YORK TRIBUNE, December 19, 1914

A woman ought to be taught just what a man is. No, I decline to be asked whether that wouldn't interfere with her becoming a good wife and mother. That question is too out of date. I am a suffragist of course! There is a club in which suffrage is debated at Smith College, and I think it is an excellent thing!

I was very happy at Smith, though my superior was a woman. Miss Jordan, head of the department of English gave me my orders and I took them, just as if she were a man. Why shouldn't I? She is a woman with a splendid brain.

BOSTON SUNDAY POST, December 20, 1914

(Q.) Is it true that college women are bearing fewer children, losing their taste for homemaking, and finding careers in professions more satisfying?

(A.) Personally, I do not believe it. Statisticians have attempted to prove that a low birth rate exists among college women, but their figures, assuming they are correct, do not prove that point. . . . The only equitable comparison between college women and other women would be to gather statistics of the birth rate among the other members of the college girl's family who do not attend college.

College life enhances all those qualities which are synonymous to women. It is a fallacy that college training produces a type that scorn the duties of womanhood. On the contrary, my observation has been that the average college girl graduate is decidedly more—let us say—winsome than when she enters. Any change that may have taken place within her is one that gives her a higher and finer appreciation of the things of life. Naturally enough her training causes her to place a greater value on the marriage relation and entertain a higher ideal of a husband exactly the same as the training causes her to hold higher standards of art and music . . .

CHICAGO NEWS, May 6, 1915

The reason why women have not distinguished themselves more frequently in the world of large affairs is because they are too conscientious. Yes, overly conscientious. By that I mean they are too literal, too hairsplitting... When a Vassar instructor asks for an 800-word paper, that is exactly what he gets.

Times are changing so rapidly that soon feminism will be but a forgotten phrase. I already see all feminist movements merging with masculine movements. In matters where brains and common interests are concerned there is no need to feel that one is dealing with women as differentiated from men. In my work I am dealing simply with minds.

The newspapers pursued other questions also relating to Mac-Cracken's appointment.

NEWS PRESS, December 19, 1914
(The *News Press* reporter apparently had an interview with someone in a position to know:)
The selection committee had four criteria: the president should be a Christian gentleman, should have had academic experience, should have won distinction in his field, and should have proved his scholarship.

KATHERINE BEMENT DAVIS (Vassar, 1892), New York's Commissioner of Corrections, said she wasn't one who thought the men should all be put out; however, women should have half the jobs. *When we become really advanced, there would be no protest if a woman were put at the head of Harvard or Yale.*

HARRIOT STANTON BLATCH (Vassar, 1878), head of the Woman's Political Union, declared it was better to have a man as president and plenty of male professors in a women's college.

ALICE BARROWS FERNANDEZ (Vassar, 1900), editor of "Vocational Education Survey," and INEZ MILHOLLAND BOISSEVAIN (Vassar, 1909), activist-suffragist and lawyer, both protested:

FERNANDEZ: I wouldn't want to do anything that would make it hard for Dr. MacCracken. He is very fine. But it does seem absurd that Vassar should calmly take it for granted that there is no woman fit for the place of president. Many of the graduates think that Professor Laura J. Wylie, head of the English Depart-

ment, should have been made president. I feel that the alumnae organization should begin making an organized effort to have women at the helms of colleges.

BOISSEVAIN: A good many of us are sorry that the Board of Trustees is so conservative. Their refusal to try to let a woman try to fill the place is very annoying.

JEAN WEBSTER (Vassar, 1900, author of Daddy Long Legs and When Patty Went to College): Julia Lathrop (Vassar, 1880) head of the Children's Bureau should have been made president. [She was approached but refused to give up her position as head of the Children's Bureau.]

MACCRACKEN:

I suppose a woman would have been chosen for president if one could have been found. I don't mean that there aren't plenty of capable women, for there are: but they are quite happy in their present positions. Miss Wooley has made a splendid success of Mt. Holyoke and Miss M. Carey Thomas of Bryn Mawr, for example.

CHAPTER THREE

VASSAR BEFORE MacCRACKEN

NOBLE MacCRACKEN AND MARJORIE had made a courtesy call on James Taylor and his wife Kate on their way to the Vassar campus at the time of their first visit in December 1914. MacCracken had previously been introduced to "Prexy" Taylor once or twice when, as a student at New York University, he had come to Vassar to date a woman friend and attend a prom with her. The Taylors, who had left Vassar ten months earlier after twenty-eight years of pioneer service at the helm of the rapidly exploding college, were then living in New York City at the Hotel Gotham and enjoying their liberation from grueling academic duties.

Taylor, as "Prexy," had been the embodiment of Victorian Vassar, the head of the Vassar "family," in the days when women's colleges still undertook to substitute the authority of the president and the lady principal for that of parents. Taylor was the fourth Baptist minister to become president of Vassar College—the fifth if the Reverend J. Ryland Kendrick, acting president for a year (1885-86) is in the count. During his administration, the college had expanded, solidified, and grown in prestige. But in February 1913, Taylor, some-what out-of-phase with the times and under considerable pressure from faculty and students to open the way to change, had notified the Vassar trustees that he wished to retire on or before February 1914. He retired as he had stipulated.

✳   ✳   ✳

FOR SEVERAL YEARS before Taylor arrived at the college in 1886, Vassar had been in a state of decline, the reasons for which were complex, and Taylor had been elected to his position to get the college back to its prime condition. In this he had succeeded admirably.

John Raymond, the second Vassar president, had died on August 14, 1878. He had actually been president since the opening of the college, having been tapped from his position on the board to take over when Milo P. Jewett, Vassar's first president, resigned after indiscreetly insulting the founder, Matthew Vassar, in April 1864. Raymond immediately had to confront the mountainous organizational task of finding a system to implement Matthew Vassar's ideas about higher education for women. The task was formidable because the staff of forty and the student body of about 353 who presented themselves in September 1865 had only very inaccurate ideas of what to expect of a women's college and what it would be like when the college was under way.

There was no universal primary or secondary education for girls or young women in the United States when Vassar was founded. In fact, Poughkeepsie, New York, barely had a high school, and public education was not mandatory in New York State—nor was it in many parts of the country. Even classifying the students caused great perplexities for the faculty and the largely unprepared administration since there were no precedents. Although the announced age requirement for candidates was that they should have reached their fifteenth birthdays, some of the women who came were in their twenties and had already taught school themselves, while others were fifteen or so and could have been the older women's pupils. One was a Civil War widow. On the other hand, many had been only superficially prepared by tutors in time borrowed from the preparation of their brothers for mens' colleges. Many of the young women could not meet the simplest standards in grammar, spelling, rhetoric, and mathematics.

Raymond had rapidly discovered that it would be necessary to start a preparatory division to bridge the gap between the inadequate previous preparation of these first students and the assumed threshold for proficiency in freshman work, if the work offered were to equal the level of attainment in the men's colleges, which was Matthew Vassar's announced goal in starting the college. In fact, it took two years before most of the original students could even be classified. The first graduating class of only four students took their degrees in 1867.

Many of the young women came to college, furthermore, not knowing what to expect of a college education, and believing in some cases that they would stay only for one year to get a taste of it. Others came with insufficient funds, since there were no scholarship grants in the earliest years to help cover the $300 yearly fee. One young woman, Laura Brownell, came to Vassar in the early 1870s from East Williston, Vermont, intending to stay for one year. (She had already been a teacher in a one-room schoolhouse at age thirteen.) She found it possible to get started on a scholarly career through the intercession of the head of the department of English and rhetoric, Truman Backus, with the wealthy patron William Thaw in Pittsburgh, who agreed to support her and some of the other students who were worthy. That young woman turned out to be the first Vassar student upon graduation to attend the extension courses, open to women, at the free university of Berlin, as graduate courses were not open to women in the United States.

Mary Whitney, a Vassar undergraduate in the Raymond years and later Vassar's astronomy professor, recalled from her early days "a struggle to keep up the standard of Vassar to a fairly collegiate level, against the unfortunate opinions prevailing in the public mind and against the pressing pecuniary needs of the time [right after the Civil War]. The curriculum was very scanty then, as the catalogues showed, and it was the character of the early professors [nine of them, two of whom were women] and teachers [about twenty women, who also doubled as corridor-mistresses] that built up the early Vassar more than a definitely formed policy of education."

Raymond died suddenly in August 1878. Following his death, Samuel L. Caldwell, a trustee board member, who was a graduate of Waterville College (later Colby College) and a professor of church history at the Newton Theological Seminary, was elected president of Vassar on September 12, 1878. He had no special qualifications for the job other than being a teacher, and he was a rather feckless administrator. After he took over, the affairs of Vassar went downhill for several reasons, chiefly, apparently, a lack of qualified students. Caldwell, a studious and mild-mannered man, did nothing to intervene or stem the tide of further deterioration.

The national competition for students was strong during these years as more women's colleges came into the field. Smith and Wellesley were each founded in 1875 and graduated their first students in 1879, not seeming to need to start a preparatory division as Vassar had done, either because the students were better prepared or resources were better managed. (Barnard and Mt. Holyoke, formerly Mary Lyon Seminary, came along in 1889, and Harvard's annex Radcliffe began to offer extension courses to women in 1893.) Coeducational opportunities for women's undergraduate work were also increasingly abundant and available at places like the University of Vermont, Cornell University, Oberlin College, and Antioch College. Even the Massachusetts Institute of Technology was admitting women to its studies in science and technology, under the aegis of Ellen Swallow Richards, who graduated from Vassar in 1870 and opened up that men's college to women. Vassar, the pioneer, seemed to be left behind. This turn of events worried the Vassar alumnae.

The graduates of the college who had first organized themselves as the Associate Alumnae in 1871 had taken some steps immediately thereafter to try to gain representation on the all-male board of trustees. They formed their first committee to work on achieving this goal. Encouraged by Maria Mitchell, Vassar's professor of astronomy (who was also head of the national Association for the Advancement of Women about the time Raymond died), and others, they maneuvered for a while behind the scenes. During the early eighties, prompted by their concerns about the college's decline, they formed an official visiting team to investigate what was happening. Caldwell and the trustees neither encouraged nor interfered with them. In April 1884, indicating their deep anxiety about Vassar's increasing loss of edge, they addressed a "circular letter" to each one of the twenty-eight trustees. (The Vassar Library has the copy that was sent to John Guy Vassar Jr., Matthew Vassar's nephew, who was a trustee.):

Dear Sir:

The undersigned, Alumnae of Vassar College, would respectfully ask your attention to the following statement:

We have long hesitated to present it, and but for the late action of the Alumnae of New York, it might now be withheld. Since, however, certain questions and assertions proceeding from them have shown us that other Alumnae share our fears for the future of Vassar College, we believe silence to be no longer consistent with our loyalty to Alma Mater. During the past year, we have endeavored to look at the facts herewith presented from every point of view. If we have failed, it has been from no lack of earnest effort among us, to solve the problem before us. The evidence which we have examined, and the conclusions it has forced upon us, have led us gradually to what is now a firm conviction. We believe that only immediate action on the part of the Trustees can make it possible for Vassar to hold that place of honor among Colleges for women of which we, as her Alumnae, have justly been so proud. . . .

They had unearthed statistics which alarmed them:

In the year 1871 & 2, there were four hundred and fifteen (415) students at Vassar; of these, two hundred and five (205) were members of Collegiate classes. Since then, the number has been gradually decreasing, until in 1883-4, there are but three hundred (300) students, and only one hundred and forty-seven (147) of these Collegiate students. The Alumnae have watched this diminution of members with increasing anxiety. It has now reached a point, where it seems to them impossible for the College to maintain the high rank which she once held, with such a shrinkage in numbers as the chief element in the regulation of her affairs.

It can no longer be accounted a result of temporary conditions, as we were, for a time, led to hope. Financial circumstances make it painfully obvious, that unless something can be done immediately to increase the number of Collegiate students, or to supply the lack with large endowments, Vassar must fall behind her competitors in the quality of her instruction, the variety of her material equipment, in all that marks the growth of a College.

These women saw a paramount problem in the continued admission not only of preparatory students, but also of others who were coming just to take a single course in art (painting, under Professor Henry Van Ingen) or music (piano or voice lessons). The number of art students had increased by 300 percent in the previous six years. This encroachment of courses offering "accomplishments" rather than real liberal arts fare should have no place, the women believed, in a college trying to stay in the running with the men's colleges.

The alumnae had canvassed the college community and the graduates as to what they thought about the Vassar education, and then analyzed the alleged causes of the decline: too many colleges, the supply exceeding the demand; too high expenses at Vassar; location of Vassar in a larger community where "the public sentiment towards education" was not favorable; and Vassar's severe entrance examinations. Having examined each one of these reasons and rejected it, the alumnae decided that management was to blame, that is—President Caldwell, and before him, perhaps Raymond.

> *In looking back over the past six years, we fail to see indications of any constructive progressive policy on the part of the administration or signs of effort in any direction to widen the influence, and thereby increase the prosperity of the College, and it is, therefore, to this lack of executive efficiency that we reluctantly ascribe the declining strength of Vassar as a College. . . . the policy of inactivity is suicidal.*

In short, the alumnae thought the college needed a more competent president who could turn conditions around. They shook the trustees up so sharply with their concerns that Caldwell was asked to resign in 1885, and he did so, on June 8. At that juncture, the Rev. J. Ryland Kendrick, trustee from 1875 to 1889 as well as pastor of the First Baptist Church in Poughkeepsie, was named acting president until a suitable successor to Caldwell could be found. The successor was Taylor, and although he had had no academic experience, he had plenty of administrative talent, apparently derived from his years of catering to parishioners. Before he was chosen president, he had most recently been pastor of the Fourth Baptist Church in Providence, Rhode Island.

The college breathed a collective sigh of relief when he was inaugurated. As his first step, at the request of the Alumnae Association, Taylor recommended to his board the election of three alumnae trustees. The addition of these women to the Vassar board constituted a watershed in the affairs of trustees across the country and, in Vassar's case, was to result in many future changes, not the least of which would be saving MacCracken from early dismissal. The power shifted only gradually within the board. But the women were, on the whole, more interested in educational policies, issues, and new directions than were the businessmen and the clergymen.

Taylor's second step was also a first: he instituted a curriculum committee of the faculty, which should begin to think about the college's educational policy as a whole. His most important goal was the immediate jacking up of academic standards.

"For the first time in the history of the College it opened, in September 1888, without any preparatory students," Taylor reported that fall. The previous spring he had told the trustees in his annual report:

*The educational world is in ferment; high schools are con-
fused with colleges, colleges with universities... Vassar College
has some peculiar obstacles to meet. Largely through the comments of the newspapers, sensational and jocular, and seldom
treating the subject with seriousness—the sentiment has been
spread far more widely than some of us suspect, that the so-
called "Vassar girl" is frivolous, fashionable, radical in social
type, and but little given to the sober work of a college life.*

The college expanded physically and economically, as well as educationally, under Taylor's administration. Many new buildings were
built, some money was raised, and relations were improved with
secondary schools and with other colleges. He strengthened the college
in other ways. Scholarships were established and graduate work was
offered, chiefly to make possible further training for women who
wanted to go into the professions, especially the profession of
teaching. Before the 1890s the universities had not opened their doors
to women for graduate work, but in the 1890s several did so, including
Yale University and the University of Chicago (which was conceived
on the Vassar campus in 1888, when Taylor arranged a meeting
between the guest Sunday preacher from Yale, W.R. Harper, and John
D. Rockefeller, a Vassar trustee). Under Taylor the quality of the
faculty was strengthened, the library was vastly enlarged, the departmental structure of the college grew more complex, and the original
nine departments of the college broke up into more specialized
disciplines. By the time Taylor retired, history (first), economics, psychology, political science, religion, and sociology had all been added,
sciences had multiplied, and many new courses had augmented the
curriculum.

Had late twentieth-century headhunters been drafting a job
description of Taylor's duties, they would have mentioned that the
presidency involved not only overall administration of the affairs of
the college, but also (until 1897): personal and family residence in
the Main Building of the college in the presidential suite; most,
although not all, of the responsibility for assigning faculty to teaching
duties; a professorship of ethics and moral philosophy which went
with the job and required the incumbent to teach those subjects to
the senior class; and responsibility for all public relations, admissions,
records, and business transactions of the college. In addition, the
president wrote much of the college correspondence in his own hand,

toured high schools and colleges, visited alumnae, and "called on rich men to beg funds."

Taylor, embodying all those accomplishments, was a *pater familias* who mixed with students in a grandfatherly way as he figure-skated on Vassar Lake; entertained students at charades; and gave serious, sometimes boring, and almost always too-lengthy talks, which the students were required to listen and respond to in chapel. Together with the lady principal, who supervised decorum and arranged for the physical accommodations of the students, and with the resident faculty members, the president created a residential environment in which the students felt alternately at home and repressed by the control exercised over student life through an overload of rules and regulations.

There was a one hundred percent turnaround in admissions by the time Taylor was ready to retire from the presidency. To take care of the new demand for admissions in his later days—by 1910 a top limit of 1000 capped enrollment—Taylor raised the money for six residence halls and persuaded John D. Rockefeller to give the college funds for the sorely needed office and classroom space.

Even though he was a rather cut-and-dried teacher himself and the students were bored in his ethics classes and with his sermons, Taylor had a gift of identifying good teachers, among them some with really revolutionary ideas about the profession and methodology of teaching. One of those was Laura Johnson Wylie, who, in 1894, with a Yale Ph.D. in hand, came back as chairperson to the department of English in which she had done her undergraduate work, graduating in 1877. Her mission was to professionalize the department and modernize the concepts and practice in the field of English. She believed that the instructor carried out an integral part of her work in a laboratory just as the scientist did. In the case of the humanities, however, the office was the laboratory, and the teacher and the student made individual contact in the office while deliberating over a composition that the student presented for consideration. This basic and simple face-to-face relationship, as MacCracken later pointed out, formed the basis of training for generations of Vassar writers such as Margaret Culkin Banning, Constance Rourke, Edna St. Vincent Millay, Mary Mc-Carthy, Elizabeth Bishop, Eleanor Clark, and others.

Margaret Floy Washburn, Vassar 1891, in psychology, which began as a separate discipline at Vassar in 1904, introduced students to developmental psychology in the laboratory which she created, where she designed experiments, invented equipment to implement them, and taught her students to do the same. Her book, *The Animal Mind*, was one of the first textbooks in the field of developmental psychology.

These and other professors, both men and women, experimented with their own philosophies of teaching and organized their curriculum within the departmental structures introduced by Taylor. He, however, increasingly resisted the free-ranging and progressive directions that the new teaching was taking in some departments and was uncomfortable with the times. Like the students, many of the faculty were no longer contented to stay in the ivory tower and maintain the status-quo. They wanted themselves to connect with the outside world, and they wanted their students to experience life outside the campus gates.

Nowhere were these developing limitations of Taylor's leadership and his paternalistic ideas about education as evident as in his dealings with Lucy Maynard Salmon, whom he invited in 1887 to come to Vassar and form a history department. Benson Lossing, the historian trustee of the college, a man who knew the field of history very well, apparently guided Taylor in the direction of Salmon. She came from the University of Michigan to Vassar by way of Bryn Mawr College. Salmon sent her students to primary sources to learn history, including places outside the Vassar campus: she rarely used textbooks and believed that personal observation and experience were as important as conventional authorities in print. Her classroom was informal and unconventional, but rigorous—a seminar to which each student was forced to make a contribution. She constantly demanded that Taylor supply the library with more and more books—not textbooks, but original sources. She very quickly became an irritant, and he did not approve of her methods once he began to understand them.

In 1890 economics had been introduced into the Vassar curriculum as a subdivision of history, with Herbert Mills in charge. Salmon fiercely contested this addition, and her enmity with Mills lasted into the future, far past 1893 when Taylor split off the economics department from the history department to solve the problem. Now Taylor, again trying to conspire to get around Salmon, introduced another factor. In 1897 he had hired as an instructor to teach in Salmon's department James Baldwin, with a fresh Ph.D. in European history from Harvard. Baldwin had been favorably urged on the president by Augustus Strong of the Rochester Divinity School, a

trustee of Vassar, whose son Charles would marry John D. Rockefeller's daughter Bessie. A more traditional historian, Baldwin was a
determined advocate of teaching history through the old-fashioned
authoritarian dissemination of facts and dates: a method pedagogically
far removed from that of Salmon. Baldwin was promoted to the
position of associate professor at a salary of $1500 at the June 9,
1903, board of trustees meeting. With the apparent cooperation of
Taylor and possibly even at his suggestion, Baldwin moved thereafter
to oust Salmon from the chairmanship of the history department, an
effort that failed. The incident is instructive in demonstrating the
indirection and secretiveness characteristic of the college administration in those years, as well as underlining the conservatism of Taylor's
views about education and the losing battles he was fighting against a
rising tide of academic freedom.

In 1905, two years after Baldwin's promotion, Taylor, as a reward
for almost twenty years of undiminished service to the college, was
granted a one-year leave of absence from his administrative duties
commencing at the end of that academic year. Behind the scenes,
Baldwin approached Taylor before he left and asked to be put permanently in charge of all the work in European history, leaving
Professor Salmon to deal with American history. Taylor agreed to this,
did not mention it to Salmon, and left for Europe. As soon as Salmon
got wind of this secret arrangement, she wrote a letter to her woman
trustee friend Helen Hadley, with a copy to Taylor, expressing her
consternation and saying that the move had been made entirely
without her knowledge. She pointed out that before he left, Taylor
had asked the faculty not to take any radical steps during his absence,
and that *she* had scrupulously observed this request. She "didn't make
any recommendations in regard to the conduct of the department and
it could scarcely have been anticipated that so revolutionary a propo-
sition would under the circumstances be made."

Salmon explained that she sought information from the secretary
of the college, Ella McCaleb, who was in on the secret and who
informed her "that the reasons have been a desire to promote unity in
the department, to emphasize the fact side of history... rather than
that of method of work, and to give greater opportunity and responsibility to Associate Professor Baldwin..." In rebutting these arguments
the outraged Salmon stated that if the department lacked unity, the
proposed remedy would destroy it, not unify it:

Were the growth of a department a mere matter of accumulating additional courses and a larger number of students, courses and students could be lopped off at pleasure and the instructors shifted at will. But on the contrary, an organic relationship exists, or ought to exist, between all parts of the Department. It is this organic relationship that the division proposed would destroy. The Department is artificially dissected and all germs of vitality and growth eradicated. A tree divided does not become two trees, but it ceases to be even one.

Other colleges, Salmon admitted—especially older ones—had "separate departments of European and American history, but this arrangement has often been due to accident rather than to a deliberate educational policy... and... some of our foremost colleges are combining their courses in European and American history and are insisting on the theory and practice of unity in the teaching of history." It had been Salmon's plan for the Vassar history department from the moment she became professor that such unity be attained. Salmon had a basic quarrel with the idea that the "fact side" of history should be emphasized over "methods." She suggested in her letter to Hadley :

... it is a 'fact' already familiar to scholars that the modern development of historical study has been distinctly in the direction of emphasizing methods of work... and... the students have been constantly encouraged to work out for themselves satisfactory methods of individual work with the view of making them independent and self reliant, of enabling them to collect and prepare material of an historical character whenever the public or private use for it might arise.

Salmon indicated to Hadley that she was ready to give greater opportunity and responsibility to Baldwin, but she certainly didn't agree with the proposals of the intruding trustee committee. One solution which she had thought might be acceptable to all would be to relieve Baldwin of the required courses in history and let him develop more electives. This she had proposed to him in an attempt to respond to the situation, but he refused to do anything until the president's return. When Baldwin refused to cooperate with Salmon, she decided to take an aggressive stand and appeal to her friend Hadley.

Later, on March 6, Salmon wrote to Hadley again saying that she had shared her problem with Laura Wylie. (Wylie and Salmon supported each other in many ways during this period, especially with reference to the issues of suffrage which Taylor was trying to keep under tight rein.) On March 10, Salmon mailed off to each trustee a copy of her letter to Hadley and indicated that there was an alumnae petition in the works which would seek to have Salmon retained as head of the department of history and to have no one advanced to equal rank with her.

The crisis then percolated. On April 2, the alumna trustee, Heloise Hersey, who was a member of the trustee faculty and studies committee, wrote Hadley to pronounce emphatically that the committee was not going to "rescind a deliberate action" just because Miss Salmon had begun to work up the alumnae. Hersey told Hadley that Taylor "greatly desired the division" and "doubtless hoped it might be achieved in his absence." Miss Salmon's resignation, she said, would certainly not be requested. "But if it should come, it would remove one of the most difficult and perplexing problems with which the President has had to deal. What he has suffered at her hands it would be hard to put in a folio! Moreover, she throws more and more emphasis on the teaching of the method of studying history, at the expense of the study of history." Convinced that Baldwin was one of the strongest teachers ever to teach at Vassar College, Hersey said that his teaching was "alive," "spirited," "vigorous," and "entirely free" from that "cut and dried midnight-oil quality so objectionable in the teaching of Miss Salmon, Miss Ellery, Miss Buck, and various others..." (Hersey went on to admit that "Baldwin antagonizes men, Dr. Taylor among them...He is arrogant and insistent. But, it seems to me good for these girls to meet arrogance for once in the balmy and 'talky' atmosphere of the feminine.")

Hadley, obviously not in agreement with Hersey, went her own way, which was to consult historians at Yale University. From what she heard, she concluded that Baldwin was on the wrong track. Trustee Strong subsequently wrote Hadley with the reminder that when Salmon had been on leave "young Mr. Baldwin had begun his instruction as her assistant. ...When she came back from Europe ...he had a greater following than she had, and his electives were chosen in preference to hers." Then *he* went to Europe for a year and *she* sought to "regain lost ground by making arrangements which would hamper him on his return." Commenting on Salmon's style,

Strong said "... she is one of those persons who enjoys everything but the one thing the Lord set her to do. She gave herself two years to investigate the problem of domestic science. Then for two years she was abroad looking up the various methods of teaching history in lycées and gymnasiums. The pedagogical aspect of her work interests her far more than the work itself." He thought that a division between American and European history was bound to come and that it ought to come sooner rather than later. Hadley responded that she recognized that an alumnae petition might be unwise, in that alumnae should not be dictating educational policy and challenging it, but she was convinced that Baldwin's teaching was not adequate. Strong responded in a subsequent exchange with her that "he does not pour water into the tub himself... he pumps it out. His pupils are made to do the work themselves." Hadley terminated her correspondence with Strong with her next letter, which contained a deleted passage saying that if Salmon were a man "she might bring suit against the college but since she was a woman, she has preferred to talk."

Taylor was back in 1907 but the matter still had not been put to rest. In fact, it was then more complex, because Taylor, pressured by the suffragists, asked Salmon to add political science to her courses in American history. "This I can not do," she wrote, "not only because I am quite unprepared to teach the theory of political science, but also because I have always believed that the development of the political system should be studied in connection with general historical development. Moreover," she added, "[t]hat history is a unity and cannot be divided has been one of my fundamental principles. That this unity should be expressed in a single headship would follow as a corollary."

The crisis ended with the board meeting. The trustee committee and the president decided against pressing matters any further about European history; Salmon remained chair of the department; Baldwin was promoted to a professorship and went on teaching in the department according to his lights; and the chair of Political Science, providing for the teaching of that subject in the curriculum, was not established until 1913, with Emerson D. Fite as first incumbent.

To his credit, in his last years as president, Taylor knew something was radically wrong. The institution's facilities were much too cramped for the number of people they served. He was so pressed for time keeping the place going that he could not give his attention to many of the reforms needed. In his annual report to the trustees for 1910, he spoke of the necessity for administrative reorganization and remarked that he thought the president's job should be redesigned. To avoid further drift, he thought the trustees should engage in a self-study and form a policy committee to establish written policy. One trustee committee didn't know what another trustee committee was up to, especially with regular meetings of the full board taking place only once a year and very few special meetings. Looking back on those times, the modern observer can see how much room there was for mis-understanding, when so many agreements were made privately and so little communication took place over important matters of interest common to certain groups in the community. It is no wonder that problems like the Salmon-Baldwin one developed in the absence of defined policy, causing resentment and hard feelings.

Towards the end, Taylor had several ideas that he never had time to explore or implement. He wanted to rid the sense of strain and intensity that seemed to have developed in Vassar's everyday com-munal life. His ideas for a new college were first presented in his commencement speech in June 1911 (in the twenty-sixth year of his presidency) and subsequently outlined and appraised in the edu-cational publication *Outlook* on July 1, 1911. The elaborate plan involved the establishment of a second group of buildings on the campus. Taylor felt that the problem of Vassar at that point was that the students' individual welfare was being neglected under the pressure of too large a student body. He wanted to return Vassar to what he called the (English) "college idea" (as distinct from the "university idea"). His thought was to build a secondary group of buildings that would accommodate 500 students, lodge half the student body in new separate residence halls, increase academic facilities, build a second chapel (the brand new endowed chapel had just been built in 1903), enlarge the library, and make it serve in common for all branches of the institution. There would be "one administration building, a common plant for heat, light, water-works and other utilities, so that the management of the college as a business could be made more efficient." Taylor further speculated that his design for a cluster-college would include an honors college, like Balliol at Oxford, where those who wished to concentrate on intellectual achievement and exclusive study would be encouraged to do so. In his *Outlook* article he wrote:

Suppose that we plan for 500 students at the beginning. Five fireproof residences ought to be comfortably built for $175,000 each; a chapel, according to its size and plainness—and here it would be well to build with a view to the accommodation of 1000, even if we should have but one college of 500, should cost from $100,000 to $150,000; a branch library ample for the general use of such an institution could be built for $175,000; the gymnasium would have to meet every necessity of the college and should have expended on it no less than $50,000; eight residences for professors and an apartment house might be built for $130,000; a power, heat, and light plant or the additions to a plant already established, might, with proper changes, be put in from $200,000 to $250,000.

Taylor stipulated that life in the second college would be identical with that in the first. There would be separate faculty, a separate social life, but intercommunications between the two colleges. Taylor ended his speculative plan by saying, "If I were ten years younger, I would try to realize this dream."

But he was not ten years younger, and the prospect of raising the some two million dollars that would have been necessary to bring about his dream college was one that he could not deal with in the midst of the growing opposition to his conservatism and the rapid cultural changes that were taking place as the great war gathered.

Taylor's attitude towards suffrage activities on campus during the period between 1905 and 1914 showed him to be increasingly out of step with the contemporary college woman of the immediate pre-World War I period. Among the causes that Taylor tried vainly to keep from the campus and that may have hastened his retirement was the movement for woman suffrage, which, especially among the faculty, became entangled with questions of academic freedom and self-governance. In a sense Taylor's vision of education for women was foredoomed in that women who chose to go to college had already departed from their traditional role, might be considering at least a career outside the home, and were likely to be susceptible to new ideas.

While Vassar students in Taylor's time were permitted to discuss controversial issues among themselves and topics of public interest in the student debate club, they were not allowed to establish a suffrage club. The faculty who were active in the cause had to go off campus, to the nearby Wagner Inn owned by an ardent suffragist who had studied at Vassar, or go downtown or into state and national organizations. When the Equal Suffrage League of Poughkeepsie was formed in 1910, many faculty were founding members, and Laura Wylie, who lived downtown, became its first president. Lucy Maynard Salmon in 1911 became a vice-president of the National College Equal Suffrage League, founded in 1908, the purpose of which was to put issues of suffrage before college faculty and students in college, and women college graduates. Ironically, she was constrained against the pursuit of the organization's objectives on her own campus. In 1907 Mary Whitney, of the Vassar astronomy department, sent Salmon money solicited for suffrage, but asked not to be associated with the cause on campus because of Taylor's "strong feeling of opposition."

President Taylor always insisted in public that he took no stand on the woman suffrage question, though in a private letter to M. Carey Thomas, president of Bryn Mawr in 1907, he admitted that he was against any extension of suffrage for men or women. His letter to Thomas was a response to one from her asking if Jane Addams, head of Hull House in Chicago, might come and speak at Vassar on the working woman's need of the ballot. He declined, saying that such a speech would be "propaganda" rather than education, and that he could not agree to any propaganda on the campus "in regard to socialistic matters . . . questionable forms of missionary effort, and extreme temperance agitators, as well as regarding this question of suffrage." Thomas, incredulous, followed up her first communication with word that Addams had been invited to Mount Holyoke, Radcliffe, Smith, and Wellesley, as well as Bryn Mawr, and she couldn't believe that Taylor hadn't misunderstood her. But he hadn't, and he didn't relent. In February 1908, a Vassar alumna doctor in San Diego who had graduated in 1877 wrote that it did not seem possible to her that anyone heading an institution of learning could have such an attitude. In her time at Vassar they had had Mary Livermore and Julia Ward Howe, and no one had suffered any ill effects from exposure.

On campus, warming interest in the suffrage cause came suddenly to a boil, the flame applied by the irrepressible undergraduate named Inez Milholland, whose family had a home in London, where she had come under the spell of the militant Pankhursts and had taken part in the same suffrage campaign there during the summer of 1909 that motivated the MacCrackens to become suffragists.

Handsome, compelling, and audacious, Milholland enjoyed enormous popularity among her Vassar schoolmates, whom she undertook, with great success, to convert to suffrage and socialism. In June 1908, while the Vassar alumnae were back on campus for reunions, she invited Charlotte Perkins Gilman, Harriot Stanton Blatch, Rose Schneiderman, and Helen Hoy to speak on the suffrage issue. The meeting was conducted in the cemetery directly across the street from the college, a place chosen to draw conspicuous attention to the fact that it was *not* being held on campus. The "graveyard rally," as it came to be called, was attended by about forty students and others and was reported in the New York newspapers, garnering exactly the sort of publicity that President Taylor most deplored.

In March of the following year, Inez Milholland, now a senior, again made arrangements for a debate at Vassar about suffrage, this time taking a poll of objections at a meeting in a college lecture hall. Milholland had gained permission from a college official to use the room, and had spoken to President Taylor, who had given permission for the meeting to be held on condition that no outsiders were to be involved and that faculty members were not to be speakers. It appears that a genuine misunderstanding occurred and faculty members did speak. Taylor was away from the campus the day of the meeting, but was greatly angered when he later heard a report of it. At a stormy faculty meeting on March 22, 1909, he accused participating faculty of flouting his policy against official discussion of controversial issues on campus and was answered sharply by several who pointed out that he had opened himself to the charge of attempting to curtail freedom of speech. In the aftermath of the meeting, Taylor sent a circular letter stating his views to participants in the discussion and received a number of replies, one from Mary Whitney of the astronomy department, who put her finger on the central issue:

> *I am afraid that if we do not come to a clear understanding of the difference between propagandism and freedom of discussion . . . rumors of repression will get abroad . . . Suppose in this unfortunate case, the instructors when asked had said, "The policy of the college forbids my speaking." The result that has so disturbed you would have been avoided, but a far greater danger in my opinion would have been incurred.*

She was troubled, as were many others that day, by the threat to freedom of speech.

On Saturday, March 20, the evening after the suffrage debate, Taylor called the student body to the chapel and spoke to them on the subject of reform movements and for the next month or so answered queries and challenges of faculty members who approached him individually. The aim of his policy, he told professor of Greek Abby Leach, in a letter of March 23, was to "encourage as serene a life as possible in college." Order had not quite been restored, however. On May 9, *The New York Times* gleefully reported that in the wake of Taylor's open discussion of suffrage on the Vassar campus, a mysterious invitation had gone out to students to come to a certain dormitory room at an appointed hour of the day. Hundreds showed up to be conducted in a long procession through a series of rooms in each of which was staged a living tableau illustrating an argument for suffrage. The Prosperean conjurer behind this display was whispered to be Inez Milholland.

Among the faculty, too, matters were coming to a head. In December 1912, thirteen faculty members drew up a resolution criticizing President Taylor and the board of trustees for their decision-making procedure. In it they expressed the view that the faculty should be allowed to make decisions about matters relating to campus life. This protest was occasioned by the failure of Taylor and the board to consult the faculty concerning a reorganization of the system of advising on campus. The names of faculty who had been active in the suffrage movement were prominent among the signatures on the resolution. Taylor considered that his methods were being "impeached" on all sides, and two months later, he gave notice to the board that he intended to resign as president within one year. He gave as his reason that after forty years of service, twenty-seven of them at Vassar, he was tired of administration and, at age sixty-five, ready to retire.

Vassar was now ready to swing wide the half-open gates to the modern age, and MacCracken would soon be waiting offstage for his entrance.

❋   ❋   ❋

INEZ MILHOLLAND
IN A SUFFRAGE PARADE IN NEW YORK CITY.

TAYLOR IN RETROSPECT:
"THE LARGER LIFE AT VASSAR"

GLADYS E. HULL HOPKINS, 1913.
(July 3, 1981.)

President Taylor was a charming man, capable, a free thinker.
(Mrs. Hopkins's class changed things socially. They went
into the common dining room and sat wherever they liked.
They overthrew the custom of sitting with the same group
of people, which had created cliques. There was no opposition to their changes from anyone.)

We all loved President Taylor. I say "all." I don't know
anyone who didn't. We all thought he was the most charming
man and very capable. And of course, he believed very much in
religion and ethics. I suppose now he'd be called maybe a con-
servative, but he wasn't for that day. We liked him very much.
All the seniors had to take ethics, and we lived in fear of being
called on, which he did once for all of us. A very fine thinker and
kindly man.

SYLVIA WOODWORTH HEATH, 1916.
President of the Suffrage Club, 1915,
the first year one was sanctioned.
(March 2, 1981.)

Henry Noble MacCracken wasn't particularly encouraging but
he allowed students to hold suffrage meetings as Taylor didn't.

FRANCES A. PLEUS, 1916.
(February 23, 1981.)

There was a direct contrast between Taylor and MacCracken.
Taylor had memorized names, tried to make a point of knowing
who you were. Taylor was fatherly, MacCracken was an educator.

HILDA TAIT HALL, 1907.
(July 16, 1981.)

Taylor was a lovable person. Understanding. He and his wife had
groups of students to dinner in 1907 and played games after-
wards.

IRMA WATERHOUSE HEWLETT, 1914.
(October 31, 1980.)

I didn't feel comfortable with Taylor: there was a rigidity about him. He had strong conservative ideas about propaganda. I didn't follow his lead very much. I wouldn't have chosen him. Many people felt Vassar was too rigid [under JMT]. It was ready for Henry Noble MacCracken.

KATHERINE FORBES ERSKINE, 1911.
(December 17, 1988.)

President Taylor was very friendly when walking around campus. He was not a 'great man.' He taught the ethics course in which there was no discussion, no questions. He was against suffrage. Inez Milholland organized an evening in which they put on tableaux in a girl's room. (It was a takeoff around the idea that woman's place was in the home and a voting booth was no place for a woman: both Taylor's sentiments.)

LUCY LOVELL, 1912.
(December 12, 1980.)

I just loved Dr. Taylor. He compared the students to girls he had known when young. "Those girls played with you."

I was in a pageant senior year, an act from David Copperfield. *Elizabeth Kittredge was David. I was Dora. I borrowed a dog. I lived in Raymond [one of the dormitories.] I was coming back whistling after rehearsal. Dr. Taylor stopped when he saw me coming along, and we talked. "Why are you whistling? Keeping up your courage?"*

I was in the library and there was a card catalogue near the fireplace. He came in and made an opportunity to talk with me. He made an effort to know different students.

MARGARET LOVELL, 1915.
(December 12, 1980.)

There was a storm of applause when Taylor spoke at Mac-Cracken's inauguration. MacCracken's comment was: "What can he do that follows the king?"

PRESIDENT JAMES MONROE TAYLOR AND
PRESIDENT HENRY NOBLE MACCRACKEN
AT MACCRACKEN'S INAUGURATION.

GABRIELLA FORBUSH, 1912.
President of the Class of 1912.
(February 15, 1981.)

Taylor was very strict. You stayed away from him as much as you could. His ethics course was dry-as-dust and we had to learn by memory. Taylor was an old-fashioned school-teacher type. I kept away from the overlords as much as I could.

Suffrage was my first serious cause. Dr. Taylor was scornful about the new fad of social service. Just nursing and teaching were acceptable to him. He sneered about social service.

MARGARET TAYLOR, 1923.
Granddaughter of James Monroe Taylor.
(October 26, 1980.)

My grandfather was extraordinarily sought after, genial, fun to be with, a family man. He was a person of enormous charm. The faculty were devoted to him.

I heard afterward that there were alumnae who felt he was too conservative. In the course of looking over his letters before giving pertinent ones to the college, I noted that he stated no one ever asked him whether he believed in suffrage or not; they just took it for granted that he was against it. He was quite clear that he did not believe contemporary issues were the proper concern of under-graduates.

He was short, stocky, vigorous. He skated a lot and walked a lot. He really liked people . . . he enjoyed everybody. His wife Kate Huntington went to Vassar. She was in '70 or '71. [She was '70, Spec.]

MARY CONNELL BRAY, 1912.
(Note to her classmates at 70th reunion, 1982.)

President Taylor and my father were friends. He was a Republican, my father Richard Connell, editor of the Democratic daily newspaper The Poughkeepsie News Press. *Dr. Taylor often dropped into his office, next to the printing press, to chat with him.*

My father used to say to me when I was in school: "Dr. Taylor's always talking about 'The Larger Life' for his Vassar girls. I want you to go there to get it." So I did, as you have done. We received from 1908 to 1912 inexhaustible resources for meeting the experiences of life with that "Larger Life."

GRACE STROEBEL KERN, 1909.
(March 6, 1981.)

It was the Depression of 1907 when I went to college. President Taylor talked about staying calm. ... When I went to college, I had an allowance. When my brother went to college, Father gave him a checkbook.

*   *   *

MacCRACKEN IN PROSPECT

WHEN TAYLOR DIED in 1917, the trustee memorial minutes summed up his career, saying, "His ministry to Vassar College was finally rounded out." The use of the word "ministry" marks the end of an era. The relations of Taylor to the board, as the trustee minutes said, were so simple and direct that "not many words were needed to describe them. ... The college never had a rival in Taylor's affection." How different would be the new regime of the young, ambitious MacCracken, who was not going to regard his presidency as a ministry, but rather as an opportunity to push women's education forward over new thresholds.

He was a modernizer. His conception of the world that women would enter in the second and third decades of the twentieth century looked forward to change and experimentation, professionalization, scientific management of households and community affairs, ever-enlarging tolerance, and, above all, increased experience. Unlike Taylor's single passion, the college he was to preside over had many rivals in MacCracken's worldscape.

There were many catalysts for change in MacCracken's early years at Vassar: the suffrage movement; the sudden impact of World War I; the shifting professional expectations of women, especially in teaching and social work; the seriousness of the challenge of social and community problems; the new internationalism; the peace movement; the rise of Eastern European countries like Czechoslovakia and Poland; and the impact of the Russian revolution. Furthermore, there were the inventions of technology—the pervasive changes brought about by the motor car, the telephone, the radio, moving pictures, and the availability of electricity. (The campus was electrified in 1912.) The push in the universities for academic freedom and professionalization of faculties—all these were clear signals that the ivory tower was being evacuated.

MacCracken saw his field in 1914 as one in which organic development could take place: his notion of a college was not of a place in which the administration and faculty "ministered to students," but rather one in which the students took control of their education, directed themselves towards their own goals, and ministered to society. In fact, with a dramatic flourish MacCracken called attention to his new attitudes in the first official meeting which he held as president of the college. He invited into his office the day after his inauguration in October 1915, the presidents of the three oldest sister colleges— Smith, Wellesley, and Mt. Holyoke—and initiated a collaboration which was to result in the changed college admission procedures which heralded the new age and were soon adopted in all four colleges, a move which shifted admissions from a first-come, first-served basis to a competitive one, where the quality of one's work really counted.

This calling of a conference to define and solve a problem was a basic building block in MacCracken's administration, and it constituted the first of many new modes of communication used by this man of many voices.

✳   ✳   ✳

MACCRACKEN, June 21, 1932, TO JOSEPHINE GLEASON (Vassar, 1914), Chairman of Committee on Admission:

> *When I came to Vassar, I found everywhere throughout the college an attitude towards students as though they were inmates of a corrective institution of some kind. Part of the attitude came from authorities, whose experience had started in schools, and part of it came from the General Manager who had been the steward of the insane asylum before his post at Vassar. You could not imagine how difficult it was to remove the attitude from our staff and to inculcate the idea that our students were our patrons and that we were in the position of endeavoring to retain their good-will.*

CHAPTER FOUR

"CIRCLE '80" AND "THE RAYMOND CONTROVERSY"

MacCracken was very soon linked imaginatively with Vassar's pre-Taylor past, and the organic development of the college connected with this past as well as with the future. He had not been long on the contemporary Vassar stage before he had developed a speaking familiarity with the philosophies, attitudes, and characteristic actions of the noteworthy actors of the past and their voices. He was at once curious to discover the nature of the drama that had already been played out and see what sort of a role was suggested for him.

The college had been functioning for fifty years when MacCracken took the helm, and the returning early alumnae as well as the older people still resident in the Vassar community could tell him stories of Victorian Vassar. He soon built up for himself a bountiful and convenient supply of reference points in the past. The nineteenth century Vassar that he recreated for himself located a pivotal tension between clashing educational forces and attitudes at work: the active and the passive; the liberal and the repressive; the encouragement given by some for the energetic pursuit of education through self-testing, self-knowledge, self-reliance, and experience; and the insulation and protection from experience and self-reliance pressed into rules by those in control of the system.

First of all, there was Matthew Vassar, the iconoclastic brewer and founding father who believed that women should no longer be relegated to the legal status of "idiots" as they were in his time. Quoting the title of a lecture given by Anna Dickinson, suffragist, at the college on April 25, 1868, Vassar wrote in a letter three days later to Elizabeth Powell, a Vassar physical education instructor:

*The subject of "Womans Suffrage" or "Idiots and Women"
was correctly quoted from the laws granting the right of them to
the ballot Box, and when I first read the Law some years ago I
was equaly supprised to find our Fair Sex placed in so shamefull
a category as 'criminals, paupers, Idiots &c,' which if the Law
was right by this classification I think it is full time my 300
daughters at 'Vassar' knew it, and applied the remidy.*

On the founder's side of the stage, also, were freethinking Maria
Mitchell, "the American George Sand," the most eminent woman
scientist of the nineteenth century, chosen first by Vassar to head the
list of nine professors invited to take a place on the faculty (the rest of
the professors, except one, were males), and certain early students,
such as Ellen Swallow Richards, 1870, and Harriot Stanton Blatch,
1888. This group of liberated and unconventional young women, the
spiritual daughters of Maria Mitchell, he referred to collectively as
"Circle '80," a tag to signify the high summer of Mitchell's career at
Vassar, which lasted from 1865 to 1888. Added to these were one or
two enlightened male trustees—notably Benson Lossing, an early
feminist and respected historian, who chronicled the Civil War while
travelling from battleground to battleground to collect oral testimony,
and who helped Mitchell in her fight to get the same pay for herself
and her one woman colleague, Dr. Alida Avery, as the male professors.
MacCracken was rather partial, too, to "Uncle Fred"—Frederick Ferris
Thompson—a wealthy trustee from Canandaigua, New York, who
liked to provide the students with outings, such as a yearly trip on the
Hudson River dayliner, and who was referred to delightedly by the
students as "the goodtimes trustee." He thought part of college should
be getting out, playing, and expressing enjoyment, and MacCracken
agreed with him.

On the other side of MacCracken's vivid mental stage were the
Baptist clergymen and well-placed businessmen who nominally ran the
place. There were fourteen clergymen and fourteen businessmen on
the original board to provide the early presidents with their rather
conservative support. Some of them, like Vassar's nephew ward—
Matthew Vassar Jr.—did not believe strongly in educating women, but
once the founder was committed, they tried to help make Vassar a
viable institution. Joining the trustees in MacCracken's roster were
other establishment figures from the early years, such as Hannah
Lyman, the first lady principal, who developed the elaborate safe-

guarding rules cloistering the campus and supervising the students; the original women "teachers," who doubled as housemothers; and the matron and other members of the housekeeping department. Mac-Cracken pegged the dramatic scenario that played out in his mind between these forces as "The Raymond Controversy."

MacCracken's drama, which he envisioned as clearly as if he had been part of the crowd on stage in the 1880s, saw Maria Mitchell as an activist who lived an integrated life embracing three worlds: the world of research, the world of reform, and the world of teaching. She came from Nantucket to teach at Vassar Female College because, like Vassar himself, she believed in the mental capacities of women to educate themselves in the most liberal ways. Denying the Victorian notion of women as domestic "angels in the house," she believed that meaningful education was active and experiential. She introduced to the college the idea of life as a laboratory, and in all of her teaching, she forced self-reliance on her students. Her instruction did not stop in the classroom or in the nightly observations of Saturn or Venus in the dome of the Observatory, to which she summoned the students out of their chaperoned gaslighted rooms in Main Building, against the wishes of the lady principal. In 1869 she took seven of her students or former students from Poughkeepsie to Burlington, Iowa, by train to witness the total eclipse of the sun. They duly recorded their observations, which were thereafter printed in a government geodetic bulletin, and they knew they were not only living in history and recording it, but making it.

MacCracken stepped on to the same stage. It was so real to him after a while that he could reach out and touch the past and pull it in to the present. But he would not dwell on the past and regret its loss. Nor would he feel superior to it. Rather, he would embrace it and renew its traditions in contemporary modes.

✳   ✳   ✳

CHANGE WAS IN THE AIR between the time of his arrival on campus and his inauguration. There were signs everywhere, on campus and off.

After the date of Taylor's prospective departure from Vassar was made known in 1913, a group of would-be reformers on the faculty, Salmon among them, wrote the trustees to ask if they might govern themselves until a new president was appointed. The trustees acceded, seemingly without reservation, and probably not aware that in granting the request, they were in danger of losing their tight grip on campus affairs. Mills, chairperson of the economics department, devoted to the college and to his students, and probably a completely trustworthy neutral figure in the eyes of the trustees, was invited by them to be chairperson pro tem of the faculty. The faculty, meanwhile, quietly divided itself up into committees to consider problems as they arose, and, in addition instituted a faculty club for informal discussion of matters later to be debated more formally in faculty meeting.

Mills was not, however, on speaking terms with Salmon for years before MacCracken arrived. Salmon had been head of the history department when Mills joined it as a young economist in 1890 before there was any thought of a separate economics department. Mills did not approve of Salmon's iconoclastic teaching methods, did not want to be associated with them, and moved as soon as possible for the division, which took place in 1893, with Taylor cooperating. Salmon never forgave him for this treason, and a line was thereafter drawn between them. (Soon after Marjorie MacCracken arrived in the president's house in 1915, however, she gave a dinner party for departmental chairpersons and, innocent of the background, seated Mills and Salmon next to each other. For the first time in years, they were embarrassed into talking to each other.) But the chemistry of their uncivil relationship was a factor in faculty dynamics in the interim period between presidents.

Now the suffrage question was broadened as both men and women faculty members began to think about their rights with respect to educational issues. In committees, and separately, members of the faculty contacted outside professional groups, of which some of them were already members, such as the American Association of University Professors (AAUP), which was in the process of working out protocol for faculty governance and was beginning to professionalize faculties. They were trying to determine how Vassar could be socialized into the larger world of institutional reform.

An "occupational bureau," harbinger of the modern career planning office, hastily organized in the summer of 1913 by Taylor in a last minute concession of his presidency, began to collect information about women's employment in various fields. A professor was appointed to a newly created and endowed chair of Political Science in 1913, which Taylor had arranged for before he left.

MacCracken later took wicked pleasure in pointing out that the man Taylor put in the chair, Emerson Fite, had been perhaps "the most conservative member" of the Yale University government department. But it was a move in the right direction.

During this superficially quiescent period between presidents, the students at Vassar also began to press for more say-so about their affairs. In 1902 a students' association had been newly chartered, but as yet it had not wrested much power from the paternalistic administration. That was largely because Taylor, maintainer of the notion of *in loco parentis,* believed that the business of students was to use their time in studying and self-improvement, and not to concern themselves with self-government.

As soon as Taylor departed, the students began to discuss ways to liberate themselves from old routines. For the most part, the faculty encouraged them to move ahead. They had ranging discussions about dress; rules for behavior; the curriculum; elective courses; the abolition of required daily chapel; the abolition of the presidential required ethics and moral philosophy course; and the need for open communication about marks. (Prior to that time the students' marks had not been made known to them unless they were in deep academic trouble.) They wanted a new academic association, no longer just a student association, but one in which they collaborated democratically with the faculty and administration, and in which they had an important voice.

The antiquated system of the lady principalship, which controlled the college's decorum and discipline, was just giving way to a new system of various wardens, which was being implemented. Under this new system, the wardens lived in the various dormitories and mixed fairly freely with the students. On the face of it, this system did not promise to be significantly different from the old one, since some of the nineteenth-century staff were still administering it, including Isabel Tillinghast, former lady principal. Still, it was another step in the direction away from the rigid controls of the past. A new feature of the warden system was specialization, so that one warden acted as adviser in the Occupational Bureau, one related to alumnae, and others were charged with other specialized responsibilities. Rules were considerably relaxed from what they had been; and although the system was still based on the concept of the substitute family, which guided, controlled, and imposed standards on the students' daily lives, the students now had comparatively much more freedom.

The students asked to graduate in cap and gown in June 1914 and the following fall there was a formal academic convocation (suggested by Salmon) for the first time.

*   *   *

MacCracken was at Vassar six months before he was inaugurated. That gave him plenty of time to feel his way. When he came to the college, he already had in mind quite a different mission for Vassar's education than Taylor had had. If Dimock and Pratt had bothered to hear him out in Glen Cove, or in Brooklyn, they might have had second thoughts about hiring him. He was definitely going to place the students first, that was clear. Before the faculty, the trustees, the wardens, or the president, came the students. They were the reason for the existence of the college. They were the young women whom Matthew Vassar wished to emancipate and sort out, with the idiots, from neglect.

PRESIDENT MACCRACKEN, MARJORIE MACCRACKEN,
AND DAUGHTER MAISRY, AT TIME OF INAUGURATION,
OCTOBER, 1915.

CHAPTER FIVE

THE INAUGURATION:
RINGING IN THE NEW VASSAR

MACCRACKEN'S INAUGURATION signalled the outstanding concerns and themes of Vassar's future. The program took place on Wednesday, October 13, 1915, following three days of events celebrating Vassar's Fiftieth Anniversary. George Lyman Kittredge, MacCracken's mentor at Harvard, testified eloquently that Vassar had an outstanding scholar—not a pedant—for a president. Henry Mitchell MacCracken, the president's father, now chancellor emeritus of New York University, implored the deity to help his son and the college work for a more just America. Commissioner John Finley, President of the University of the State of New York, pronounced Vassar a place where students could explore the mysteries of the mind, and reminded the audience that a Vassar professor, Henry Seely White (the head of the Mathematical Society of America), had recently found a "new eternal theorem to add to those of Euclid."

After he was installed as president by William Plunkett Rhoades, new chairperson of the board of trustees, in the Vassar Chapel, MacCracken looked out over a large, friendly audience, which consisted of educators from around the country; Vassar alumnae, curious about the new man; and students from other campuses as well as Vassar students, who had attended a student conference on the campus (the first one ever held at Vassar) during the anniversary celebration. MacCracken speculated that the college of the twentieth century was to its students what Dante's medieval synthesis had been to his age—"the genius of life." Vassar's particular appeal to "young women seeking higher education might be determined by what would be called a stratum of interest, an idealism underlying the whole land

and not confined to any section." He asserted that to maintain its position,

> *Vassar College must drive down until it taps this vein, and there are signs from past experience that, once tapped, this flow of goodwill throughout the country will be no less continuous than that of the old Franklin oil wells which have been flowing now these forty years. . . . What is to be this vein which, running through the great resources of national life, shall constantly and continuously feed. . . this college with a never ending stream of devoted students?. . . It is that current of present thought which magnifies the cause and sinks the individual in the great purpose for which the individual may strive. To convince our students early that they are all part of a great plan is to provide the interest which is the critical element in American education.*

Thus MacCracken articulated for the first time as Vassar's new public spokesman, even if in somewhat grandiose and hyperbolic language, a view that college education for women had a socializing purpose and a mission, which was to prepare its graduates for dedicated participation in human affairs.

Two Vassar alumnae, Julia Clifford Lathrop, 1880, and Ellen Semple, 1882, and two distinguished guests, Lillian Wald of the Henry Street Settlement House in Manhattan and Emily Jane Putnam, Associate in History at Barnard College, issued a challenge to MacCracken to redirect the education at Vassar to fill a new bill.

Making different points, all four speakers addressed the new demands placed on the college for women in the modern era. To educate themselves for their new, unforeseen, and certainly unpredictable prospects in a world of uncertain future, they needed to be offered new opportunities for graduate work. Julia Lathrop, who was head of the Children's Bureau in Washington, envisioned a wide-open field for research on the family. She said that the old questions about equality for women were satisfied—women had been assimilated into the higher educational system and had taken on the cultural training, the unspecialized training of liberally educated persons. But this no longer could be considered adequate training for citizenship in the twentieth century world. They needed now to specialize and learn to become professionals and trained leaders, not followers. In short, they needed to "arm themselves intellectually" to remake the world, not just to accept it as it came. Ellen Semple, a distinguished geographer, called her specialty "anthropo-geography," which she described as the investigation of the influence of geographic environment upon human development. Both of these speakers emphasized that women were equipped to make breakthroughs into all manner of new professions. The frontiers opening up challenged women to call on their liberal educations to solve human problems. On all sides, there was a need to put human brainpower, especially the brainpower of women, to work.

Emily Putnam took a somewhat different direction, emphasizing the need for women to redefine themselves; to minimize the differences between themselves and men; to demonstrate their aptitude for entering professions and pursuing careers by making their work intelligent; and to take up their role in society, facilitating their own progress by demanding of themselves real excellence. There was no one formula for rising to the peak of their potential, and if necessary, they should limit themselves to smaller, but deeper, fields of action. The fourth speaker, Lillian Wald, directed women to familiarize themselves with the new disciplines, arts, and technologies that could put them at the service of their communities, and get them beyond the selfish and limited purposes of merely furthering their own domestic lives.

With one voice, but many accents, these four women so successful in their fields, called upon Vassar, as they had not been able to do before, to deliver women opportunities for higher education that would improve the quality of life for the human family and that would put them on an equal footing with men in a democracy that was about to offer them the vote. Others echoed their sentiments at dinner and at receptions:

ELIZABETH WOODBRIDGE MORRIS, 1892
then teaching English at Wellesley:

Begun as the women's colleges were in the face of keen challenge, they were always held bound to prove a close and practical connection with life. Even the students at Vassar of the nineties felt obliged to prove this connection, but although they were more conscious than is the modern student of the present day of the need of such proof, they did not begin to offer it as does the modern student. They were living on the fringes of the Victorian era, and the Victorians made the mistake of thinking that a good

heart and good intentions were all that were needed. . . . Good
hearts and good intentions must not be underrated, but for most
occasions it is also useful to have a good head.

MacCracken was readier than the speakers could have guessed to
accept their challenge, even without so much as a day's delay. Before
the inauguration, he had worked out in his head a scenario for future
action. He had formally by letter summoned the presidents of Mt.
Holyoke, Wellesley, and Smith to his office on October 14, the first
working day after the inauguration, with the intention of leading the
collective group into a radical change in admissions standards. He had
already served notice to the alumnae in New York on his way to the
Vassar job that students were going to be his first concern. When he
first arrived, he had shocked his hosts across the street from the Vassar
campus—the William Bancroft Hills, professor of religion on the
Weyerhaeuser chair and his wife, who elegantly housed him in their
mansion—with his incautious statements about putting the students
before the curriculum and his belief that the end of the college was to
empower the student. "To put it in a phrase," as he wrote in *The*
Hickory Limb, "I would try to make every Vassar woman a citizen of
the world, as well as of her college, state, region, or country."

CHAPTER SIX

BEGINNING FROM THE EGG

*There was heat as well as light in Vassar's culture, and
one could not tell where the volcano would erupt. It was
no wonder that Dr. Taylor destroyed all his correspondence before turning his office over to me, and I had to
begin from the egg to feel my way into the conflicting
tensions. But I was hardly prepared for what I found in
the president's otherwise empty desk on the day that I
took over. In the right-hand drawer was a cardboard box,
with the printed label "wax candles." When I opened it,
I found a loaded revolver. This was Prexy Taylor's only
bequest to his successor.*

— The Hickory Limb

A S MACCRACKEN began to explore the traditions and history of
Vassar and to determine its identity in 1914, and as he began to
think about how he would relate to it, he turned for help to those in
the community who were already working for progress and reform. In
this enterprise, he was aided and abetted—in fact goaded—by Lucy
Maynard Salmon, the ringleader on the faculty of other activists, who
also joined in at every possible point.

The yeast of Salmon's ideas had been rising ever since she was an
undergraduate at the University of Michigan, and by the time Mac-
Cracken arrived at Vassar, as we have seen, she had put her ideas in
motion in many places, helping to create dissatisfaction with the
limited status-quo of women and the restrictive conditions prevailing
in the teaching profession. From 1888 on, she had taught history to
many of the students who now constituted the growing alumnae body.
When they left the college, or perhaps remained in it to have a career

as teachers, many of them were prepared to go to bat for issues which she had taught them to care about, by giving them opportunities for experiential and self-motivated education while they were her students.

She had been mulling over, writing, and speaking publicly about her ideas and suggestions for developing a college organization which was "organic" in nature, with a democratic governance through which each segment of the college community would be empowered to uphold its own role and do what it was equipped to do. To her way of thinking, the collective faculty should be in charge of drawing up and integrating educational policy. Similarly, the students should take the primary responsibility for directing their own education, according to their personal preferences and abilities. The trustees should be responsible for providing the general financial welfare and budgetary means of the college, but no longer be in charge of the daily minutiae of decisions about expenditures of small sums, or of educational policy. Above all, they should have a vision of the mission of the college.

MEMORANDA EXCHANGED
BETWEEN MacCRACKEN AND SALMON:
YESTERDAY'S E-MAIL

FOR THE FIRST ELEVEN YEARS that MacCracken was at Vassar, until Salmon's retirement in 1926 (when she was three years past Vassar's official retirement age), her electric presence and freely offered advice—sometimes unwelcome because he didn't need it—had a positive effect on MacCracken's successful efforts to turn Vassar into a more progressive institution. There were, of course, many other factors and many other people involved in the transformation of Vassar from a Victorian institution to a modern one. Some of the other faculty members had sharp daily differences with Salmon and her modus operandi and even those who were in accord with her views of modernization and the need for change, found her to be a bit bossy and somewhat outrageous in her ways. But the few years at the end of Salmon's career that coincided with MacCracken's first years at Vassar created an important bridge between the college's past and its future.

❋   ❋   ❋

These days they would communicate by E-mail. They would both probably have rejoiced in it, had it been available in 1915, for they were each communicators, and took to their pens, to convince each other of strongly held or tentative views. Even though their offices were less than half a block apart and they probably ran across each other in daily life, nevertheless, according to the etiquette of the times, Salmon and MacCracken communicated with each other through the college unstamped mail, or even had letters delivered to each other by messenger. They often tried to feel each other out.

The correspondence revealed a remarkable unanimity of thought between two determined people who almost, but not quite, hit it off. MacCracken no doubt appreciated what a remarkable help Salmon was in running interference for him—she loved to interfere—but there must have been times, too, when he had to bite his tongue at her presumptions, and felt their pressure a bit too acutely. They always had something to say to each other. Salmon felt that she bore the weight of the institution on her shoulders and that it was up to her to indoctrinate the new president, not so much in the ways of the past (although they were fun to reminisce about) as in the possibilities of the future. She sent him 142 personal letters of advice and information. MacCracken knew she was on the "Circle '80" side of Vassar College actors and that her sympathies lay with the students.

Excerpts from the MacCracken-Salmon correspondence enable us to see the nature of their exchanges. The preserved group of letters began with a polite note written from MacCracken to Salmon, apparently responding to a welcoming note from Salmon, which he received in Northampton after his first visit as president:

> *Hampton Terrace*
> *Northampton*
> *January 15, 1915*

My dear Miss Salmon:
I find your very friendly letter awaiting me on my return from Poughkeepsie. Let me thank you for your offer of helpful cooperation, and join with you in the desire which is implied in your words, to continue and further the high record of Vassar in the field of education.

> *Faithfully yours,*
> *H.N. MacCracken*

Sincerely yours,
Lucy Maynard Salmon.

LUCY MAYNARD SALMON.

The next letter sent to MacCracken, including a report to be forwarded to the board, was apparently matter-of-fact and routine, but gave MacCracken a chance to tell Salmon she was welcome in his office. The report communicated to the trustees some of the progress made by the faculty committee during the interim period, as this would be the first meeting of the board after the arrival of Mac-Cracken:

> *Vassar College*
> *February 1, 1915*
>
> *Dear Professor Salmon,*
> *The report for the Trustees' Committee on Faculty and Studies which you have submitted, has been carefully read and will be presented for action at the meeting of the Trustees Committee late in February. If there are any parts of your report which you wish to discuss privately with me before the meeting, will you kindly make an appointment in the near future for conference in my office.*

Salmon wrote MacCracken on February 15, 1915, with the suggestion for reform of the governance. In her letter given here, she reported that the faculty believed a search should be made of all the enacted legislation of the past governing both the faculty and the trustees, and that the body of material gathered should then be evaluated and revised. In his response, MacCracken seems to have interpreted the suggestion for faculty discussion as a suggestion for an open forum. *The Vassar College Statute of Instruction,* drawn up between 1921 and 1923, and adopted and published by the trustees in 1923, was the end result of these beginning deliberations. Both Salmon and MacCracken could take credit for the finished governance, which became an acknowledged model for college constitutions throughout the country:

> *February 19, 1915*
>
> *My dear Mr. MacCracken:*
> *Many of us have long hoped to have a codification both of faculty regulations and of the rules of the board of trustees. May I suggest in connection with the first proposal that an admirable person for doing the work would be Mrs. Catteral.*

It has occurred to me that if Mrs. Catteral could do the codi-fications of the rules it would then be possible for a committee of the faculty to present recommendations in regard to the revision of these rules. There is undoubtedly much dead wood in the faculty minutes and the necessity of faculty revision would seem to be imperative.

February 22, 1915

Prof. Salmon:

Your suggestions with regard to planning Vassar College campus have been received and will be referred with other matters on the same general line to the proper time.

The idea of an open forum which you suggest is one which has been adopted with some success elsewhere, but it is my under-standing that these forums have not maintained themselves for any length of time unless they confined themselves to a single definite object. This matter might well be brought up, I think, in Faculty.

I note that Mt. Holyoke has recently created an open forum for discussion, I believe, of public affairs. My own Alma Mater, New York University, has long had an open forum for the discussion of all sorts of political topics.

After his inauguration and the separate celebration of the Fiftieth Anniversary of the college, MacCracken told Salmon that he had already followed up on the ideas of one of the speakers, Julia Lathrop, who made a suggestion which interested him and which would be, as it turned out, of importance in future debates about new directions for the Vassar education. He and Salmon also seem to have exchanged views about the possibility of getting out a publication concerning Vassar's education, which would use departmental reports of the previous years' curricular developments:

October 28, 1915

My dear Professor Salmon,

Your interesting suggestion of October 27th is in line with some thoughts that have been in my own mind for some time. While I hesitate to add anything to the labors of the depart-ments, especially at this season when everyone has been working extra hours, nevertheless the advantage of such a volume might well outweigh the cost of the work, and up to a certain size I should be glad to see the expense of printing is borne.

I should like to add that a great deal of the departmental reports last year was material which would properly go in such a volume.

I have already called upon the departments of Psychology, Economics, and Physiology, for an expression of opinion concerning the work which Vassar College could do within the undergraduate curriculum along the lines proposed by Miss Lathrop in graduate work [in her Inauguration speech] with a view of using this material to interest some of our generous alumnae in the laboratory in Psychology and Physiology. Possibly these articles could be incorporated in such a volume . . .

Before he retired, Taylor had put in motion a suggestion that new housing be built for women faculty members, for whom no housing other than dormitory accommodations was available. By late November 1915 MacCracken had already taken up that suggestion. The final result was the building of Williams Hall (1924), a faculty residence hall.

November 23, 1915

My dear Miss Salmon:

Your suggestion in relation to the new faculty house is in accordance with my own ideas, and a sketch has already been drawn up along that line. As for the name, that is a matter for the donors to consider.

Let me thank you for your suggestion regarding the endowment fund: I shall try to arrange something to meet this need.

As time progressed, Salmon recommended publicized procedures for applications by scholarship candidates, a suggestion which led to MacCracken's discovery of the fact that not only were there no publicized procedures, but there were no official procedures to publicize. Lists in the treasurer's office were haphazard. He promptly called for such a list to be drawn up. Here was one more piece of evidence of the college's need for a coherent budgetary and fiscal policy.

In this letter, MacCracken referred to Burges Johnson—a new and certainly symbolic addition to the Vassar administration—a friend whom MacCracken lured from the New York publishing world to take a position as press officer at Vassar and straighten out the college's official communications with the outside world. Taylor for the most part had had a negative and defensive relationship with the press, and tended to think that outsiders should not be told about the internal functionings of the college. The lines between information and propaganda were also very blurred in his dealings with the press, as was, even more, the college lecture program—another arm of communication establishing contact between the college and the outside world. Visiting clergymen were safe enough as speakers, as were trusted poets or classicists or visiting ambassadors from other countries. But Taylor stood fairly much on principle against permitting speakers on controversial contemporary, social, or political questions to occupy the Vassar podium. For MacCracken, accustomed to openness of communication, an enormous burden was placed on him initially by such secretiveness. He wanted the outside world to know about Vassar, and having a press officer indicated that.

April 8, 1916

My dear Miss Salmon:

Your letter of April 3 lies upon my desk upon my return from a trip through the west. I have already on the docket for today a letter to our Treasurer asking him to prepare a definite statement of the scholarship and fellowship funds, with respect to his office. So far as I can learn, there has never been a formal method of procedure. I have been trying to straighten out the difficulties this year, and think that we have now arrived at a procedure which can be properly published. A pamphlet such as you suggest would be most helpful, and I will discuss it with Mr. Johnson at once.

The next three letters to Salmon gave further testimony of their common desire to relate more effectively to the world beyond the college.

October 18, 1916

My dear Miss Salmon:

Carrying out your suggestion, I am inviting the teachers of the city schools, Putnam Hall, Glen Eden, New Paltz Normal, and

PRESIDENT MACCRACKEN ON THE LIBRARY STEPS
WITH AMY REED, LIBRARIAN, AND AN UNIDENTIFIED MAN,
CIRCA 1916.

Eastman College to a lecture by Dean Frank B. Graves on "Great English Public Schools" on Saturday afternoon, Nov. 11, at 3:30 in Taylor Hall. There will be an informal reception afterward, at which I hope the Faculty will greet our visitors.

Let me thank you for your recommendation.

November 3, 1916

My dear Professor Salmon,

It will be a great satisfaction to me if you can accept membership on our Lecture Policy committee, to work with Professor Drake and myself on plans for another year.

June 8, 1918

My dear Miss Salmon,

I know that you are just as busy as I am, but you have been associated with Vassar College for so many years that your description of our plan of organization would be far more helpful than mine, and I am wondering if you could do me the courtesy of answering the enclosed letter for me. I would suggest that such a letter contain not only the data of our present organization, but the plan towards which, in your opinion, we seem to be working. Please be perfectly free to criticize the system and the organization of the college in any way you desire.

The correspondence began to dwindle after MacCracken got his new staff in place. By 1923, in the last letter to be preserved, MacCracken displayed some degree of irritation in what he wrote Salmon:

October 27, 1923

. . . Would it not be better for you to talk these matters over first with Dean Thompson? It is my hope for her as an educational expert that she may fully acquaint herself with just such problems and be able to lead faculty opinion to a decision. I say this not because I would not welcome a talk with you, but your History Department has laid such a heavy load upon me that with the ordinary routine of my office and the outside engagements which the trustees wish me to make, my time is more than occupied just now. I have already put in ten hours this week in

preparation for next Tuesday's lecture, and must put in an equal amount, and I do not know where I am to find it.

While I am writing, may I say that I am asked to convey to you the protest of a colleague against what your colleague heard as coming from you—that you had suggested to the student curriculum committee that they should ask for the establishment of courses in translation of the classics and the history of science. Your colleague claims that such a suggestion by members of the Faculty would defeat the very aim for which the student curriculum committee was supposed to exist, viz. as a means of communicating to the Faculty student reaction to the curriculum. I pass this protest on to you as requested and should be glad to be the medium of exchange in forwarding your reply should you wish to make one.

Abrasive though she might be, Salmon at the end of her life would be able to count the many ways in which she had been kingmaker of the modern Vassar.

CHAPTER SEVEN

ADMITTING THE NEW STUDENT

*Well, of course, one of the big problems was . . . the early
registrants were so numerous that you had to cut off the
line before you could take any new applicants. This
meant that the new applicants—and they might be very
brilliant girls—couldn't be taken, and that's the thing
that Dr. MacCracken was set on doing something about
when he first came. He was instrumental in establishing
a waiting list for the late applicants—a limited number
of places reserved for them and they were called the
Honor Group—and there was an Honor Group of ten
which later became an Honor Group of 20 or 25, and
later larger, and finally by that time the number of early
applicants had dwindled down, and they just had it
competitive for everybody except for a few places that were
there for the early applicants.*

— Vera B. Thomson, first Committee on Admission secretary

E VER SINCE THE BEGINNING of the college, the admission procedures
had been changing, and what happened at Vassar was paralleled
in other places as other women's colleges of its stature grew and
matured. In September 1865 when the college opened its doors to just
over 350 women students, these students for the most part had heard
about the college from Baptist magazines, from *Godey's Lady's Book*, of
which Sarah Josepha Hale was the editor, or by word of mouth. Few of
them had any notion at all of what a college education equal to that
for men would be like, and many came along to the college simply

because they had been entered on the admission rolls by their fathers, mothers, or other relatives. A set of requirements analogous to those in men's colleges was publicized in the college's original prospectus, and no doubt many prospective students, daunted by the list, did not apply.

Public education at the secondary level was not mandatory in the middle of the nineteenth century, although it was sometimes available, especially in large cities. In many cases male candidates for college were tutored privately. And as entrance records have come to light revealing the credentials of earliest candidates for women's colleges, and for Vassar in particular, which had a ten year start over most, it is clear that the preparation and state of readiness for college among the early candidates were mixed.

In the earliest days, provided that the applicant was fifteen years old, one of her parents or adult relatives wrote a letter of application to the college, and requested two character testimonials for the prospective student from respected clergymen or friends. However the student had been prepared, "certificates" and "testimonials," as they were called, of academic accomplishment were requested from the teacher, clergyman, or tutor who had educated her. In those first years most of the testimonials that were sent to the college on behalf of students touched much more heavily on character and virtues than they did on scholarship and aptitude. Only after the young women arrived in Poughkeepsie were they tested, and those who could not meet the standards were sent back home in disappointment or, as it turned out more frequently, put back into preparatory classes, which the college almost at once found it necessary to offer because so many students were ill-prepared. Many early candidates who came under-qualified remained at the college for more than four years, first finishing their preparatory work, and then their requirements for the college degree.

Over the years the admission process became more complicated. More colleges opened their doors, as more students entered high schools or preparatory schools in the 1880s after public secondary education became available and mandatory. College graduates of the women's colleges, many of them feeling an individual responsibility for extending the privilege they had had to others, went into teaching, which was the leading profession for women of the nineteenth century. Some of them started feeder preparatory schools for their own colleges. By 1890, Taylor gave up Vassar's preparatory division, and

credentials from secondary schools had at last become more standardized as expectations became clearer, and forms, acceptable to more
than one college, and requests for specific rather than generalized
information, were developed. Standardization was implemented, also,
by the formation of national testing services, such as the College
Entrance Examination Board, and more local ones, such as the Regents
examinations in New York State. But even so, practice in admission
varied from college to college, and it was not necessarily uniform over
the years in a given institution.

The custom had developed of parents registering their daughters at
birth for admission to Vassar. The story is told of one Vassar family
with two nineteenth century Vassar grandparents, both of whom
journeyed to Poughkeepsie to ensure registration of the same female
granddaughter shortly after she was born. Registration at birth—or at
any time prior to the probable year of admission—had resulted in a
backlog of applications accumulating over the years, and naturally,
parents and candidates alike failed to remove names from the list until
the last minute even if the candidates had no intention of taking their
places.

The student population at Vassar had grown by leaps and bounds
to 1000 students by 1905 when, because of the swelling population,
the trustees decreed that Vassar should grow no larger. It was this
crowding that caused Taylor in 1910 to think seriously of proposing
his second college for students on the Vassar campus. But that he
never got to do.

Instead, following the trustee restriction of 1905, and beginning
with the group of students seeking admission in 1906, the first
students to have registered for entrance that year were the students
who were admitted, provided they were anywhere near meeting
entrance requirements. Those who registered nearer to the time of
prospective admission ran the risk of not getting a place, even though
their records were better. To many students the college essentially
had to say, "We can't admit you this year; there are too many candidates. We'll put you on the waiting list for a place next year." Some
of those students waited and never were accepted. Some waited and
were accepted. Some gave up in disgust and went elsewhere. (Edna
St. Vincent Millay, who did have some deficiencies in her preparation
even though she was uniquely brilliant, was put on the waiting list of
students seeking to enter the college in 1913 but fortunately
persisted. She solved her problem by going to Barnard for a half-year

as a non-matriculated student before proceeding to Vassar.) In spite of these uncertain conditions, numbers of candidates waiting to be admitted continued to grow. According to C. Mildred Thompson, a history professor who had graduated from Vassar in 1903 and who was selected by MacCracken to become chairperson of the Committee on Admission when he initiated it in 1916, "For entrance in September 1916, the number of applicants reached the six hundred mark on February 1, 1915, that is, one year and nine months before entrance; for 1920 the same number was registered three years before entrance." The bottom line of the practices in admission procedure during this period was that the best candidates for admission might never have been admitted.

MacCracken knew these practices had to be changed and that admission had to be made competitive. The best students would clearly be the ones who would profit from the education. He had become familiar during his Smith College experience with the analogous complexities of the procedures there, had thought about them, and was ready for action even though he had not yet set foot on the Vassar campus in his capacity as president. He could guess at Vassar's situation on the basis of what he knew about Smith because it was obvious that several women's colleges faced similar problems. MacCracken's solution was to propose joining forces with the other women's colleges and adopt analogous policies.

This, then, was the subject of his first working meeting with the presidents of those colleges who were gathered for his inauguration, a meeting which found all present of the same mind about the need for action. They each regarded the situation as a crisis in the relationship between the colleges and their clientele, and also a crisis between the colleges and the preparatory schools, including high schools, from which their students came. Under the circumstances of a climate of urgency, general agreement was reached and changes followed closely on the heels of the meeting.

In Vassar's case, MacCracken proposed that the college as an interim measure immediately move to the use of two lists in admission procedures: one list would record date of application, and the only candidates on that list to be removed from consideration would be those who did not meet the college's standards, however mediocre their passing record was; the other list would reflect the evaluation of the quality and promise of the applicant, as judged by several factors, including certificates and testimonials, letters of application, examinations, and school records. Ten students from the second list, Mac-Cracken proposed, would experimentally be given places on the basis of merit for the class entering in 1916. That new procedure was instituted and carried out, and since the experiment was successful, twenty-five students were then chosen by the same method in 1917, and by 1921, one hundred. By September 1918, advance registration increased over fifty percent. The college was rapidly developing a reputation of democratic admission and efficient instruction. The admission committee continued to use the new method until, in 1928, the college was fully committed to competition for all places in the student body, and all students were admitted by the same method.

From the beginning, forecasting the success of this new system, MacCracken believed that the college would now be in a position to make the students much more self-reliant, and to free them from the shackles of the traditional safeguards which had been set up to control a student body in which not all students were strongly motivated. He further thought that the students who were most eager to enter Vassar and were sufficiently equipped mentally to succeed in the competition would undoubtedly constitute a clientele the likes of which the college had not previously known. These would be women who were personally ambitious and who were not coming to college simply because their parents wanted them to; by and large they would be a newer breed, thinking about empowerment for a future for which they were preparing themselves. In some cases, their future plans would include the active pursuit of a career, perhaps in teaching, social work, or one of the developing new fields.

Vera B. Thomson, reflecting on the way admission had functioned, said:

> It [going to college] was the thing to do. . . . Some grand-fathers even registered an early applicant as a baby. [They] wouldn't like it if the child didn't want to go when the time came. Some of the grandfathers were trustees of Vassar. People weren't particularly interested in education, but they had some connection with the college.
>
> I don't think most of them—there were some of them, but I don't think most of them—had in mind a profession. Some of them got interested in it later, and some got interested in something that their families were very much set against, but they just went ahead.

C. MILDRED THOMPSON
PRESIDING OVER VASSAR'S MATRICULATION BOOK.

MacCracken believed this apathy would change. In many cases, he knew these students would still be anticipating marriage and motherhood as had their own mothers before them. But much more often, he forecasted, graduates would leave college committed to undertake responsibilities in civic leadership and problems in their communities, and often to continue in graduate work either in older disciplines or developing new ones. This was MacCracken's perhaps overly optimistic notion of the possible rapid shift in role among a more motivated, new generation of college women.

The new admission system was first implemented in the summer of 1916. Earlier that year, in January 1916, MacCracken informed Ella McCaleb (since 1913, dean of the college, and, before that, longtime associate of Taylor in an administrative capacity) that the admission system was going to change. McCaleb had been struggling prodigiously and practically singlehandedly on the admission front for the previous thirty years, since Taylor's arrival at the college. Very reluctant to give up any part of her job, even though it was a backbreaker, she thought MacCracken was moving much too fast. But he was determined to make this significant step in modernization work as smoothly as possible and to forward admission into an entirely new arena.

Beginning the first year that the new admission procedures were in effect, he undertook to give a mandatory course about the liberal arts to the freshmen. That course was his philosophical equivalent of the course in ethics, compulsory for seniors in their last semester under Taylor, but now abandoned at their request. He hoped to reach the individual student at the beginning of her career, and help her find for herself her motivated direction into the curriculum. This was his way of giving each person the sense that she was in control of her own destiny.

CHAPTER EIGHT

DECENTRALIZING
THE GOVERNANCE

S HORTLY BEFORE Taylor resolved in 1913 to retire, several incidents occurred to unsettle his mind and shift it in that direction. Constantly pushed by the liberals on the faculty to make concessions that would empower them to be consulted about decisions that would affect them, he started to gather information about how other presidents of colleges were managing their relationships with the faculty. He was encouraged to find out that Nicholas Murray Butler at Columbia for one, urged caution and restraint lest the faculty be given too much power. The most liberal response that he got at the other end of the spectrum was from Ellen Pendleton, president of Wellesley, who said that while the Wellesley board of trustees had not been asked whether they would welcome a larger faculty role and direct conferences between faculty and trustees, she suspected the answer would have been "yes" if they had been asked.

When Taylor had come to Vassar in 1886, he had found a green pamphlet entitled *Laws and Regulations of Vassar College* which had been drawn up by the trustees as a kind of constitution of social regulations in 1880, replacing an earlier one created in 1866. Those "laws" in codified form remained in place, essentially unamended until Mac-Cracken's governance was adopted in 1923. Even though Taylor resisted the way the changes were occurring, in 1913 he began to think seriously about the inadequacy of the social regulations. The copy of the "Green Book," as it was known, which he annotated in October 1913, shows that he had begun to question many of the parietal rules and overly fussy regulations. So, without consulting the faculty, he recommended to the trustees the abolition of the lady-principalship, and the institution instead of a pluralistic system, in which there were wardens as heads of houses. He did not take any steps, however, to withdraw the rest of the regulations in the book. That left somewhat in limbo the question of what regulations were in effect just before MacCracken came.

Unfortunately, while Taylor's recommendation was a definite move in the direction of modernization and one that the faculty could endorse, he made it in the same old-fashioned way that presidents had employed since the beginning of the college. He didn't consult the faculty. While he probably would have admitted that the new warden arrangements would significantly affect the life of the college, especially that of the students, neither he nor the trustees saw anything wrong with proceeding the way they always had and announcing a *fait accomplis*.

Taylor hated petitions, which he thought unfair when coming from students, faculty, or alumnae, for they seemed to misrepresent his position no matter what they were about. In 1912 he received such a petition from one hundred members of the senior class, requesting permission for a chapter of the National Equal Rights League on campus. A year later, just before he resigned in distress, he received a petition from some members of the faculty expressing discontent over a communication from the trustees "by which radical changes in educational policy were thereafter to be referred" to the board. Even worse, the faculty complained that "legislation affecting the educational interests of the college was constantly announced to the faculty as already accomplished." These trustee moves, the faculty petitioners wrote, "would seem to indicate that the faculty may be left without any ultimate responsibility for the larger educational policy of the college." They wanted—"demanded" might be slightly too strong a word for 1913—consultation in the future when important steps were to be taken by the trustees.

At the time of Taylor's resignation, then, the mechanisms for governance had not changed since the nineteenth century. During the period without a president between February 1914 and February 1915 the trustees made no special provisions for communication with the faculty, but they asked Herbert Mills, professor of economics, to chair faculty meetings and resolve any problems that might come up, and William Bancroft Hill, professor of Bible, to take charge of the chapel services usually conducted by the president. The faculty engaged in their daily business without event, and met as a faculty as routines

dictated, but they decided, in addition, to have informal sessions off
the record as a faculty club, and through that organization, to pursue
some of their concerns about suffrage and self-government. The club
divided itself up into various sub-committees, chiefly to investigate
what was happening in other places and report back to their
colleagues, but also to exchange their own ideas. They kept no official
records of what transpired at these meetings. As part of this research
and study, Salmon, who proposed the project, undertook to assess the
needs of the faculty for standing committees and to write up a
proposal for introducing them and establishing their procedures that
could eventually be sent to the trustees through the new president.
The proposal also urged suffrage for the faculty, stating that they be
permitted to vote on the matters forwarded to them for consideration
by their own committees. When MacCracken arrived, they invited
him a few days thereafter to a club meeting and told him of their
concerns. MacCracken made it clear that he was wholeheartedly in
favor of getting grievances and questions out in the open and doing
something about them.

In the next few years he encouraged the students to develop a new
student government with a constitution allowing them to manage their
own affairs to a much greater degree. By 1923 this constitution went
into effect and was accepted by the trustees. The constitution
established a principle of conference between students and faculty.
Similarly, by 1923, the faculty, after thorough deliberation, had newly
defined itself as a body with rights of suffrage and self-determination,
whose rank and qualifications were set forth and categorized. It took
incessant committee meetings and conferences to iron out these
questions. (There were faculty holdouts who shared Taylor's views.)
But by 1923, the year when an official modern governance was
adopted by the trustees and put into effect, a very satisfactory set of
arrangements had been agreed upon.

The trustees brought up the rear during these deliberations. The
board that wanted to dismiss MacCracken in 1918 would probably
not have agreed to them even then. But between 1918 and 1923,
there had been many changes in the faces and attitudes on the trustee
board—with more female faces. The governance approved and adopted
by the trustees in 1923, and at once put into effect, was a modern
document, which provided generous rules for the institution to live by
in a changing world. Overhauled and modified every now and then, it
has remained in effect to this day.

MacCracken was highly gratified at the success of this enterprise.
He had been thinking about these questions of governance ever since
he had observed the way Smith College operated during his brief but
instructive stay there. Indeed most of the colleges that after 1925 were
to make up the Seven Sisters group were in a similar state of turmoil
with respect to their governance during and after the war. Taylor's
answer from Butler was not a true indication of the real conflicts that
were emerging, and MacCracken's many inquiries of others reflected
an academic world in transition. Issues promoting change differed
from college to college. At Radcliffe, for example, the big questions
had to do with how it could find a viable relationship with Harvard.
At Bryn Mawr, the difficulties were located in the tensions between
the strong and authoritarian president, M. Carey Thomas, and the
awakened faculty who wanted power. At Smith, when MacCracken
arrived, Burton, its first secular president, was already overhauling the
structure of the administration.

When he had to justify himself to the trustees during his career
showdown in 1918, MacCracken drew up a statement which he called
"The Policy and Record of My Administration, 1915-18" to explain
his position. He described those three years as "a period of training for
the president to learn his own trade"—years during which he learned
how to "direct a modern working office." Excerpts from this seminal
document define MacCracken's theory of decentralized governance
and make clear his notions that an ideal college community is organic
in nature, with well defined relationships between its constituents and
an implied recognition that it is part of a larger world, to which it also
has connections and responsibilities. MacCracken wrote this document in his hotel room in New York City while considering his next
move in his battle with the trustees in 1918:

> *The President's theory of administration, in brief, has been
> that of decentralization with responsibility, from the highest to
> the lowest throughout the college. . . . The policy of decentraliza-
> tion is democratic because it gives to every individual the fullest
> freedom in the administration of the duties of his own office. It is
> progressive because it assigns the specific problems to the attention
> of those who are competent by training and by interest to deal
> with them. And it is sound because it places responsibility upon
> the shoulders of those who should carry it, and encourages each to
> work for the whole, knowing that his own sphere is appreciated*

and recognized. Decentralization with responsibility is not only [a] sound principle in the conduct of the classroom, and the accepted rule of the most modern financial administration, but it is also the only possible method, among members of a Faculty, of opening opportunity for self-development and self-expression which will make them independent, vigorous, self-respectful and loyal scholars and teachers. The President has endeavored at all times to promote an atmosphere among members of the Faculty, students and alumnae, as well as Trustees, of confidence and trust, to make all feel that free discussion and suggestions are encouraged, and that it is possible for all to share in the development of the college policy. . . . The modern American college may be regarded as a complex, of many factors. . . . 1) The parents of prospective students; 2) The prospective students and their teachers; 3) The under-graduates; 4) The alumnae; 5) The faculty; 6) The trustees; 7) The sister colleges; 8) The local community; 9) The general public interested in college education.

MacCracken said he had taken a score card and marked himself for his accomplishments in carrying out this new concept of decentralization. He pointed out that he had incorporated "the system of admission at the college as an educational function, not a primarily administrative one." This and other measures—like "frequent visits of the President throughout the country to meet parents, through alumnae hospitality, to talk with them on Vassar matters"—had provided a new base of decentralization with the parents of prospective students. He had reached out in new ways to prospective students and their teachers through visits, and "substitution of the comprehensive examination system for the old certificate system." The students had been given, in the agreements between the administration and the Students' Association, the "authority to initiate (their) own activities." Their course of study had been intensified as the principle of sequential study had been confirmed and the old system of required courses in a multitude of fields had been abandoned. The degree requirement had been increased to 120 units; open marks had been established. In peripheral developments for student life, the college newspaper had been broadened as an "organ of information and opinion"; a "Faculty Freshman Board" had been instituted "for the special consideration of the problems of freshman year"; the War Work Council had begun, with farm work at the college during the

summers of 1917 and 1918, and two new clubs had been organized—
the Good Fellowship Club, to further employee-student relations, and
the Christian Association.

Reaching out to the alumnae, a division of the wardens' office was
now concerned with their problems and relationship to the college,
including keeping their records and helping them look for jobs.
MacCracken had helped the alumnae groups raise their Fiftieth Anniversary Fund, designed to assist the college in improving faculty
salaries (although some of the trustees had tried to divert its use to
repairs of the power plant); and *The Vassar Quarterly,* a periodical
linking the alumnae to each other, and to their college, had been
formed, with the first issue appearing in 1916.

By 1918 MacCracken had implemented faculty suffrage and introduced a new system of chairmanship into the departmental structure,
so that faculty in a department could elect their own chairman and
run their academic affairs. The college now encouraged a much
stronger lecture policy through the establishment of a lecture committee; now the college cordially invited lecturers of all persuasions to
come instead of sometimes rebuffing them. If they preached propaganda, it was a way for the students to learn to sort out their own
ideas. Planning had been completed for the operation of an alumnae-
faculty house, the actual building of which had not begun. Instead, by
1924 two buildings were built, one for alumnae and one for faculty.

MacCracken, in his document, then directed attention to the
reformed relationships between the trustees and the rest of the college
organization. The number of alumnae trustees had been increased
from three to five; for the first time in 1915, a formal budget had been
adopted for instruction (although, alas, not for the business side of the
college). MacCracken had also made suggestions to the board that had
not yet been executed. He urged them to modernize their governance
to encourage the election of new trustees. This could be achieved by
substituting rotation in office for life tenure and would involve shorter
terms of service (and avoid the traditional problem of trustees hanging
on to their places on the board as if they owned them). He had also
urged the trustees to formulate objectively, and to codify, their
statutes and bylaws; to complete the "definition of powers of all
college officers;" to adopt a budget to cover the whole operation of the
college; and to open themselves to a system of conferences with the
various constituencies of the college. He further encouraged trustees to
engage in a searching survey of all aspects of the Vassar internal

systems, such as the operation of the Vassar farm as a provider of food, and the heating plant (which had been in continuous, but increasingly inefficient, operation since 1865).

During the first years of the decade of the twenties, MacCracken did manage to urge along many of his recommended organizational modernizations to the trustee board, which in turn enabled him to implement ideas that could not possibly have been passed by the board in power when he became president.

At a later time, in 1964, MacCracken looked back at the nature of the board of trustees when he had first come to the college. He said that the way they conducted finances was careless and gave him concern:

> *The Trustees of Vassar College held one meeting a year which lasted about 2 hours and consisted of reading short reports of antediluvian committees written perfunctorily for the committees mostly by the Dean, who had been the Pres's Secretary in years past. The Executive Com. met monthly. It chiefly consisted of a devoted alumna Florence Cushing, Mr. George Dimock, an insurance agent, and three local members. Of these, Mr. [Edward] Atwater, a banker, managed the investments; Mr. Adriance, a retired plow manufacturer, managed the college, and signed all contracts for food, coal, etc.; Mr. Pelton kept the minutes, managed the machinery of the trustees themselves, and voted "no" on all suggestions of the Faculty or anyone else.*
>
> *Several members of the Board had not the slightest interest in women's education and at least two were bitterly opposed to it. A small group of Baptist clergymen . . . preserved the putative affiliation with the Baptist denomination which Matthew Vassar had forbidden but which had grown up. My reform of the Board took 9 years to complete and of course earned me distrust and opposition.*
>
> *One of the principal reforms and the earliest, was in the business administration. It was never made public and so has never been mentioned in my administration, although I was the only person to carry it out.*
>
> *The transfer of the securities from the Farmers and Mfg. Bank to the Bankers Trust Co. in N.Y. met violent opposition from the president of the local bank, Mr. Atwater. Aided by some private conditions among some trustees affected, I was able to put*

the securities on a strictly accounting basis, establish a proper comptroller's office, and put the college management in capable engineering hands. The local accounts were still kept in Pough-keepsie but transferred to the Pk. Trust Co., then the largest local bank. I was elected a director to insure good accounting.

The banking with students and employees, however, still went on at the college, until with cooperation with some members of the Pk. Trust Co. I established the Vassar Bank on Raymond Avenue in 1925. After difficulties with the first and second presidents of the bank, both of whom resigned, I was compelled to take the presidency, just as the panic of 1929 came on.

The responsibility for carrying the bank through the Depression fell upon me alone, the other banks in town refusing to help.

MacCracken's reform of the internal business administration of the college dug as deeply as the other reforms just described. In 1925 he employed Keene Richards, a management engineer, to reorganize the business side of the college from top to bottom. The important difference was that the general manager, as he was called, reported to the president, who in turn reported to the board of trustees. Never again, under the decentralized governance, could an inexperienced president get caught in a financial cross-ruff as MacCracken had.

MacCracken envisioned the full use of the campus, summer and winter. He wanted to offer alumnae and other adults continuing education. (This was not a completely new idea, as earlier Vassar graduates had taken postgraduate home courses directed by Vassar faculty, and had later transferred that credit into masters' degrees.) In the summer of 1918 the college, subsidized by the American Red Cross, under the direction of Professor Herbert Mills, successfully ran a training school for nurses, preparing college students, Vassar and others, for effective service during the war. This kind of preprofessional work provided a unique opportunity for upgrading skills and testing employment, and MacCracken felt it could be implemented on a larger scale, without interfering with the regular undergraduate liberal arts curriculum.

In his position paper MacCracken also discussed his undertaking to establish cordial relationships between the four colleges—Mt. Holyoke, Smith, Wellesley, and Vassar—and to form an association to promote cooperation among these similar institutions. Once this organization, of which MacCracken was president, had been formed, the colleges could proceed to develop a "uniform system of admission and of intercollegiate relations," and subsequently, fund-raising efforts. As MacCracken pointed out, just in the three years he had been there, the college had reached out to participate in the national educational forums in new ways—in fact, had become something of a leader in its ideas for collegiate reform.

He had encouraged the faculty to invite conferences and meetings of learned bodies to the campus and fostered the participation of members of the Vassar community—both students and faculty—in meetings elsewhere. During his inaugural festivities, male and female student delegations had visited the college and held discussions of mutual concerns, marking the first conference of that sort. (In that case, the Vassar tables were turned on M. Carey Thomas, who saw no point in students exchanging that kind of information away from their campuses and felt it was a distraction from studies because it would take students too long to settle down afterwards.)

CHAPTER NINE

MacCRACKEN'S
"VIOLENT CHANGE IN ATTITUDE":
THE ORGANIC INSTITUTION

A T THE ENTRANCE of America into World War I, April 6, 1917, MacCracken went to Albany from Vassar and asked John Finley, Commissioner of Education, what his duty was as college president. Finley suggested that he stay in Poughkeepsie and make Vassar an information center for the community. The next day he received a telegram from Governor Charles Whitman of New York State appointing him chief of the Division of Instruction of the New York State Council of Defense. As part of his job, he assisted at Chautauqua in June 1917 at the American War Aims Conference, which lasted a week and created much interest. There the leaders decided to organize popular preparation for war by a series of conferences. Ten teams with four speakers each addressed audiences on six days in six counties. Approximately a million people attended these meetings. MacCracken also prepared—in his office at Vassar—a manual for the Second Liberty Loan. Working with Frank Vanderlip (later Secretary of the U.S. Treasury), he distributed seven million copies of this document.

He received permission from the Vassar trustees to take two-thirds time off without salary to engage in this war work. By fall he had become involved in the planning of a much larger project—the national development of the American Junior Red Cross. The national War Council approved a preliminary plan for the Red Cross in September on condition that MacCracken would head up the organization and take full educational responsibility for it. Vassar agreed to give him two-thirds time off during February through June 1918 to be in Washington, D.C.

Meanwhile, on the local front and before America entered the war, MacCracken, who had followed a similar path at Yale, took steps to begin service to his local community. His first move involved working with the local authorities in Arlington, near the college, to establish a public health nurse service. That led very soon to his founding of the Dutchess County Health Association, together with Joseph Wilson, an agent of the State Charities Aid Association, who helped implement his idea. It was the first county health association in the United States; he agreed to be the president of this organization, a position that he held for seven years. Through this connection, he was first introduced to the Franklin Roosevelts since Mrs. Sarah Roosevelt, Franklin's mother, was the organization's vice-president. The meetings were frequently held at her house at Crum Elbow, New York.

Also during 1917, Noble and Marjorie MacCracken, with a handful of interested Vassar students, started what was to become Lincoln Center, a settlement house in downtown Poughkeepsie. Josephine Voorhees, 1917, the Vassar student president of "Downtown Work," a student activist movement which collaborated with the MacCrackens to organize this settlement house, recalled during an interview:

> *Dr. Taylor's administration thought that students should remain behind the hedges and the stone wall. He thought they should make contact with the outside world only after graduation.*
>
> *The "downtown work," pitifully enough, pertained to just a handful of students who wanted to go downtown once a week and read to the old ladies at the Old Ladies Home or the YWCA. And it was very sporadic and very small.*
>
> *Dr. and Mrs. MacCracken had joined with Poughkeepsie citizens to raise money and seek out the potential in the community, and if they were to find a worthy project, the college students would rally to it. One of the things that was decided by the joint committee was that a community center down in the Italian community would be very helpful. There were a great many children whose parents couldn't afford to send them to the YWCA. It was almost free but they thought it was a little grand and all the rest of it. The directors and the students decided that a community center [in the Italian district] would be highly desirable: it would afford opportunities for the children and also for their parents who had language problems and so forth.*

So, Dr. and Mrs. MacCracken took me under their wing, and we went hunting for a possible locale.

We found a place half-way down the hill towards the river as I recall, and it had a lot of floor space. We could get it for a very modest rental, and it lent itself to group activities and had space for classes. So arrangements were made, and a group of us went down with mops and pails. The accumulated dust and debris were tremendous, so we had to plan to go back for several sessions prior to the grand opening. Then something dire happened. There was a faucet out in the street which was a source of water for a number of people. About this time a young Italian girl went out one evening with her pail for some water and she was murdered by a disappointed lover. Dr. and Mrs. MacCracken thought on the basis of that experience that it would be just as well if their Vassar girls found some other place to exercise their philanthropic enterprise. So we had to start all over again with a vacant store on the other side of town.

Eventually the place was found and the big event of the opening was advertised for three o'clock in the afternoon, or whatever it was. I carried a huge bag of lollypops in my arms, together with the key to this place and thought it would be just as well to get there a half an hour early. I had great trepidation as to whether anybody would turn up. As I approached the building, not only was I made aware that more than a few people had turned up, but that they had broken into this place, and that the entire floor was crowded with enthusiastic young people. We finally got it calmed down, and we went on to have classes and programs there supported by faculty members and members of local organizations.

There was a place called Riverview Military School nearby and with a stunning blow one day during the winter, the roof caved in. That put an end to the use of the building as a boys' school and military academy. However, that was a wonderful piece of property, and Lincoln Center, which was the name of our group, took over the Riverview Academy. It went on a number of years before it disappeared from the landscape. I remember visiting it several times when I came back to reunions, and it really proved to be quite a useful enterprise with its neighborhood playing fields. One of the professors who was most violently opposed to this change brought about by MacCracken was

Professor Mills, who was a wonderfully fascinating teacher of economics, as I am sure is well remembered. But he thought that Dr. Taylor was absolutely right, and not only did he oppose this violent change in attitude but he got one of his most distinguished alumnae, who had a job on the east coast somewhere, to come up and try to stop it. She tackled me and I was somewhat overcome by her excellent reputation, and her presentation of her own point of view. But I did the best I could in sticking to my own belief.

By the end of 1918, then, Vassar students were involved in two settlement operations—the "Good Fellowship Club," already mentioned, and Lincoln Center. MacCracken and his wife had become conspicuous links to the outside world—local, state, and national.

In this context of community building in 1917, Minnie Cumnock Blodgett, 1884, a great community builder herself in Michigan, became an alumna trustee, and immediately began to set her own agenda in trustee affairs for connecting Vassar with issues of social service. She believed that the college should use its property in the summertime to aid the war effort. Through her auspices and those of Vassie James Hill, 1897, chairperson of the Associate Alumnae, together with the enthusiastic cooperation of MacCracken (who by the late fall of 1917 had begun his own affiliation with the Red Cross), the American Red Cross financed the training camp for nurses on the Vassar campus during the summer of 1918. Herbert Mills, professor of Economics, was a logical choice to be the head of the school and to give it substance and credibility. He apparently did not have the same negative attitude towards training work on campus as towards work "down town."

Four hundred and thirty-five college graduates came to the program on the Vassar campus during the summer of 1918 from 110 colleges. It was a first; the campus had never had anything like it. Under Taylor virtually no outside groups had been invited into the campus. Mrs. Blodgett was greatly involved in making the project work. During the course of the training sessions, laboratories and workrooms were set up in somewhat makeshift fashion in the basement of the Assembly Hall (formerly, the Museum), since there was little other available space. Mrs. Blodgett saw the difficulties and began to think what to do about them.

In addition to this summer venture of 1918, in the previous January a Vassar Relief Unit was sent abroad, with a Vassar graduate,

Major Julia C. Stimson, 1901, chief of the A.E.F Nursing Service, as its overseas adviser. Members of the unit served in Red Cross recreation huts for convalescent soldiers at an American Base Hospital Center in France. Some of the graduates of the Vassar program were already preparing to become part of this unit, when the armistice was declared. Meanwhile, Vassar nurse graduates were also filling nursing vacancies, occasioned by the war, in American hospitals. Twelve Vassar students also worked eight hours a day on the Vassar farm that summer to supply food for the Vassar community in line with the war effort, and other students worked in canning factories in Poughkeepsie. As never before, Vassar was visibly linked with the community, with an eager president taking new steps every day to put not only Vassar students, but college women in general, conspicuously under the public eye.

Soon after the sequence of war-related events, Mrs. Blodgett asked MacCracken about the possibility of setting up a chair at the college in child welfare. She also let it be known that, as a consequence of the success of the 1918 summer program, and the college's pressing need for another classroom building to alleviate overcrowding, she and her husband would be interested in donating a building to the college for the implementation of a new curricular program training women for the social services. There the matter rested for a year or so: she did not at the time formally offer the building or press the program.

In June 1919 MacCracken, who had been studying the past for precedents, made a speech in which he reminded his college audience of Matthew Vassar's unfulfilled wish in 1868 to see domestic science incorporated into the Vassar curriculum and housed in a specially equipped building. He cited the founder's wish that Vassar be fearless as a women's college in administering education with a view to empowering the needs of the lives of women. But the trustees in Vassar's time had rejected this particular idea because it seemed to detract from the notion that women's education could only be made commensurate with that of men by offering an identical set of courses.

MacCracken thought that the college now no longer needed to worry about that issue; education of women in the liberal arts had been firmly established. He had come to the conclusion that the college ought now to provide new opportunities for a new era, with a special purpose of educating graduates for positions in newly developing professions, still in their infancy, relating to family and

HENRY NOBLE MACCRACKEN AND
HERBERT F. MILLS, PROFESSOR OF ECONOMICS.

public welfare: public health; nutrition and sanitation; the environment; child development; and other allied subjects. This program would encourage women to enter professions especially suited to them, but in which training in liberal arts colleges had theretofore been unavailable. It would provide research and graduate opportunities for women who wanted to enter professions pertaining to the newly developing social, biological, and physical sciences and their applications, and provide a curriculum which would cross over single disciplines to study areas and combined fields. MacCracken envisioned that such a program would give new vitality to the scope of education of those who wanted to head in the new directions opening up, but it would in no way replace more classical studies in the traditional liberal arts curriculum. He saw a spectrum of enhancements for understanding contemporary culture and its problems. The program and its impact would serve as the modern equivalent of the founder's idea of possible far-reaching effect of research in domestic science. Only now the impact would be global rather than merely domestic.

Two years later the prominent alumna Elizabeth Kemper Adams, who had been assistant chief of the Professional Section of the War Emergency U.S. Employment Service during the recent world war, added her voice to MacCracken's. She wrote a book about changes occurring in women's professional interests as a result of the war, pointing to the fact that:

> the detachment of the liberal arts college from professional concerns has for a good many years been more theoretical than actual. It has been yielding gradually and for the most part unconsciously to prevalent ideas of the social and civic as well as the economic responsibility of the liberally educated. This change reveals itself clearly in the education of women because of their recent emergence as wage-earners and citizens...

She believed that liberal arts colleges should be organizing to accommodate the new vocational restlessness of women, a product of their wartime activities and experiences as breadwinners which had terminated with the end of the war.

By 1921 MacCracken decided to invite the whole alumnae body to evaluate the experience of education at the college, and to offer their ideas and recommendations about future directions for Vassar education. They convened in June 1921 and, before the meeting was over, elected a committee of five to work on an agenda for the future. Mrs. Blodgett was elected chair of the committee.

Salmon made a speech at the joint trustee and alumnae meeting at which events were wound up. In this speech she too linked the college's post-war search to find a new educational creed viable for educating the modern woman to Matthew Vassar's search sixty to seventy years earlier. In one of his early addresses to the trustees, he had stated that he had devoted three years to this cause alone—years of gleaning information, advice, and suggestions from almost every source and every variety of experience and mind.

> *What Mr. Vassar's ideal was for [the college's] future he stated most explicitly in his last address to the Board of Trustees [1868] when he wrote: "If we only follow on in the old beaten path, we will make no progress. We do no more than others have done before us. We are only copyists and not progressionists. My motto is progress." How far have we realized the ideal thus set forth by the founder must therefore be the searching question that we must all ask as we take stock of our progress during the last half century. Has the contribution Vassar College has itself made to education been commensurate with the contribution made by Matthew Vassar in founding it and in working out its early plans? If it is one of the functions of Vassar College to train leaders, has it itself been a leader in education? If Vassar College has presumably given its alumnae what they have desired, do we recognize that desires and needs change as new conditions arise and that these new desires and needs of the present and of the coming generation of college students are not perhaps fulfilled by means that have been adequate in the past? Do we as college graduates desire to anticipate these needs, to give coming students opportunities other than those that have been ours, perfect as we have deemed them?*

Salmon had fault to find with three contemporary aspects of college education, especially Vassar's. In the first place, she believed that for many years in most colleges what she called a "Chinese wall" had separated what faculties termed "education" from what students called "college life" or the "extra-curriculum." Quoting a then recent article in *The Freeman,* she described the life of the average student body of the American college as devoted to action rather than thought, and the life of the faculty as "an effort to repress the actions and to induce the thought." She averred that it ought to be possible to work out a plan that would "unify all the mental and physical activities within its boundaries [that is, unite thought and action.]"

She next criticized the gap between the college and its environment. In that connection she thought that Vassar should be able to develop a system whereby it could extend its educational enterprises to the adjacent communities, setting up a field experiment station of some sort, an offshoot department of education, where research could be done and from which conclusions reached by Vassar educators could find practical uses and redound to the benefit of all concerned.

Her second criticism led to her third one: that the problems of Vassar as an institution were the problems of life and of the world. "At the very doors of Vassar were all the questions of the larger community." This aspect of Vassar's situation could be met, she thought, "through the erection of a building on the campus which should be an experiment station in devising means for meeting all these problems of daily life that confront every human being in this wide world..." Salmon felt that a "concentration on reunification—of the college within itself, of the college within the community, and of the college with the world" would allow both students and faculty to "replenish the sources that maintain the intellectual life," which in turn would give "vision" to the future. The college could, if it wished to do so, and were brave enough, unfasten "its own ball and chain—prizes, marks, grades, outworn husks, and invent a truly modern mode."

In this speech she summed up problems and remedies, and her thoughts and MacCracken's reverberated.

INTERNATIONAL OUTREACH:
GLOBAL AS WELL AS LOCAL CONCERNS

AS A RESULT of his wartime position in organizing the American Junior Red Cross in Washington, D.C., during the winter and spring of 1918—that position which had caused him so much grief on the trustee front back in Poughkeepsie—MacCracken had become extremely interested in the international movement of the Red Cross and in the principle on which it was based—group action to solve pressing problems.

The summer of 1920 found MacCracken first in Paris attending the international Red Cross conference, and then in Czechoslovakia, where he collaborated with Dr. Alice Masaryk, the daughter of Thomas Masaryk, first President of the newly established republic of Czechoslovakia, his American wife, Charlotte Garrigue Masaryk, and Julia Lathrop, his Vassar alumna colleague. They worked to institute and develop the Czechoslovak Red Cross, modelled on the American predecessor, now "transformed from a war to a peace footing." The Czechoslovak Red Cross was faced with a prodigious problem of post-war reconstruction and complex needs in national social welfare projects, especially since Czechoslovakia had not had organized charities under its pre-war regime. The new organization was arranging for the care and upbringing of orphans and foundlings, and expanding social services in every direction. It was in Prague, where he spent the latter part of the summer that year, that he also made the acquaintance of Czech students and officials who were "struggling to found a university without buildings or without books."

As one consequence of the visit to this country, MacCracken invited five Czech women to come to Vassar College the next year as students, and arrangements were made by the new cosmopolitan Vassar trustee Stephen Duggan, head of the Institute of International Education (IIE), for some of their expenses to be paid by an American donor, Mrs. Willard Straight. Vassar students contributed the rest of the scholarship funds. From that year on, MacCracken invited as many foreign students as he could to enroll at Vassar. Subsequently Vassar students also enrolled in European universities for a year taken off from Vassar and received credit towards the degree for doing so. This mode of sharing cultural and educational values built an international and global dimension into the Vassar education.

Further following this foray into Eastern Europe, in the summer of 1922 MacCracken began a leave which extended through the first semester of the 1922-23 academic year. He had just helped complete an endowment campaign which had raised three million dollars, presided over the college's reorganization, and was ready for a holiday. Never one for idleness, he took the holiday best known to academics— he did research. His subject was a field study in Eastern Europe of newly restored universities.

It seemed to me that as a college administrator I could do no better than to study college and university administration in what was, from an educational point of view, the most in-

teresting place in the world—the new provinces and republics of central Europe.

Here, in an accessible ring near the Baltic shores, had sprung up the greatest renewal of old universities and integration of new ones that had occurred since the Renaissance. Here, too, were great disparities between prosperous Scandinavia and war-torn nationalities.

For the next five months, in the fall and early winter of 1922, MacCracken visited eighteen institutions in Eastern Europe, staying long enough at each place to get his bearings, and in some cases to establish the groundwork for friendships that would be carried out by exchange and correspondence in future years. In each place he volunteered to give a lecture on American education and ended up giving thirty-five lectures, all-told.

MacCracken was truly moved by the degree of interest in American education that he found everywhere, and he vowed that he would do something to make it possible for institutions in the United States to develop relationships with their Eastern European counterparts. He was, nevertheless, troubled by the appalling conditions in which, in some cases, these universities were operating.

> *On the morning I arrived in Konigsberg one of the students died of starvation. I went through every hospital in all the cities where I visited, and I saw much suffering. And the isolation! None has enough money to buy American books or magazines, save Scandanavia. Others are cut off as if America does not exist, from the great scientific world of research and culture over here. In that, surely, we Americans can to some extent aid them.*

Although he claimed that the experience of visiting was enjoyable from beginning to end, MacCracken noted both good and bad political developments in the movement for university education. In the case of faculty, he saw that they were developing positions of power in government, as well as at the national universities: the universities were establishing national languages, "to tell the truth about their history . . . to record permanently their customs and their social life . . . to serve the state by training civil servants and leaders." University professors, for example Dr. Thomas Masaryk, were becoming leaders in various countries. This progress seemed favorable to restoring ethnic awareness and integrity. The student politicization which seemed to be omnipresent, however, he regarded as "mostly bad." He had come to the conclusion that the students suffered from being active participants in political life, and he felt they would do better to be observers of the principles of history and law:

> The European student is first and foremost a member of a political party, second a particular race and family, after that a student . . . The incessant agitation resulting from being the center of great racial and political issues must inevitably take much time from studies and must prevent an impartial consideration of the principles of history and law.

(He encountered this politicization again at the time of the Second World Youth Congress on the Vassar campus in 1938. In that case he was seeking to draw a line between every delegate's right to freedom of speech and belief, and the intractable positions of certain national delegates.)

MacCracken further noted with alarm anti-Semitism in the developing eastern European universities and was awakened to and disturbed by its virulence:

> In Lemberg the students of the university went on strike because they did not wish so many Jews in the university. They wanted the number reduced from forty-nine percent to eleven percent, corresponding to the total population of the Jews in the whole country. The anti-Semitic question is the greatest difficulty obstructing university life. In Germany, for instance, the students passed a law that the front seats in each auditorium should be reserved for those of pure German blood; they would not allow foreigners to sit in them. In Vienna they struck against the University because of a supposed favoring of Jews.

MacCracken returned to the States after his semester away much excited by these diverse experiences. He was considering a new philosophy of education for colleges and for schools alike. He had witnessed the efforts of Masaryk, whom he greatly admired, to infuse social ethics into his university, so that ". . . responsibility for the well-being of one's fellow citizens was no longer a personal matter, as religion taught, but something for the state to recognize and control."

"All of this great new development of the control of the environment, which had been loosely defined as the sphere of Euthenics by Ellen Swallow Richards of the Class of 1870," he wrote in 1969, "now became not only the legitimate but actually the central pivot of the new education." MacCracken saw it as the new gospel—it would call upon science, religion, social sciences, the arts, and social culture to improve the present and future quality of human life. He observed in retrospect that the old disciplinary studies resisted this new multi-disciplinary intrusion. Masaryk and other Eastern European educators, however, had seemingly grasped the concept and used it as the basis for their new society.

MacCracken viewed his trip as having illuminated his perspective. The "light of the rising sun," as he put it fifty years later, shone on his duty as an educator. He remained determined and deeply committed after that trip to "enlighten the college upon the likeness and unlikeness of its own with other cultures, indeed with all cultures." As he began to see it, the continued development of the modern liberal arts college "would be guided through the fire zone of unreason—the new curriculum enormously enriched from the treasures of the new history and the discoveries of the new science, as well as the vast treasures of the past." Life would serve as the laboratory to which the education would be applied. The problem was that there was much resistance to this kind of radical openness everywhere, frequently on the emotional levels of bitter prejudice.

The original five Prague students came and subsequently graduated. MacCracken reported on them—and the Polish alumna—in an article in *The Vassar Quarterly* in the fall of 1925. Their influence on Vassar and Vassar's on them, were exactly what he had in mind:

> *We may well be proud of our Czech alumnae, and our Polish alumna. Of the five who graduated in 1922, three have been at work under Dr. Alice Masaryk, helping that great social pioneer in development of the Czechoslovak Red Cross as a national welfare organization. Marie Doskova has created the technique of social case work, while her husband, Dr. Krakes, has been in charge of the International Migration Service, and has given legal service to the Red Cross. Marie Podzimkova has organized nutrition classes in both Czechoslovakia and Moravia, and developed the whole technique of its instruction. Vlasta Stepanova was secretary of the Junior Red Cross, and editor of its bulletins; and since her marriage to Dr. Jaroslav Kose of the International Labor at Geneva has managed, in addition to her household and small daughter, to translate from the French a textbook on public*

health for Dr. Masaryk. The other two are also at work in Prague. Julie Matouskova as a national Y.W.C.A. secretary (the organization is called the Student Christian Movement), with an office in the Student Home; while Marie Novakova has passed her State teacher's examination and is teaching languages in a gymnasium for boys. She is working at present on a new textbook of English. Our Polish alumna, Joan Kossak, is director of the International Migration Service.

The two younger alumnae are still students at the Karl University, Marie Schindlerova in history, Rokyla Kucerova in law. The latter has passed preliminary bar exams.

All of the group agree that their two years in America have profoundly affected their social viewpoint, helped them in obtaining a technique of social contact, and broadened their sympathies. While they recognize the value of what they have learned, they place still higher the hopes and desires created to realize for their country, especially among women, some of the experience they have had. They believe that future scholarship holders should be either younger students, getting a full American college training and postgraduate course, or else older women, with special fields of interest, getting the social outlook for their work. In particular, in view of the great program of social reform in which Dr. Alice Masaryk is giving her whole life, they believe that American-trained women would be of greatest value, especially in the field of sciences that we call euthenics.

CHAPTER TEN

THE DISAPPOINTING
FIRST THRUST OF EUTHENICS

T HE STORY OF THE IMPACT of a group of Vassar women trustees
and professional social scientists on the vulnerable, receptive,
and eager Henry Noble MacCracken between 1915 and 1925, in his
early stage of formulating and executing his forward-looking academic
policies, revolves around a floating, much misunderstood, and (to
some on the faculty at the time) alien idea. It called for modernizing
women's liberal arts education and training women in a scientific and
interdisciplinary way for a life of active citizenship and community
participation. The objective of skill in community participation was
not at all unfamiliar to the Vassar alumna: from Maria Mitchell's day
on, Vassar graduates made themselves known and did things in their
communities. But the way this new interdisciplinary program was
supposed to lend itself to the established curriculum rankled too many
of the faculty at the time for it to be thoroughly successful.

✳   ✳   ✳

IN JUNE, 1894 Ellen Swallow Richards, 1880, alumna trustee,
coiner/inventor of the word "euthenics," had sat in the trustee
conference room on the first floor of Main Building at Vassar and
listened as her colleagues—male, except for the two other elected
female trustees—introduced a drastic but old-fashioned plan to cope
with Vassar's nasty contribution to a local sewage crisis. James
Renwick Jr.'s design for the disposal of sewage from Main was
considered in 1865 to be "as nearly as may be" the "perfect system of
sewerage and drainage" for a college:

> *The sewage from the College [was] carried through pipes to the ravine, four hundred feet east of the building, and there discharged into a large covered brick tank, from which, after the settling of the more solid portions, the comparatively clear liquid [was] conveyed through sewer-pipes underground nearly two thousand feet, before it [was] discharged into the united Casper Kill and Mill-Cove Brook. The portion retained in the tank, rich in phosphates and other fertilizing elements, being then drawn off into the muck-heaps prepared to receive it, [was] at once deodorized and converted into a valuable manure.*

What may have been on the cutting edge of sanitation in 1865 was in 1894 vigorously complained about by Poughkeepsie authorities, who proposed then that Vassar by-pass the creek and build a sewage line to the Hudson River, six miles away. Hearing this, Richards immediately proposed a non-polluting waste disposal system, which would amount to one-fifth the cost of the proposed six-mile pipeline. It was to be a double drain-field spreading southwest over Vassar farmland from the Vassar farm buildings, south of the main campus in an undeveloped area. Her plan was subsequently adopted, put into effect, and written up in a national scientific journal as exemplary procedure in providing sanitation. Richards summed up her plan commenting:

> *This is a valuable record of the possibility of sewage utilization without offense, and of the right principle in taking care of the wastes of an establishment by itself, instead of fouling a stream, to become a menace to the health of others, and an expense to helpless dwellers further down. It is thus in the line of modern economic and sociological investigation, a line which must be followed up if the land is to remain safely habitable.*

This professional intervention of Richards into questions about Vassar's sewage disposal was an example of the application of technology to a practical community problem, in this case Vassar's pollution of waters passing through other neighboring properties. Richards was able to solve the problem because of her understanding of public health and water pollution problems, gained at the Massachusetts Institute of Technology. M.I.T. did not call the discipline she practiced "euthenics." But Richards did. "Euthenics" was a word she herself had coined from the two Greek stems, *eu*, well; *the*, root of *tithemi,* to cause. Hence the word "euthenics" meant to be in a good state. Richards began the foreword of her book *Euthenics, the Science of Controllable Environment,* originally published in 1910, with these words: "Not through chance, but through increase of scientific knowledge; not through compulsion, but through democratic idealism consciously working through common interests, will be brought about the creation of right conditions, the control of the environment."

Having entered Vassar at age twenty-six in 1868 and graduated two years later in 1870, Richards was, in 1894, a scientist of note, specializing in water pollution and the quality of water as a resource. On her twenty-eighth birthday her application to enter M.I.T. (founded for men five years earlier) had been accepted and she was admitted as a special student without charge, a device around the fact that she was a woman and that the institute was chartered to accept only men. In 1884 M.I.T. had established a separate laboratory for "sanitary chemistry," the first in the world, and Richards became its head. The laboratory carried out water testing and analysis for the state of Massachusetts from 1884 to 1897, when it was replaced by a laboratory opened in the state house. Richards was concurrently employed by the state to examine and report on foods.

She paved the way for women to become engineers at the institute, and later became its first dean of women, advising them about their programs and careers. When she married Robert H. Richards, who was a mining engineer in the first class at M.I.T, she went with him on their working honeymoon to Nova Scotia, dressed in field equipment, wearing short skirts and heavy boots, and ready for scientific exploration.

Under her leadership, too, the new discipline of "home economics," one aspect of many in the larger field of euthenics, came into being at a meeting in Lake Placid in 1899. The concept of "home economics" had broad implications for the American home and family. It was much different from the simpler notion of "domestic economy" promulgated by Matthew Vassar in his 1868 speech. It concentrated on the "management of the home on economic lines as to time and energy as well as money." Like the broader term to which it was now linked—"euthenics, the science of controllable environment"—the home economics concept envisioned environmental reform through concentration on application of scientific principles to the protection of air, water, and food, and the elimination of pollutants of the environment. Richards believed that the future quality of life lay in the hands of parents of children, and of those children turned adults, who, having been brought up with applied scientific awareness, would raise the level of the environment through management of these basic resources for the good of the whole.

By and large, however, her movement failed to have an impact in the right quarters at the time. As Marcia Yudkin said in *The Vassar Quarterly*, "her broad definition of the environment failed to catch on." Yudkin explained that the outdoors was considered man's sphere: the Ecological Society of America, founded in 1911 by male scientists, largely "ignored her contribution." Yet Richards and her theories and practice had not been ignored at all by certain advocates among the Vassar alumnae, nor by the women's networks that were growing up among collegiate alumnae at large.

Beginning with Maria Mitchell, Richards's undergraduate astronomy professor at Vassar, who invited her as a distinguished alumna to speak to a woman's group in Poughkeepsie, many women who were listening had a keen sense of her contributions to reform in the sciences and her interest in the potential for interrelated development of the social sciences and the applied sciences. Lucy Maynard Salmon, who had arrived at Vassar only after Richards had graduated, had separately come to conclusions somewhat akin to hers in pursuing systematic historical research into the subject of domestic science. Louise Fargo Brown, in her book *Apostle of Democracy, the Life of Lucy Maynard Salmon* comments in connection with the publication of Salmon's book, *Domestic Science* in 1891, which preceded Richards' book by eighteen years, that it was the "first scientific study that had ever been made of the subject and was immediately acclaimed." By sending out questionnaires and gathering information, of which they then analyzed the results, her students found out what went on in the great households of the wealthy gentry in America in the nineteenth century. Information was collected about the economics of the household: the pay of servants; working conditions; housing conditions; use of leisure; the description of tasks; and employer-employee relationships. The book, a "scientific study," was the result of that research.

Richards was dead by the time MacCracken arrived on the scene. But the speakers at his inauguration were worthy protagonists of her cause and had taken him by storm. In his later years when MacCracken wrote *The Hickory Limb*, he recalled that Lillian Wald's speech at the Fiftieth Anniversary celebration of the college had hit him "like the sound of a trumpet" as he sat in the audience that day. She spoke of the growth in her time of "a new consciousness" in women, which she linked to the fight for suffrage in that it was part of the evolution of self-government.

> As a result [of this new consciousness], many more women than ever believe that they can best represent themselves in those measures that immediately concern them and for which tradition and experience have fitted them.

Julia Lathrop who also gave a clarion call for a new educational agenda at MacCracken's inauguration, had first addressed the reuning alumnae on the subject of euthenics at a meeting in the Assembly Hall on campus two years earlier in June 1913. Just before the meeting, she encountered one of her classmate friends, Louise Stanwood, in the hall of Main Building and made modest disclaimers about whether her speech would be worth listening to. Stanwood met her again the next day and asked her what the reception of her speech had been. Lathrop said she didn't know about the impact on alumnae in general, but that one alumna in particular had taken her aside and expressed great interest in and support for what she had to say. Over a private dinner that evening, perhaps at the Wagner Inn near the campus—a spot where returning alumnae tended to gather for sociability—Julia Lathrop and the supportive alumna, Minnie Cumnock Blodgett, hatched a plan to press for redirecting and reinvigorating certain aspects of the curriculum at Vassar with the development of an interdisciplinary program in euthenics, which would be an add-on, and would include a new amalgamation of courses from the applied sciences, arts, and social sciences, directed towards solving problems involving the betterment of human life in the home, in society at large, and in the environment.

Inventor of the birth certificate and heir-apparent of Richards' ideas after her death in 1910, Julia Lathrop was one of Vassar's most distinguished alumnae and the first woman in the country to be appointed to a position as a governmental bureau chief. President William Howard Taft asked her to be the head of the U.S. Children's Bureau of the U.S. Department of Labor in 1912, a position to which she was reappointed under two succeeding U.S. presidents, before retiring in 1923. In her seminal 1913 speech to the alumnae, Lathrop mentioned that the first difficulty she had encountered in the

Children's Bureau was the lack of documentation. "We do not pay enough attention to ourselves in this country to know how many of ourselves are born." She continued that "in only eight states were the statistics sufficiently accurate to enable the Bureau to carry on its investigation."

Lathrop's first move as chief of the bureau was to launch comprehensive surveys of infant mortality, procedures which resulted in a summary of the results in *The New York Times* of February 7, 1915, under the caption "Poverty Kills 300,000 Babies Yearly." During the course of her subsequent career in government, Lathrop initiated and supervised many new approaches to child welfare, especially with the implementation and passage of laws against child labor, the establishment of juvenile courts, and the improvement of management of institutions affecting the lives of children and parents.

Lathrop told *The Chicago Sunday Record Herald* in 1912, the year she was appointed to her government position, that she had had to invent her disciplinary training—there were no such studies as statistics, sociology, institutional history, and training in community organization when she was in college. History as she had been taught it (before Lucy Maynard Salmon's time at Vassar) was "dry as dust and without purpose. ... You cannot get the right sort of government till certain types are trained for it, as we are training young men now for the consular service. We need orderly training for those going into public work." It was this missing interdisciplinary training for work in the complex contemporary social environment, either in paid or voluntary positions—or simply in scientific household management— that prompted Lathrop's interest in persuading the new president to establish a program in euthenics.

Minnie Cumnock Blodgett and Julia Lathrop were a formidable team. Blodgett, based on her own experience, thought that women in general, including college graduates in her generation and afterwards, too often lacked access to information necessary to child nurturing and family welfare. She had herself nearly lost her first baby, she said, through ignorance of infant feeding. "Although I had a classical education and was a college graduate, I had no information whatever along the lines of motherhood and child training." In 1908 she had founded clinics for infant feeding in her native city of Grand Rapids, Michigan. "That led to reconstructive community problems such as the re-writing of the milk ordinance, advocating of more school nurses, interest in playground movements and city housing schemes."

Blodgett, together with her husband, John Wood Blodgett, was in a position to offer financial support to begin a program of euthenics at Vassar, which would address these growing problems of contemporary society and offer women graduates an opportunity to tackle them professionally or on a voluntary basis after graduation.

MacCracken had not run into the concept of "euthenics" as such before his exposure to these determined women. Nevertheless, the philosophy of social science and activist reform that it represented, and that they advocated, was entirely familiar. His father, Chancellor MacCracken, had imbued his children with the idea that college undergraduates during their educational experience should be actively concerned about social betterment of the community. The elder MacCracken had made it clear in his inaugural address in 1884, entitled "Relation of Metropolis and University," that the city university and the city were mutually dependent on each other. Through the informed study of social statistics, students could feed results into a reservoir of information useful for the development and carrying out of social policy for reform. To that end, for example, the older MacCracken instituted a course in sociology to be required of sophomores at New York University around the turn of the century— a course in which students would begin to learn what the urban community around them was like, how it functioned, and how it could be made better. He was at this time an officer of the American Institute of Social Service, which prepared an annual Baedeker of social progress in New York City. In a newsletter for 1903, the institute indicated that it would that year publish statistics about labor unions, arbitration, child labor, civil service, cooperation, divorce reform, housing problems, social settlements, wages, public ownership, institutional churches, and education. So the general field of community planning was a concept familiar to the younger MacCracken as he exchanged views with his father during the period of his own undergraduate education at New York University and in the early years of his own presidency.

MacCracken soon decided that euthenics was a viable framework through which to put forward a new educational mission for the college and that the time was ripe for such a fresh emphasis. He believed that the offering of the multidisciplinary subject of euthenics would add new purpose to the Vassar curriculum and would usher in a new day in education, a new way for women to link their undergraduate training with professions undertaken after they graduated. He was not thinking of this program as a requirement, or as universally appealing to all students. The regular disciplinary curriculum would continue to develop and expand through normal channels as well. But a program in euthenics would provide one distinctive and direct medium for the student to equip herself for a life of service in the postwar community. There were others.

In his introduction to the third edition of Richards's book, reissued in 1929 (presumably to honor the inauguration of the Minnie Cumnock Blodgett Hall of Euthenics, just constructed on the campus of Vassar), he gave his own definition of the usefulness of euthenics:

> *[E]uthenics is coming to mean the immediate conditions of physical well being; hygiene, physical and mental; sanitation and public health, preventive medicine and social work, and the contribution of the arts to the same immediate end.*

He continued, saying that the rapid advance of applied science, such as the kind given in these examples, was jeopardizing the inherent value of pure science, which was in danger of being forgotten in America. The pure and applied sciences, the social sciences, and the pure arts and the applied arts must foster each other, not compete with each other. This would be achieved when they were taught as one interdisciplinary subject, with many disciplines interrelating with each other to make up the field.

❋   ❋   ❋

DURING THE COURSE of the Alumnae Association study of college programs to meet new needs in women's post-graduate lives—the study headed by Mrs. Blodgett—MacCracken took a daring leap forward. In May 1922 he proposed the establishment of a euthenics program to the faculty. He handled his introduction of the idea in a curious (and probably harmful) fashion, however, first summoning the faculty to a special meeting, and then putting the meeting in charge of a temporary chairperson, as he himself would be out of town on the particular date. It looked to many as if he were afraid to commit himself. No one on the faculty was really enthusiastic about the idea, and many members actively opposed it in the debate that ensued. No action was taken that day, however, except to table the discussion until fall.

Why he went about his purposes in this fashion, especially after he had put such emphasis on the faculty's prerogative in curriculum-building and self-government, is a question that may never be answered. Looking back, it can be surmised that he anticipated heavy criticism from the faculty—which he got—and that he thought it could best be deflected by an oblique introduction, and a waiting period. Since the Vassar faculty had only recently gained control over educational policy, MacCracken certainly might have predicted that they would not give it away so freely to a coalition of the alumnae.

The following fall was the one during which MacCracken was on leave for a semester visiting eastern European universities. Acting president George Nettleton, a trustee of Vassar, who was Mac-Cracken's former colleague at Yale University, probably in keeping with the same stalling purpose, did not raise the issue in MacCracken's absence. The matter was introduced again, however, in due course—this time at a curriculum committee meeting in April 1923 when MacCracken had returned from his leave. This time he was present, and he reported to the committee that there was a gift in the offing of $250,000 for a euthenics building. He recommended the recognition of a group of courses called "euthenics," which would comprise that field of study that "considers the improvement of social and physical conditions by conscious application of the arts and sciences." Many of the courses were already in the curriculum, he noted, already offered by various departments as part of their discipline. Some would be created anew—such as nutrition, applied physiology, and new courses in child psychology—to supplement the single course on the subject already taught in the psychology department. By and large, MacCracken indicated, the euthenics program would be a revamping and restructuring of subject matter already in the curriculum to concentrate on complex social problems of contemporary society. The students would learn how to think about them, and actively deal with them. MacCracken emphasized that euthenics was but one optional opportunity in a large and flexible curriculum: it would not replace anything. Still the faculty was only lukewarm.

Following that curriculum committee meeting, he recommended to the appropriate trustee committee that Mrs. Blodgett's offer of a gift for the purpose of housing euthenics be accepted. (The acceptance of buildings was a trustee concern, over which the faculty had no control.) The building, as designed, would provide space for the department of physiology and hygiene, as well as research rooms and laboratories which could be used in cooperation with the psychology department and zoology department. There would be provision also for a social museum, with plenty of space for exhibitions concerning the researches of the euthenics program—the impact of planned change and problem-solving on communities, the documented history of the need for change, and the study of change in particular instances.

This trustee committee in 1923, as it happened, stalled and voted to defer deliberations, presumably until the faculty had spoken. The program may well have sounded too vocational in educational thrust to some on the board. It is hard to know whether they were worried about the radicalism of the "application" aspect of the program, or about the negative reaction of the faculty to this new idea, or both.

At a subsequent meeting of the faculty, where discussion of the issue was to be continued, MacCracken was again absent, sick in bed. (In retrospect, three absences from a total of four meetings seems to indicate MacCracken had lost his nerve, caught between opposing positions.) In his absence, the euthenics idea was attacked by its opponents at this meeting. They said it was vague, not scholarly, and contained courses not worthy of study. It threatened to return women to domesticity, and again shut women's doors to the outside world, which had only just been pried open. But the president, anticipating that there would be unfavorable criticism, guessing what it would be, and perhaps thinking that he could be more persuasive and better ward off the attack on paper than in person, had sent along a letter to be read at the meeting.

In the letter, he explained that euthenics was no vaguer a term than sociology, or anthropology, or psychology. He insisted that his own interest in euthenics had preceded Mrs. Blodgett's, and then—not too subtly—he added that she helped raise the money for their salaries (the million dollar endowment that the college received from an alumnae drive in 1917). He notified the faculty that he was going to recommend to the trustees at their June meeting that they accept the building, together with an endowment from the Blodgetts to keep it up. The implication was that it would be a shame to accept the building without having accepted the program tailored to go in it.

Euthenics squeaked through the faculty vote by a narrow margin in June 1924, and became an option in the undergraduate curriculum the next year. It set up certain applied and multidisciplinary courses, such as nutrition and child psychology, and linked a few departments in disciplinary experiments. But it fell far short of the rather grandiose reform notion on which it was predicated—that of preparing students across the board for a better society. Not many students braved the general opposition of the majority of the faculty to what some considered to be a fringe experiment. The publicity surrounding the introduction of the program called a great deal of attention to it in alumnae circles, but the undergraduates, with a modest number of exceptions, scarcely considered it, except for availing themselves of the opportunity to take child-study, the single aspect of the program which attracted general interest.

Some members of the Vassar faculty thought the whole movement had been railroaded through, and never forgave MacCracken for getting Vassar involved with euthenics. Badly as she needed space for her psychology students, Margaret Floy Washburn, partisan to Mac-Cracken when he first came, refused to move her psychology laboratory, for which she had invented both equipment and concept, out of its quarters in Vassar Brothers Laboratory, the ancient out-of-date science building. She stubbornly hung on until her retirement and would never cross the threshold of Blodgett Hall of Euthenics after it was opened in 1931. She believed that euthenics was neither a science nor a social science, and she thought it did not belong in the Vassar curriculum. (When he wrote *The Hickory Limb* in 1950, MacCracken could make light of the situation in which he had found himself in the 1920s. He quoted Washburn, "'You are driving women back into the home, from the slavery of which education has helped us escape, Dr. MacCracken.'") Mabel Newcomer, a distinguished economist with an office in the same old building as Washburn's, didn't want to leave for Blodgett either, and stayed in Vassar Brothers until it was razed in 1936. There were quite a few other holdouts like these.

MacCracken did not see his program as returning women to domesticity and thought that as it expanded it would liberate them to have an enhanced impact on social change and to improve the quality of lives in home, community, nation, and on the globe.

While the program continued as a viable major for more than a decade, the only part of it that ever took hold was Child Study, which, after a few years became a separate major and remained so until 1965, long after MacCracken had retired, when it was assimilated by the psychology department. Since it seemed fairly clear that euthenics was not going to thrive among more than a handful of undergraduates in any given year, MacCracken and the alumnae trustees decided to introduce a variant of it as summer adult education, an idea forwarded also by Blodgett's committee. The first summer school of euthenics took place in 1926, and the summer school program continued until 1959, thirteen years after MacCracken's retirement. Participants included, but were not limited to, Vassar alumnae, and were taught by a faculty, with members from both Vassar itself and other institutions, especially Sarah Lawrence, which as we shall see, was MacCracken's substitute venture into the field of experiential education, conceived as his earlier dreams for a modern program of euthenics at Vassar itself aborted.

The open curriculum of the summer institute addressed such subjects as social welfare, nutrition, child psychology, early childhood education, and psychiatry. Its concentration on contemporary questions, problems, and attitudes of American culture, and specifically on the American family, served to focus the attention of those on the campus each summer on the value of working positively at questions by the give-and-take methods of an institute, and of arriving at good solutions. Eleanor Roosevelt sometimes slipped into the sessions and even taught for one week. In 1942 the often misunderstood term euthenics was temporarily dropped from the title of the institute, which was renamed "The Vassar Summer Institute for Family and Childcare Services in Wartime." It gained new importance during World War II as one of several war institutes sponsored by the state and federal government. Later, it resumed its previous title.

The building with a purpose was elaborately designed by the firm of York and Sawyer. It was a one-of-a-kind edifice, with sections reserved for various aspects of the euthenics program. Unfortunately the space-hungry college could not afford its elegant luxury and it was soon adapted to more generalized use. One section of the building, however, which had been planned to be devoted to the household arts and interior design—the most objectionable part of the program to some—was used to house an experiment in cooperative living throughout the years of the depression. And the space of the Social Museum, a modern gallery for visual presentations of research in the social sciences, was used quite broadly by departments in the social sciences and the arts for several decades. When Eleanor Roosevelt and Harold Ickes participated in a symposium at Vassar on municipal housing in 1937, an exhibition of materials on housing was displayed in the Social Museum.

In 1931 MacCracken hired a sociologist, Joseph Folsom, to replace the retiring Herbert Mills, professor of economics (and sociology). By 1936 Folsom had developed an academic program in field work in the social sciences, which was reported as thriving in the published "President's Report to the Trustees" in October, 1936. Folsom, two years later to become president of the Eastern Sociological Society, by then was teaching several courses which based the students out in the community—one of the courses was entitled "The Community," and another was "Seminar in Social Problems." Students taking the seminar were doing research theses in such areas as "Social Mapping of Communities," "Mapping of Social Phenomena," "House to House Surveys," "Studies of Social Agencies and their Functions," "Studies of Individuals and their Families," and "Studies of Nationalities and Racial Groups."

Folsom cited as objectives for this field work that "education in the social sciences [should] be made more vital and [should] prepare students with both the knowledge and the enthusiasm to serve their own communities as leaders...that the college [should] serve the community around it and make information researched available for community leaders" and "that the program should also serve to educate the general public in principles of social science and pro- motion of social-mindedness." He noted that the implicit danger in such a program was that the community might reject its intellectual paternalism as snobbery and elitism.

The broader Folsom expansion, as it might be called, was more popular with students than the original euthenics courses. (These were clearly all courses which might have been included in the original program, but were not. Had they been available five years earlier, the narrowness of focus of the earlier program would have been avoided, and the amplified program perhaps would have sharply altered the Vassar curriculum.) The euthenics program did not jell into the initial mold planned, and MacCracken could only have been disappointed that his first venture in curricular innovation had not been much of a

MINNIE A. CUMNOCK BLODGETT
IN FRONT OF THE BLODGETT HALL OF EUTHENICS.

success. But within the next two decades in his administration many of the ideas latent in the program cropped up again when the times were ready for them and took hold. The activist field work program of the college, always in the air from the time of Maria Mitchell on, became increasingly important during the forties and fifties and remained an accredited permanent part of the curriculum. Mac-Cracken would in 1925 immediately have been at ease with almost any of the multidisciplinary courses taught in the college of the 1990s. He might have opened a 1990 catalogue and picked one at random, such as: "Perspectives on the Global Village," an introduction to the varied perspectives from which an interdependent world can be approached, and have uttered: "Ah, just what a euthenics course should be!"

A major problem in the aborted curricular life of euthenics was that it came too early to a traditional faculty which had just gained autonomy over its own role in developing single disciplines and was not ready for a multidisciplinary approach. And it came as a conspicuous outcome of alumnae and administrative pressure. Perhaps more important than either of these defects was that MacCracken pulled the wrong stops in his campaign to introduce the program. With his instinct for the language, it is puzzling that he chose to make use of Matthew Vassar's imagery about domestic economy in order to impress his liberated modern listeners, calling the program an embodiment of the founder's unfulfilled dream to start a scientific program in domestic economy and erect a building to house it. He tried to graft a futurist movement onto a concept whose time was past: the term was too old-fashioned for the 1920s undergraduate or faculty member, emitting vibrations of "domesticity" instead of "community organization."

MacCracken had already succeeded in rapidly executing so many of his ideas for reform and change in those early years, that his loss on the acceptance of an academic program of euthenics was disappointing and unexpected. Fortunately he was involved with many other progressive curricular changes which did succeed from 1923 to 1928, instituted through the modernized procedures and carried out as part of the faculty's overall charge. Those changes were overseen, with his enthusiastic cooperation, by the efficient new dean, C. Mildred Thompson, whom he chose in 1923. So the forward movement of the curriculum transpired, in spite of the initial setback. In fact, in due course, many of the disciplines added to their offerings courses which brought their students to confront the changing contemporary world.

CHAPTER ELEVEN

"THE OPEN ROAD TO THE FUTURE"

M ACCRACKEN'S REMARKS before the Second Annual Congress of the National Student Union in 1926 showed how wide open was the sphere of undergraduate education in the twenties, and, in particular, the education of the woman student.

MacCracken used this occasion in December 1926 to air his dissatisfaction with the excessive traditionalism of higher education in America, and to encourage students to study the American college, especially each one his or her own, to discover and propose ways in which the range of opportunities at college might better meet the needs of post-war students. His speech summed up many of the discoveries he had made in trying to open up the Vassar structure and revealed more than a little of the frustration that he had experienced along the way in trying to rid Vassar of paternalism and conservatism. In his speech he offered criticism of the status-quo:

> My chief criticism of the American college executive is that he does not sufficiently trust the students. His own distrust is the starting point of a vicious circle. From his distrust arises the paternalistic system of college government. From the paternalistic system there comes the postponement of important decisions by the student. From this postponement of important decisions there follows immaturity, irresponsibility and preoccupation with trivial rather than important issues. I firmly believe that if the American college will adopt a different attitude toward the student this circle will be reversed.

MacCracken emphasized that "faculties and students should be colleagues rather than master and man" and that "the way to get a respectable attitude toward study is to grant responsibility" in its conduct and choice. He urged the convention's delegates to "vitalize" their lives as students by investigating "the student and his support...his choice of work...his political status...his academic and non-academic life...faculty research and undergraduate instruction...the choice of the college and the choice of the field of work...[and] the college student and other college students."

He likened the disconnected American college of his time to "one of the American states ten years [earlier] before 'the good roads movement' had struck its citizens. Only at certain seasons of the year was contact possible at all along the highways. When the good roads movement began, highways were flung out from this center and that, most of them without leading anywhere and not linked up with any major systems of the continental traffic. Now the good roads movement [had] learned to think in continental terms, and traffic [was] continuous." Accordingly, in the 1920s there could be a good roads movement in education, through which students could improve and understand the cross-links and fertile interconnections between themselves and others, and among hitherto parochial and insular institutions. Certainly MacCracken's Vassar and some of the other Seven Sister colleges had already established some byways into the network of the college good roads movement by prompting women students to be more self-aware and more conscious of their own educational goals. But, even so, there was not yet in American colleges a rising movement to promote student rights. This, MacCracken thought, there should be.

In his discussion of this proposed study, MacCracken suggested that students needed to revolutionize their conduct to take command of their own education. First, they had to know themselves. To that end, he and Dean Thompson had introduced psychological testing to the Vassar campus with the appointment of Dr. Austin Riggs, of Stockbridge, Massachusetts, in 1924, as visiting college psychiatrist. This new discipline of personal guidance of the student to enable her to explore her own personality was in its infancy. So far, MacCracken suggested, students had not made sufficient use of it for results to be understood. The movement would enable students to stop wasting their time in false career moves. "Life is so short," he said, "and preparation for it so long, that students ought to take this matter to heart, and, in the use of their new responsibility, to see to it that their talk in college bears now and then upon the choice of their life work, and that a great definiteness [then] crystallizes."

MacCracken acknowledged that this idea of taking direction in one's own hands as early as possible had met with almost universal resistance, and that the application of psychological testing to the analysis of individual personality traits had produced "hostility" and a generally negative reaction. The first year he arrived at Vassar, he had instituted a system of lectures for first year students to help them see for themselves what they wanted to do with their educational opportunities. But that was a non-threatening, non-psychologically oriented option which could be sloughed off, and which was not taken too seriously except by the strongly motivated. As one Vassar freshman of 1928 put it, "It was wonderful to start college by taking a course with the college president." The course offered by MacCracken was of an academic and scholarly nature, suggesting the rich traditions and growing body of knowledge in various fields. MacCracken's attitude toward student input into education was definitely non-traditional and to the left of center. He was trying to stir students to take the responsibility for themselves and become self-directed and self-motivated.

As has been indicated, the curriculum that his post-war Vassar inherited had slowly changed. By the 1890s new departments and new disciplines had evolved or begun, more often than not, under the direction of faculty members and department heads who were innovative. But before MacCracken, the college had not engaged in any such rigorous analysis of the curriculum as it did in his first years. The student's choice of electives in the early 1920s could take her in one direction or another, and might change the whole thrust of her education.

The implementation in 1927 of a new curriculum enacted by the faculty as a result of its corporate prerogative to rethink and re-establish educational policy completed the first round of changes in the modernization of the college. MacCracken was very eager to have this reform take place, and as soon as Thompson had assumed her office in 1923, she led the faculty in its study, ending with the legislation of 1927. (As an unpublished critique of the curriculum by Professor Evalyn A. Clark clearly demonstrated, the Vassar curriculum "swung like a pendulum" thereafter during MacCracken's administration, and on towards the present, but within a rationalized framework, as the educational movements at Vassar and elsewhere responded to contemporary societal needs.) The 1927 curricular framework, which

On their way to the dedication of the Helen
Kenyon Hall of Physical Education, in 1933
(left to right): Stephen P. Duggan, trustee; Dr.
William Darrach, trustee speaker; President
MacCracken; and Helen Kenyon.

required for each student a concentration in a major to give depth, distribution requirements in related fields to give breadth, and the obligation of the individual student to lay out her own interests and follow them, essentially has lasted through the century until the present.

Between 1923 and 1927, MacCracken, Thompson, and the faculty had done the work. The new curriculum was the result of conferences, committee discussions, and debates that had been ongoing since the war. The alumnae had had their say in the 1921 conference, the students had been consulted through their newly-founded curriculum committee, and then the faculty and the administration, their research and opinions buttressed by cross-fertilization from their colleagues in other institutions, had drawn up a working plan for changes. They met late into the night in each others' houses figuring out the details. The faculty, voting in the new plan on May 2, 1927, with only four members in opposition, had been impressed with the need for redefining the role of the student and how she made her way through her college education.

MacCracken communicated to the trustees on May 31, 1927, that the new Vassar plan successfully answered the many voices that had been raised to point post-war directions for the liberal education of women. He believed that a whole range of contemporary issues had been taken into account. The new curriculum would meet the needs of the new student. (By 1928 admission procedures were at last—after twelve transitional years—fully competitive.)

MacCracken explained:

> *The unanimity with which the faculty voted on these proposals . . . indicates the interest of our teachers in the experiment, and their wish to give a fair trial to the principles outlined in the plan. Except for the two semesters of orientation in freshman year in personal hygiene and the theory of education, for the first time in the history of Vassar no single departmental course is prescribed; students may elect any course in each of four groups in freshman year—the arts, literatures, natural sciences, and social sciences. With this limited restriction on undue specialization, the remainder of the course of study is chosen by the student to fit her own needs. Such a degree of liberty would not be safe unless protected by the adoption of a principle of guidance considerably more direct than that now provided. A new faculty*

Board of Elections is created, with departmental directors of elections cooperating, and it is expected that by conference with every member of the freshman class and with students in the upper classes who need such assistance, a study of plans of elections will be made which will secure the values inherent in a tutorial system of supervision, while still retaining those virtues that come with contact with many minds in the teaching staff through courses of study and progressive work in special fields.

His report continued:

On the whole the plan is a step in the direction of specialization, but leaves still free one-half of all the hours of study above the freshman year, while still requiring distribution in the freshman year. The plan is, therefore, a compromise between the traditional American view of a college course as a general survey of knowledge, and the European university course of specialized and intrusive study. There have always been in the student body at Vassar groups of students entirely capable of organizing their own course of study and carrying it forward independently. The question as to whether the present student body is now selected with sufficient care to warrant the extension of this principle to the whole group is one that can be answered only after a fair trial for several years of the present experimental plan.

MacCracken and Thompson had managed to direct the transformation of the curriculum into an instrument through which individual students could pursue their own interests, largely free of irrelevant requirements. The major encumbrances of the past were gone.

CHAPTER TWELVE

VIGNETTES

C. MILDRED THOMPSON, 1903,
MacCRACKEN'S DEAN

JAMES BALDWIN wrote a history of MacCracken's time at Vassar without ever once mentioning C. Mildred Thompson, first Mac-Cracken's choice as secretary (dean) of the committee on admission in 1916, and then college dean from 1923 until her retirement in 1948. For whatever reason she was omitted, it was the loss to his book (which was never published) of a colorful and important player in MacCracken's academic administration. Their association began as soon as he came to the college, when she was already a young history instructor, fresh from Columbia with a doctorate in American history and a thesis on the Reconstruction period.

She grew up in Georgia, and, modern, open-minded, but strong-willed, was one of the new wave of professional women ready to find places for themselves in academia. Hand in hand with her colleagues at Vassar and alumnae in the Vassar contingent, she marched in the big suffrage parade in New York City in 1916. She had been one of the participants in the Town and County Club, an organization founded in Poughkeepsie by Laura Wylie of the English department, to unite area women with college people in the common quest of the right to suffrage. She was a collaborator with others on the faculty in preparing the way for the modernization of Vassar, and MacCracken immediately sized her up as someone who could be a help with the plans for bringing Vassar into the twentieth century. She knew the college very well, having graduated in 1903 under Taylor and having started her teaching career in American history under Salmon in 1909. Yet her horizons were outside Vassar; she was a woman of the world and an independent thinker.

When MacCracken arrived, Thompson's predecessor, Ella Mc-Caleb, 1878, had just been promoted to dean from the position as Taylor's administrative assistant which she had held since 1887. McCaleb's work admitting students to Vassar increased each year as the idea of young women going to college rose like yeast. But the times had overtaken her and she could not do for MacCracken what she had done for Taylor because she did not really believe in the changes that he was trying to bring about. She was old-fashioned. "What she had done," MacCracken wrote in *The Hickory Limb,* "that she would do. So in my first days I found all my mail had been opened and read by the dean before I received it. In addition, it seemed her prerogative to handle all general college correspondence. 'What will the dean do to him?' asked my somewhat fearful sister-in-law, Marion Dodd, '03. The battle was short and sharp, and Miss McCaleb retired in good order."

Thompson did believe in MacCracken's modern notions and took over where McCaleb left off, as chair of the (newly formed) committee on admission. She also continued to teach history. To negotiate that administrative change, MacCracken wrote McCaleb that he was re-structuring the college's admission procedures and that she would have to step down from her dean's job, even though she had just stepped up to it, and retire.

The schools from which the college drew its candidates were in-creasingly upset by the necessity to prepare students to meet the college's newly-shifting entrance requirements, and it took all the tact MacCracken and Thompson together could muster to cope with hinterland ruffled feathers. MacCracken travelled to the schools across the country and talked with teachers, principals, students, and alumnae, but it was the admission office back on the campus that had to deal with the increasingly voluminous correspondence and the range of both important and picayune issues. Standards were agreed upon and set by the four cooperating colleges, but the individual adaptations of the colleges to the standards had to be carefully worked out between the institution and the outside world by the individual deans. Nothing was automatic: everything that had been routine had to be reconsidered. The background work for MacCracken's forward planning was capably managed by Thompson.

By 1923 McCaleb was fully retired, and Mildred Thompson was nominated dean of the college, a position which she did not surrender until 1948, two years after MacCracken retired in 1946, and his successor, Sarah Gibson Blanding, arrived.

Thompson went home to Atlanta to spend the Christmas holidays with her family the year that she was appointed dean. There she was interviewed by the *The Atlanta Constitution* on her views on college girls and modern women. She gave a glimpse of her thoughts as to how things were changing.

> *The modern woman must do something and be of use even though she is unmarried. If she does marry, she who has had the career or the urge for it, will be all the better fitted to manage her home. ... In the last analysis... vision is the biggest thing the modern college girl gets from her college. More and more, she is learning to grasp the big things in life and to let the rest go. More and more, she is learning the value of real work and real service.*
>
> *The modern college girl, whatever her outward marks of emancipation, has shown that she is a serious individual with a good aim. ... She is very straight with older people. ... [Modern girls are] less inclined to consider themselves as a class apart. ... You can talk to a girl as man to man and expect her to be square with you. ... She isn't afraid of reality.*

Thompson and MacCracken made a coherent team in those years and learned from each other. Together they began to implement the remodeling and reformation of the curriculum and to articulate changes transferring the major responsibility in the liberal arts education to the students themselves. They both wanted to prepare the Vassar graduates to be modern women, ready to take their places in the community and in professions, as well as in the home. MacCracken's notions about education, however, were distinctly more experiential than Thompson's more conventional views.

As the years went by, Thompson resisted some of the developments that MacCracken, if left to his own devices completely, would probably have supported, such as the installation of more multi-disciplinary courses and more vocationally-directed programs. As it was, there were two major revisions of the curriculum—the one in the '20s and another in the '30s. However, the two worked vigorously to adapt Vassar's curriculum and requirements to the wartime realities of World War II, cooperating to introduce a three-year program so that students could respond to wartime needs for women in the labor force, as well as to family upheavals.

In 1926 *The Vassar Quarterly* said of Thompson:

> *The second Dean is an educational expert. To her, education is an intellectual policy. Her task is not so much to carry out the votes of the faculty, as to report upon them critically, to suggest their emendation, to bring the progress of the college and the school world to the doors of Vassar. Her office is most simple in organization. Three trained college women direct the school girl to the gate, the college girl through the mazes of the curriculum, and the young alumna-to-be to her job or graduate study—past, present, or future. The Dean is on all important faculty committees, which meet more rarely as the rules work with greater smoothness. She arranges grants of scholarship aid. She confers with physician and psychiatrist, makes all assignments of academic rooms, controls the schedule and the calendar. It is a task of intricacy and difficulty. Yet she slips off to Europe for a summer of medieval chateaux, or to New York for a weekend of opera and theatre. She reads. She talks.*

While the professional relationship between MacCracken and Thompson grew more complex in time, it had its light sides. MacCracken was a family man, and Thompson was a pivotal member of a group of women faculty members who were good friends, which included Dr. Jane Baldwin, college physician; Rose Peebles and Edith Fahnestock, housemates and professor of English and Spanish respectively; Eloise Ellery, professor of history; and Anna Kitchel and Helen Sandison, professors of English. These women, among others, exercised a certain amount of behind-the-scenes control and influence over the affairs of the college and each other in those days, and there was very little happening on campus that escaped their attention.

Both Thompson and MacCracken moved back and forth in their dealings with their counterparts at the other sister colleges. Meetings were held regularly to discuss issues of common concern and to determine joint projects, for example in fundraising. From the mid-1920s on, many fundraising and public relations projects were undertaken cooperatively by the various presidents and deans, and they all became quite intimate with each other, and knew each others' strengths, weaknesses, and temperaments. They reached into each others' alumnae rosters and into each others' faculties for their teaching replacements and fresh hires, and they shared problems and prospects, and gave advice to each other. They also enjoyed each others' gossip and relaxed with each other during the "Four" and "Seven" College meetings. The group as a whole was a functioning network. Together they exercised a great deal of control and influence over the education of women, and over each other, in the Eastern, single-sex women's colleges in the twenties, thirties, and forties.

The meetings of the colleges were usually held on an appointed host campus. In one of the earliest meetings, MacCracken was to speak in the—to him familiar—Smith chapel, and at the same time, Thompson was to present a plan to representatives of the sister colleges relating to admission. The president decided to drive the dean to Northampton in his automobile the afternoon before the meeting. (He had been over the same route earlier, in 1921, with Madame Curie as a passenger.) But this was a time when the ground was covered with snow. The day of the drive there had been a thaw, and there was mud everywhere. Late afternoon, probably a Thursday, and somewhere between Lakeville, Connecticut, and Great Barrington, Massachusetts, the car skidded off the road in a river of mud, and MacCracken had to get a farmer to pull his car out. That took two hours amidst much embarrassed negotiation.

By seven, when we should have been dining in Northampton, we were rolling over the upper part of Jacob's Ladder, the steep road leading from the Berkshire hill-top down to Springfield.

There they slipped out of control again, this time into a snowdrift.

They were pulled out again. They slipped a third time and had to abandon their car and take a train. They never got to Northampton until five a.m., when their "colleagues looked at each other, but said nothing."

VERA B. THOMSON
Administrator in Admissions office and house warden:

MacCracken was very much interested in students. For instance he would telephone a few minutes before lunchtime, when I was a warden at Strong and say "I'm coming over for lunch today and I'll sit with a group of students." He wouldn't give people any warning, nor had he collected the students. But the students would find that there was this sixth place at their table, and that

UNDERGRADUATE HENRY NOBLE MACCRACKEN *(above, first row, right)* AS STUDENT CAPTAIN OF A NEW YORK UNIVERSITY ATHLETIC TEAM, 1890S. *Below:* PRESIDENT MACCRACKEN, PROFESSOR PAUL NORTHROP, AND TWO VASSAR STUDENT TENNIS PLAYERS ON THE NEW COURT IN KENYON, 1930S.

*was where he was going to sit, and he would have great dis-
cussions with them. . . . And then he used to come and work
sometimes in the evening. He'd talk with a group of students—
have coffee and talk with them. One evening he was singing
Kentucky ballads: he was interested in that and loved to tell them
about [them]. He loved to teach in that way. He was very good
about working with students. He and Mrs. MacCracken had an
at-home every other week. He would try to invite—or she would
try to invite—a little nucleus, so that there would be sure to be
some similar folks there, and then the others were free to come,
and they'd come. One day Mrs. MacCracken was delayed down
at Lincoln Center, and he had to do something about it when it
was time to serve tea. But he served it himself to the students
and then he just sat down on the floor and talked with them,
about the kind of students he had when he was a young man, and
then about the foreign students who came to this country.*

JULIA COBURN ANTOLINI, 1918:

*Henry Noble MacCracken came in the middle of our fresh-
man year [January 1915]. He was very young at the time. I
think he was about thirty-four. He seemed rather dignified, a
little bit distant. I guess it took him a while to get acquainted
with us, and it took us a while to get acquainted with him.*

CAROLINE WARE, 1920
(later professor of economic history
under MacCracken during the 1920s):

*Back to my student days—there is an episode which to me
was self-revealing of what my education meant to me. We came to
college in the midst of war, and World War I hung over our
heads as a constant, hung over us and engulfed us and moved us
in many ways. Seeing the BBC revival of Vera Brittain's
"Testament of Youth" on TV recently, I was reminded of how
much difference the four years between her age and mine made—
she was nineteen when the war began, I was nineteen when it
ended. We were just too young to be directly involved, though a
couple of my school classmates went to France with ambulance
crews. And we in the U.S. were distant, not just across the*

English channel. And only a few of our men were killed, not our whole generation. But Vera Brittain spoke for us all—the youth of those years. I recall my response to the book when it was first published and my feeling that it captured a sense of urgency which we felt in spite of our remoteness. In the summer of my sophomore year I had expressed some of that urgency by working as a farmerette on the college farm with a stint in a local canning factory, and had taken a brigade of students around to local farmers to help harvest and shuck corn.

Then came the armistice. The bells rang, and everybody rushed out to shout and celebrate. The tension broke and emotions flowed like a river in flood. I was as explosively relieved and overjoyed as the rest but I did not join the shouting throng. As I started for the door another thought caught me. "This isn't the end, though the fighting has stopped. So much remains to be done. But the motivation of war is gone now. We have to supply the motivation and drive to carry on ourselves."

I was in the midst of working on a paper that was due the following morning. Knowing that no one would be expected to come to class prepared the next morning, I went back to my desk, wrenched my mind back to the subject on which I was working, sat up most of the night, and handed in a good paper at the morning's class. It seemed to me the only way to register my commitment to Vassar's objective: the free and responsible application of knowledge and talent to the advancement of mankind.

RUTH DILLARD VENABLE, 1924
(later professor of French under MacCracken):

They were very exciting years. C. Mildred Thompson was a very exciting Dean. She was a vigorous person—a person of strong opinions, a person I think of a fundamentally liberal commitment . . . who also rose up in opposition that made itself felt to the further swings to the left of center in the student political opinion. The Miscellany News in those days was quite left wing, and I think that the Dean was probably as responsible as anyone for the beginning of a rival campus newspaper called The Chronicle *which was not a right wing newspaper, but was certainly not a left wing newspaper.*

EDNA ST. VINCENT MILLAY,
PORTRAIT FROM *VASSARION*, 1917.
(Photograph by E. F. Foley)

Every year the Dean and President would choose among the faculty eight members who would become part of Potluck. Your responsibility was to entertain the group once and give a paper once. . . . In that way, they were trying to get to know some of the younger, newer members that they thought might stay on or not. I just happened to benefit very much from that because it so happened that I gave a paper on something that I had done at Columbia. We were on leave during the war [World War II] and couldn't stay in France and came back and spent a year at Columbia. I gave a paper on the Italian Vico, historian and philosopher. The paper was on how the French historian Michelin happened to become acquainted with the work of Vico, who was not then one of the most thought of and talked about people. I gave this paper, and Mr. MacCracken had brought to the meeting a Polish historian, a friend of his, whom he admired very much. It so happened that that man was interested in this subject and obviously must have said something to MacCracken, and that sort of was a feather in my cap. MacCracken believed that in art, music, language—where there was a skill along with scholarship required—that you could waive the Ph.D. for instance . . .

EDNA ST. VINCENT MILLAY, 1917
a protégée of MacCracken:

Edna St. Vincent Millay, twenty-three years old when she arrived at Vassar, had grown up as an eccentric genius in Camden, Maine. But because she challenged the authority of one too many teachers in her local high school, she was barred from attending classes and had to complete her secondary education by herself. Besides that, she lacked the training to construe Latin prose and to present certain other traditional credentials required for Vassar admission in 1913. To prepare herself for Vassar, she attended Barnard College in New York City from February to June 1913 as a non-matriculated student and was conditionally admitted to Vassar over the summer of 1913 into the class of 1917.

Millay and MacCracken were drawn to each other. The play in his honor during the festivities surrounding his inauguration and the celebration of the Fiftieth Anniversary of the founding of the college, was entitled *The Pageant of Athena* and written by Millay. As soon as he made her acquaintance, he paid special attention to her, encouraging her to use her talent as poet and playwright.

Not that she needed encouragement: she had the fresh breath of genius. C. Mildred Thompson, still a history instructor in 1913, recalled after retirement that she flunked Millay in her entrance history exam. She had to, because the answers didn't bear any particular relation to the questions asked. But, said Thompson, "The extraordinary information given at the beginning made me especially interested in the writer who was then unknown to me." When Thompson encountered Taylor on the way to McCaleb's (admission) office to report the result of the exam, and told him she had just read a most remarkable exam even though she had to flunk it, Taylor said, "Oh, our poet!"

Millay was fortunately a student in MacCracken's Shakespeare class, and he allowed her to make creative innovations in her assignments. She took a course he taught, "Drama 220," the history of dramatic literature. As a substitute for the more conventional final exam taken by the other students in his class, MacCracken encouraged her to compose a play that would reflect her comprehension of the course. She wrote a moral interlude called *Two Slatterns and a King*. "She wrote during class for three weeks and finished it," according to a reporter, looking into Millay's life as a student for the undergraduate paper *The Miscellany News*. The reporter, Muriel Crane, 1953, observed:

> *Drama 220 was a lecture course. ... However, this did not deter Vincent from getting up and spouting Shakespeare when the occasion moved her to it. Physicians considered women frail in those days and sick excuses could be sent to class for almost any reason. Miss Millay used this convenient means to cut her eight o'clock drama class one morning. Dr. MacCracken saw her performing splits and all sorts of fantastic capers about an hour afterward under Main gate. He remarked teasingly when he saw her later in the day on her "quick recovery from illness." She replied, "It just so happened that at the time of your class I was in pain with a poem."*

MacCracken found ways to keep Millay from making too many waves in faculty waters. She was constantly in trouble with the wardens who monitored the rather strict social regulations of the college on behalf of the faculty. MacCracken's more relaxed attitude towards the regulations had not yet begun to prevail: possibly he would have dismissed them all as counter-productive. He was too politic that early in his career, however, to make such an exception to rules.

But in the spring of 1917, Millay would not have graduated had it not been for MacCracken's intervention.

"It was all because of Caruso," she later told a reporter, Jerome Beatty, in 1932, who wrote:

> *During Easter vacation in New York, an elderly woman had invited Miss Millay to hear Caruso in* Aida. *It was to be a tremendous event. Vincent knew* Aida *by heart, could play every note of the score, but had never heard Caruso.*
>
> *The elderly woman did not know that the date when Caruso was to sing was two days after Vincent was supposed to be back at Vassar, and Vincent did not tell her. She went to the opera, had a glorious time, and returned to Vassar to take her punishment.*
>
> *The punishment was that she could not leave campus overnight for the rest of the term. Remember she was 25! Towards the end of May . . . she went driving one Saturday with her roommate and two Vassar graduates, one a minister's daughter. They had luncheon at a tearoom at the Ashokan Reservoir, wrote some silly things in the tearoom's guestbook, and drove to the minister's house for dinner.*
>
> *At dinner she suddenly recalled that she was illegally away from the campus. . . . The last ferry was gone. She stole in her room at nine o'clock the next morning. . . . "A week later the warden of my hall happened to visit the tearoom,"* she told the reporter *"and all was lost."*

Just before graduation, Millay was told that she could not receive her diploma with her class and she was banned from the premises. The faculty met in solemn session and voted against leniency. The students in her class were affronted and defiantly demanded that she be allowed to participate in the final festivities for graduation, but she missed both class day and baccalaureate ceremonies, for each of which she had written a song. MacCracken, later saying that it was the only time in his career as president when he had exercised his right to overrule a faculty decision, granted her permission to return to the campus, and she graduated with the others. He repeatedly referred to her during his administration as one of the most talented students that had ever studied at Vassar.

CALVIN COOLIDGE
Vice President of the United States in 1921:

Coolidge expressed fears that Vassar students in post-World War I days were in too radical an environment at Vassar. *The Delineator* (June 1921, XCVII) featured Coolidge's article on reds in women's colleges, from which these passages are drawn. First the magazine's editor introduced the article by writing:

> *(This is the first of a series of three articles written for* The Delineator *by the Vice President of the United States in the interest of our country's common weal. Nothing in the scheme of civilization transcends in importance the subject to which Mr. Coolidge has here addressed himself with his characteristic calmness, terseness, clarity of expression and abiding faith in American institutions. In the preservation of this Republic lies the hope of mankind. Yet the Republic can be destroyed, and all about us active and insidious forces are working toward that destruction with the sheer strength of obsession.*
>
> *Conscious of* The Delineator's *audience the Vice President stresses and emphasizes the appeal of his facts to the women—the mothers and mothers-to-be of America. But the case he submits is not, we feel, for mothers alone. It is rather a case for mothers and fathers. It is time for them to put their heads together and ascertain exactly what manner of instruction their children are receiving in school, in college, in university. It is time, too, we think, if investigation discloses such an atmosphere or such results as are herein recorded, to have a thorough house-cleaning. Better a sane hewer of wood or drawer of water in one's family than a university graduate who has nothing more than antagonism to contribute to the service of society.—The Editor.)*

Coolidge remarked about Vassar:

> *... The spirit of this radical element is all too clearly expressed by a student in the* Miscellany News. *"I know what I am. I'm not pessimistic. I'm not optimistic. I'm just antagonistic." There one has it. That is not a sporadic incident of a*

sophomore conclusion. There are graduates not confined to those who may have imbibed them from the home influences surrounding some of the new elements of the American environment, who express similar views. An examination of recent publications shows a friendly familiarity with that antagonistic attitude towards our institutions and not without support by some faculty members, who permit its exercise under a cloak or claim of academic freedom.

In another copy of the Miscellany *we find that Miss [Winifred] Smith of the Vassar faculty during the 1920 Spring vacation was in Washington where she went to various hearings before the Senate committees. The most interesting was the Martens hearing, where Miss Smith was quite favorably impressed by the Soviet ambassador and struck by his moderation and intelligence compared to the narrowness of some of the committee.*

A Warning

... There can be no objection to the study of any development of radical thought or any social or economic movement or the hearing of radical speakers. Such activities by students, however, ought to be pursued under competent direction and instruction, as appears to be done in some of the colleges cited...

... It is not merely a question of economics, or of a larger humanitarianism expressed in profounder realization of a brotherhood of man. It is not progress or reform that is to be criticized. It is the breaking away from the old faiths. Where one of these goes, the rest are likely to follow.

Adherence to radical doctrines means the ultimate breaking down of the old sturdy virtues of manhood and womanhood, the insidious destruction of character, the weakening of the moral fiber of the individual, the destruction of the foundations of civilization.

JUDITH OGDEN HENRY, 1941
a skilled creator of double acrostic puzzles

Like other students, Judith Henry noticed MacCracken's restless energy and affectionately depicted it in the puzzle on the following pages.

A DOUBLE ACROSTIC PUZZLE
INSPIRED BY HENRY NOBLE MacCRACKEN

by JUDITH OGDEN HENRY

Directions for Solving: Guess the words defined on the next page and write the letters over their numbered dashes. Then transfer each letter to the correspondingly numbered square in the pattern below. Black squares indicate word endings. The filled puzzle will contain a message reading from left to right. The first letter of each guessed word will form an acrostic with further information reading vertically.

■	1 C	■	2 X	3 C	4 P	■	5 L	6 D	7 B	8 S	9 J
10 A	11 B	12 C	13 J	14 E	■	15 N	16 I	17 X	18 J	19 C	■	20 Q	21 L
22 X	23 R	24 C	25 W	■	26 Q	27 B	28 L	29 K	30 I	31 A	32 V	33 N	■
34 P	35 H	36 E	37 A	38 M	39 Q	40 G	■	41 X	42 L	■	43 B	44 U	45 K
■	46 L	47 X	48 U	49 S	50 G	51 K	52 Q	53 R	■	54 T	55 D	56 O
57 N	58 Q	59 T	60 Y	61 R	■	62 F	63 Q	64 E	■	65 C	66 A	67 Y	68 E
69 T	70 U	71 D	72 J	■	73 N	74 E	■	75 B	76 C	77 F	■	78 N	79 X
80 K	■	81 B	82 X	83 U	84 F	85 V	86 S	87 R	88 T	89 W	90 M	91 V
92 P	93 U	■	94 L	95 O	96 F	97 V	98 S	99 H	■	100 D	101 C	102 J	103 O
104 S	105 M	106 W	■	107 G	108 R	109 P	■	110 K	111 T	112 O	113 B	■	114 I
115 C	116 E	117 C	■	118 V	■	119 B	120 E	121 X	122 W	123 H	124 X	125 R
126 X	127 E	■	128 Q	■	129 J	130 T	131 G	132 H	133	134 V	135 Y

(Solution on page 304.)

A. An informer (Br.)
$$\overline{10}\ \overline{37}\ \overline{66}\ \overline{31}$$

B. Entertainment spectacle of swimmers
$$\overline{11}\ \overline{119}\ \overline{7}\ \overline{75}\ \overline{27}\ \overline{43}\ \overline{81}\ \overline{113}$$

C. The dearth of mirth
$$\overline{12}\ \overline{3}\ \overline{76}\ \overline{1}\ \overline{117}\ \overline{65}\ \overline{115}\ \overline{101}\ \overline{24}\ \overline{19}$$

D. A holler mockery
$$\overline{71}\ \overline{100}\ \overline{55}\ \overline{6}$$

E. Small white scales trying to get a head
$$\overline{64}\ \overline{116}\ \overline{68}\ \overline{14}\ \overline{36}\ \overline{120}\ \overline{74}\ \overline{127}$$

F. Money for the needy
$$\overline{62}\ \overline{77}\ \overline{84}\ \overline{96}$$

G. Affectionate
$$\overline{107}\ \overline{50}\ \overline{131}\ \overline{40}$$

H. A gait
$$\overline{132}\ \overline{99}\ \overline{35}\ \overline{123}$$

I. A sign used to make other people believe you know more than you do
$$\overline{16}\ \overline{114}\ \overline{30}$$

J. A hermit
$$\overline{18}\ \overline{9}\ \overline{129}\ \overline{102}\ \overline{133}\ \overline{72}\ \overline{13}$$

K. Equipped with weapons
$$\overline{29}\ \overline{51}\ \overline{110}\ \overline{80}\ \overline{45}$$

L. A cockroach, for instance
$$\overline{94}\ \overline{46}\ \overline{28}\ \overline{5}\ \overline{21}\ \overline{42}$$

M. Something that grows stronger with age
$$\overline{90}\ \overline{105}\ \overline{38}$$

N. 0°
$$\overline{57}\ \overline{73}\ \overline{33}\ \overline{78}\ \overline{15}$$

O. Nobleman
$$\overline{56}\ \overline{95}\ \overline{112}\ \overline{103}$$

P. Flock of ducks
$$\overline{109}\ \overline{92}\ \overline{34}\ \overline{4}$$

Q. Marine invertebrate
$$\overline{128}\ \overline{20}\ \overline{52}\ \overline{26}\ \overline{58}\ \overline{63}\ \overline{39}$$

R. Ponders moodily
$$\overline{23}\ \overline{125}\ \overline{87}\ \overline{108}\ \overline{53}\ \overline{61}$$

S. Lowest in rank
$$\overline{49}\ \overline{104}\ \overline{98}\ \overline{8}\ \overline{86}$$

T. Implant
$$\overline{130}\ \overline{69}\ \overline{88}\ \overline{111}\ \overline{59}\ \overline{54}$$

U. An impression
$$\overline{48}\ \overline{83}\ \overline{70}\ \overline{44}\ \overline{93}$$

V. Lifts
$$\overline{134}\ \overline{118}\ \overline{85}\ \overline{97}\ \overline{32}\ \overline{91}$$

W. Ireland
$$\overline{25}\ \overline{89}\ \overline{122}\ \overline{106}$$

X. Fear of strangers
$$\overline{47}\ \overline{124}\ \overline{17}\ \overline{82}\ \overline{2}\ \overline{79}\ \overline{126}\ \overline{22}\ \overline{41}\ \overline{121}$$

Y. Long-haired bovine
$$\overline{135}\ \overline{67}\ \overline{60}$$

HENRY NOBLE MacCracken.

RAMIFICATIONS: MacCRACKEN'S VASSAR, MARCHING TO A DIFFERENT DRUMMER FROM THE OTHER SISTERS?

T HE FORMAL ASSOCIATION of the Seven Sister colleges was anticipated when MacCracken in 1915—the day after his inauguration—called into the joint meeting in his office the three presidents of Smith, Wellesley, and Mt. Holyoke to discuss and find a solution to the admission problems common to all those colleges. (Bryn Mawr, to join later, appears not to have been invited; M. Carey Thomas, its president, probably did not feel that it shared the admission problem. Barnard and Radcliffe, the other two colleges in the group, were in slightly different situations, both being attached to universities.) Calling this group together was the first formal act that MacCracken performed as Vassar president.

That first conference in October was the precursor of many others which MacCracken initiated with different groups on all sorts of subjects. He was beginning to perceive that the best and most democratic way to solve problems at any level—local, regional, national, international, or global—was to let those involved talk issues through and try to arrive at solutions. The use of association by conference to solve mutual problems of groups was perhaps MacCracken's most innovative practice as an administrator. This was true both inside the orbit of the college—within the framework of the mechanisms established by the governance for committee action and conference— and outside the periphery of the college, such as with the National Conference of Christians and Jews, the Kosciuszko Foundation, the

League to Enforce Peace, the American Junior Red Cross, and the Community Chest—all organizations which he founded or co-founded so that particular relationships could be developed and problems solved.

The informal association of the four colleges in 1915 produced successful common solutions in that first instance, and also led thereafter to the more formal association of an enlarged group, which included Radcliffe, Bryn Mawr, and Barnard, and was called together by Virginia Gildersleeve, Dean of Barnard, in 1926. The new Seven Sisters association, as it was then called, tackled an enhanced agenda, the chief item of which was the common difficulties of the women's colleges in raising money for endowments. At their first joint meeting on September 15, 1926, members of the new group discussed how to gain financial backing for women's liberal arts education "from wealthy men not previously involved in supporting education."

A memorandum that was prepared soon thereafter for circulation to potential donors suggested that women's colleges had to compete with men's universities for teaching staffs, salaries, leaves and equipment, and money for the endowment of special kinds of research projects, where women workers were in the majority. As women in American society merited "dowries" for marriage, but incurred debts for their education, the women's colleges needed much larger sums of money for scholarship funds than those then available to them, especially for "loan funds and self-support." The underlying fact-of-life for the women's colleges in the 1920s was that their alumnae were dependent upon money drawn from the males in their families, especially their husbands, for financial support to their colleges. Many of the jobless alumnae had no money of their own, no checkbooks, and no financial clout. Accordingly, they had to ask their husbands to untie the pursestrings for contributions if any money were to be forthcoming for their alma maters after graduation. As the husbands' colleges usually came first, their own came second. Insufficient finances were troublesome realities for the Seven Sisters in those early years.

Thomas W. Lamont addressed the Seven Sisters administrators on "Increased Endowments for Women's Colleges" at a dinner held in Philadelphia in November 1928. At the meeting, Gildersleeve reported that of seven male colleges named, individual colleges had endowments in the high millions—for example, Harvard, $82 million, and Duke, $27.5 million in 1928, which, added to the large sums amassed by the five other leading male colleges totaled $318.5 million for the seven colleges. Whereas among the women's colleges, of which Vassar was financially on top in 1928 (only because MacCracken and the alumnae had raised money several times after his arrival), the range was from Vassar's $6.5 million down to Mount Holyoke's $4 million, for a total of $36 million for all Seven Sisters.

The colleges established a joint office in Manhattan, with an administrator to carry out their newly conceived development plans. Each college put $1000 into the kitty, and the money was used to promote the public relations and development of the colleges through a series of public and private, joint and separate moves. The colleges set as a goal the raising of $50 million among them. They talked together continuously about how to attract the money and fired memos back and forth. The presidents, singly or in pairs, made calls on wealthy people. As soon as they could, they tackled officers of the new educational trusts and foundations just coming into being, such as the Commonwealth Fund, the Penney Foundation, The J. M. Foundation, and the General Education Board, set up by John D. Rockefeller. In April 1930, for instance, Vassar presented to the General Education Board a request for $6 million.

This idea of raising funds cooperatively through group appeals was a new wrinkle in money-raising in the 1920s. During Taylor's administration, he singlehandedly raised all the money. He invited onto his board of trustees John D. Rockefeller, Frederick Gates (Rockefeller's top administrator), and Charles Pratt. Between the gifts of Rockefeller and Pratt, most of Vassar's urgent money problems were resolved by direct appeal before MacCracken came.

In 1888, for example, soon after he assumed his duties, Taylor wrote Rockefeller, telling him of the difficulties he was having in raising money:

> *I have almost finished another month of labors for the "endowment." College business calls me away for a few days—a meeting of school principals at Syracuse. Important as this is, I should not go if I knew of any work I could do hopefully toward completing the $100,000—but though I have followed trail after trail, with hope and without hope, I seem to have reached a point where advance is checked.*
>
> *Let me tell you briefly how I have worked. I have written eighteen more letters to people in New York, Springfield, North*

Adams, Wellesley, Seattle, and Detroit. Among others I tried your brother again. He writes me that he cannot give now. . . . One or two have not answered me yet: all who have have declined to help.

I have made a good many calls on men and women reputed to be very wealthy . . . I have not received the slightest encouragement, save the promise to "consider and write." I suppose that means "no," as they have not written, but I am perfectly willing to "follow them up" if it seems best, but I think they mean to decline as gently as possible. . . .

This whole month then has resulted merely in interesting people in the College, in making them acquainted with its works and its wants. It has taught me that we cannot force that sort of intelligent interest which gives. People must come to know us and what we do. . . . The discouraging thing to me is that I seem to already have exhausted the list of those intelligently interested. For while I raised $10,000 last month, I have utterly failed this month though I have worked very hard. . . .

At the end of the letter, Taylor pressed Rockefeller to make another contribution to the college, and the appeal was subsequently granted.

Between 1926 and 1935, the Seven Sisters organization formulated a bevy of fund-raising plans in a concerted effort to put the financial needs of the woman's college before the public. They tackled the wealthy men through a series of formal dinners held in prominent places and much publicized in the newspaper press, as well as over the radio (on stations WEAF in New York and WOR in Newark, New Jersey). The newly created motion picture newscasts captured some of these events, and enabled the women's colleges to find a place on a brand new communications map. MacCracken may very well have been responsible for this frontier project; in 1915 right after he had come to the college he was already investigating the possibility of making a movie of Vassar students going about their daily life on campus.

Memorandum from MacCracken to Louise Sheppard (warden in charge of alumnae relations), March 1, 1915:

In conversation with Professor Wood, the suggestion was made by me that students of Vassar, under the supervision of the English

Department, should get Professor Shattuck and his moving picture machine to make a moving picture of Vassar life which might be shown for an admission fee.

While some on the Vassar faculty were deploring the development of the new art form of the motion picture as a waste of time, MacCracken immediately connected with its informational, theatrical, and visual potential and may well have talked his presidential colleagues into its use. Although apprehensive ahead of time, the presidents were delighted when in January 1930, Paramount News, in theatres across the country, showed a delayed picture of the newly appointed Chief Justice of the Supreme Court, Charles Evans Hughes, at a formal dinner at the New York Astor Hotel with Eleanor Roosevelt and the five women and two men who were presidents of the colleges at that time. It is amusing to realize that in the 1920s MacCracken and the others were doing their best to place an accurate visual picture of life in the Seven Sisters colleges before the press, whereas a decade earlier Taylor went to the greatest lengths imaginable to keep Vassar's name out of the press in the case of suffrage meetings and other contemporary causes.

Still, traces of the Taylor attitude—a feeling of the necessity for aloofness—kept cropping up among the old guard. Cornelia Raymond, President John Raymond's aged daughter, was working as publicist in the Vassar press department in 1930, and she sent a complaint to Mrs. Maud Steward, coordinator of the Seven Sister's office on January 20, 1930. A prying woman reporter from *The New York Post* had just come to the campus to do an article on Vassar. Raymond wrote:

The people she interviewed felt that she had a preconceived idea of what she wanted them to say and that when they answered their questions in a different way she twisted their meaning to almost the opposite of what they said. . . . She frankly said she was not interested in the educational side of the college but only wanted to know what they talked about when they were alone in their rooms. She asked a great many questions as to their opinions on marriage and sex and even asked the chairman of the Community Church [the Vassar religious organization] how many girls at Vassar knelt down and said their prayers before going to bed. The girls cannot believe that we are going to allow her to use their names in her article and that we are not going to see the article before it is published.

This scene, and others like it, were repeated in the days to come as Vassar, and other colleges, became more accustomed to scrutiny in the national press.

During the formal presentations at the big joint fund-raising meetings, MacCracken, an engaging raconteur, was one of the presidents most in demand at the podium. At the Hughes affair, he shared the platform with the Chief Justice and several other presidents. The substance of the addresses that evening ranged over the desirability of an education for women comparable "by every educational standard" to the education of men.

On that and other occasions the presidential speakers repeatedly tackled educational goals for women from their varied points of view, some emphasizing the uses to which the education should be put, such as the preparation for a life as a parent, or for a life of leisure, made possible by modern technology. Others advocated increased attention to vocational preparation for a limited number of professions, and the sharpening of the mind to deal with whatever life brought.

MacCracken's unique theme, then and always, was the social uses of women's education, and he invariably made a pitch for women's roles as community leaders, their responsibility to seek knowledge and techniques to improve the environment in which community life was played out, and their work for a higher social order—all the themes of euthenics. Other presidents seemed most often to speak about more classical curricular issues, such as the tutorial system of teaching at Radcliffe, or traditional graduate work for women at Bryn Mawr. MacCracken gained his reputation in the Seven Sisters league for being less interested in the intellectual life of the woman undergraduate than in the ways she spent her time after college. To him, her mission, more often than not, was one of causes and community, involving national and world citizenship.

The various members of the Seven Sisters group may have had their disagreements, but in general they shared common ideas about women's education. Many of the women faculty members who began their teaching careers at Vassar got their advanced degrees at Bryn Mawr, either before they started teaching or along the way. (This was, of course, because Bryn Mawr along with Yale University, was among the first institutions to offer women the Ph.D.) It was not uncommon for female faculty members to move from one of the Seven Sister colleges to another, moreover, especially from Vassar to Smith and Wellesley or vice-versa, gaining initial teaching experience at one, and carrying it over to another, where they settled down to permanent positions. They spread a mantle of the prototype experience of the nineteenth and early twentieth century woman's college from one institution to the next, making their own subtle modifications and adaptations as they passed. The effect on the texture of women's education was cumulative, interwoven in the shuttle of time, and making for commonality rather than disparity. Administrators—the executives—also moved back and forth: Vassar to Wellesley, President Millicent McAfee (Horton), 1920, and Dean Keats Whiting, 1918; Smith to Barnard, Dean Marjorie Nicolson, and Smith to Radcliffe, President Ada Comstock; and Radcliffe to Bryn Mawr, President Marian Park. Many of the internal organizations of the colleges were similar; guest lecturers often passed from one institution to another, where they gave the same guest lectures. For example, MacCracken drove his automobile to Smith in Northampton to pick up Madame Curie, whom he had met in Paris, and drove her from there to Vassar, where she would also give her lecture.

In essence these colleges were not all that different from each other if compared with other women's colleges in other places. Because they cooperated in implementing similar policies, their students were of comparable quality and had been similarly prepared, their curricula were cut out of the same general liberal arts cloth, with certain variations, and their economies were more or less analogous—the Seven Sisters resembled each other more than they differed.

Privately, however, some of the women administrators resented certain aspects of MacCracken, especially early in their association, in his first years as president. They thought he was a smart aleck. Ada Louise Comstock (dean of Smith 1912-23, president of Radcliffe 1923-43) early observed to her colleague Bernice Cronkhite that she found MacCracken to be a "very disturbing man." M. Carey Thomas, who had deemed MacCracken's predecessor Taylor much too stodgy and conservative for her taste, thought MacCracken quite the opposite: a "Hotspur Harry," "impetuous," "excitable," and "changeable," according to her colleague Helen Taft Manning, former dean and acting president of Bryn Mawr during a year-long leave of M. Carey Thomas. Manning recalled in retirement that MacCracken struck them at Bryn Mawr in the early twenties as pursuing what seemed to them to be "half-baked ideas." He did not at first seem to have the earmarks of a real educational leader. They did not think

Vassar was a very intellectual place under MacCracken's leadership. He seemed to be trying to pull away from the Taylor Vassar in too great a rush.

They were right about the rush, if not about the place. His chief interest was in rapidly modernizing the liberal arts—transforming them into something more pertinent to post-war needs, causing the students to look ahead beyond the saxophones and speedometers of the jazz age at what they wanted from their futures around the corner, making their pursuit of life more conscious. In his annual report to the trustees of 1921 he spoke of a reconceived trivium on which he hoped to base the Vassar education: he had a consistent and steadfast purpose in wanting to maintain classical scholarship and a continuing interest in science (the old components of the medieval quadrivium with new additions) he said, but, besides those two traditional aspects, he wanted admitted to the liberal arts the study of human relations as a third branch of intellectual discipline.

A revised mission for the Vassar education, he said, would not make everything over and everything new: the curriculum would continue to be grounded in the past and to give students opportunities for many full backward glances. But it would seek also to break down boundaries, compartments, and unnecessary walls which made false separations, and to change the patterns of the future lives of its students. MacCracken thought that the liberal arts should be studied in a more interdisciplinary context. Students, no longer having to take a set of required courses, should find their own interests and hone them, both in depth and breadth; their education should be actively participatory, grounded in observation, seeking and finding in the present as well as in the record of the past. The rapidly shifting conditions created new expectations and opportunities that Vassar should prepare them to meet and accept.

In the stenographer's report of the Fiftieth Alumnae Anniversary conference held on the campus in 1921, MacCracken declared that education for him was:

> *...the economics of experience. ...What we wish to do is to make as much experience available as can be digested by the individual student. ...we regard the twenty-four hours of the day and every single point of contact of the student with the world as an educational opportunity. Play or recreation of all kinds and everything else, sleep, household living, the social*

ideals, the Chapel worship, as well as the classroom, all of these are educational opportunities, and we have the opportunity here of making this free to the students.

✳   ✳   ✳

HELEN D. LOCKWOOD, Vassar 1912, was a stunningly innovative professor who taught English during MacCracken's presidency from 1926 to the late 1950s. She was an iconoclast who had herself studied under Lucy Salmon, and who upheld and reinterpreted her mentor's views of education. In 1967 in retirement Lockwood wrote a pamphlet that was never published, summing up the essence of the Vassar experience developed under MacCracken. The occasion for her pamphlet was the possible removal of Vassar College to New Haven, Connecticut, to join with Yale University, at the time also a single-sex undergraduate college, in a coeducational enterprise. (The move, because of opposition from alumnae and for other reasons, never took place.) In her pamphlet, she pointed out why she thought it would be an act of alienation and abstraction to remove Vassar from its roots.

. . . Students at Vassar shared in the development of participation in the community. The vision of social responsibility and public service whether volunteer or paid, has pervaded the climate of the college.

From the time a student entered to her graduation, she heard it expressed by the leaders of the college, she saw them often acting it themselves in Poughkeepsie or the nation, and she found it assumed in her courses. She volunteered in the social centers in Poughkeepsie and helped them [through fund drives] financially. She expected to take part in making the college community. . . .

There was a world vision in a local one. The Vassar social sciences approached the natural sciences in their emphasis on laboratory work in the field. At every level of education, the college and the community have made the beginnings of relationships. MacCracken started community forums in Poughkeepsie and presided over them. Students participated in them. These were designed to uncover the many sides of any public issue and to make sure that each was coherently presented by someone believing in it. The college reached out to the community through local radio programs: "Poughkeepsie Speaks."

In 1937 President MacCracken, with a fund given by the Alumnae Association, opened the Social Museum as an experiment in curricular research in visual education. It displayed provocatively the results of social research or relationships between the sciences in artistic form, using the visual arts in combination with language.

Helen Lockwood, herself a maker as well as a follower of this philosophy, sent her students to the streets and backyards of Poughkeepsie to find out what was there, who the people were, and what they wanted. So did Hallie Flanagan, head of Vassar's theater, in her "Living Newspaper" plays, which chronicled the Depression. So did Caroline Ware, who sent a thesis student to the City of Beacon nearby in Dutchess County to dig into its history; so did Mabel Newcomer, distinguished economist who served Franklin Roosevelt at Bretton Woods, whose students went to Poughkeepsie neighborhoods to conduct surveys that could be used in making civic and governmental decisions.

There was a new and unique drumbeat in the Vassar marching music. The Bryn Mawr presidents were not the only ones to hear it.

CHAPTER FOURTEEN

MacCRACKEN'S "DREAM CHILD":
SARAH LAWRENCE COLLEGE

THE YEAR IN WHICH President MacCracken founded the Vassar Summer Institute of Euthenics, 1926, was the same one in which he led a group of persons in the application for a temporary charter for a junior college in Bronxville, New York, to be called Sarah Lawrence College. The two events were closely connected, and both stemmed from MacCracken's desire to further "socialize" women's education and to educate more women to the issues of their changing times and needs.

The story of how MacCracken got together with the aging millionaire William Van Duzer Lawrence of Bronxville, to give him advice and help him implement his plans for founding an experimental new educational enterprise, adds still another example to MacCracken's restless initiatives to change and improve the quality of educational opportunities for women after the war.

At the time of MacCracken's inauguration in 1915, the Vassar alumnae announced that they would raise a million dollars as a present to the college in honor of its Fiftieth Anniversary. Their new president eagerly joined in the enterprise, never dreaming that among other things, the timely success of the campaign would nearly lead to his own downfall because of unsure fiscal policies within the board. The president of the Vassar Alumnae Association during the financial campaign was Louise Lawrence Meigs, Vassar 1891, William and Sarah Lawrence's daughter. MacCracken enjoyed working with Meigs while cultivating potential Vassar donors, and through her, he very soon got to know her father, "a gentleman of some means," as he later described him. In an interview which Constance Warren, Sarah

Lawrence president between 1929 and 1945, conducted with Mac-
Cracken in 1961, he recalled that the first time he saw Lawrence, he
"marked him down in his mind's eye, as a college president inevitably
does," and it wasn't long after he made this mental note that he
actually solicited Lawrence for funds for Vassar.

Lawrence said "no" to the request, but for an unusual reason:

> *No, I have made up my mind to do something. I do not know
> what. But whatever I do, I shall leave it in Bronxville, where I
> made the money. I believe in leaving the money where I made it,
> and not putting it in to something else. That is only fair.*

MacCracken recalled that that was where the matter was left, on
the surface of it, for the next few years, but that sometime in 1924 he
wrote Lawrence a letter with an idea. In fact he apparently wrote not
one letter but many, and the subject of the correspondence was Mac-
Cracken's suggestions about what Lawrence should do with his money.

MacCracken must have felt an uncanny link to Vassar's past as he
took up the subject of Lawrence's projected Bronxville gift to posterity.
Certain aspects of the Lawrence-MacCracken situation seemed to be
repeating history—the lead taken by an educator from out of town,
Milo P. Jewett, in persuading Matthew Vassar to found a college for
women, rather than spend his money in other ways, had enormous
parallels to this Lawrence situation.

✳   ✳   ✳

MACCRACKEN'S OWN ROLE in keeping the memory of Matthew
Vassar's creative genius alive in the twentieth century was a persistent
activating force in his consciousness. He wrote and spoke about the
founder, and his ideas and relationships, on many different occasions,
and made himself extremely familiar with all of Vassar's recorded
thoughts and dilemmas about the college's beginnings. He was very
impressed with Vassar's ability to incorporate the best thinking of
others, which had enabled him to actualize his plan although he started
from a zero base of understanding about women's educational needs.

MacCracken had especially studied the crucial role of Milo P.
Jewett, the first president of Vassar (1861-64), in the formulation of
Vassar's educational philosophy, and had come to the same conclusion
as an earlier trustee, Benson Lossing, that without Jewett, "there
would have been no Vassar College." He was closely interested in the

king-maker aspect of Jewett's performance, and looked back at what had happened between Jewett and Vassar more than fifty years earlier as a kind of collective act of creativity, in which both persons had a chance to fulfill their desires.

Jewett, a Baptist minister, had arrived in Poughkeepsie shortly before the Civil War from Alabama, where he had been the president of a women's seminary. A serendipity of timing enabled him in 1855 to take over Cottage Hill, a girls' school in Poughkeepsie founded by Vassar's feminist niece, Lydia Booth, who died in 1854. Matthew Vassar, who had come back to his home from a grand tour of Europe in 1846, had determined, while mulling over his affairs when abroad, that he wanted to found an institution which would be "of benefit to mankind." He also had in mind that the institution would necessarily involve a monumental building, which could serve as a memorial to the Vassar name for all time in Poughkeepsie. For the years between 1855 and 1861—after which plans for founding Vassar College were actualized through application for a charter—Jewett skillfully steered and advised Vassar, and helped him arrive at what finally seemed to him an inevitable conclusion that he must found not a hospital, not a secondary school, but a college, where women could get an education equal to that available for men.

MacCracken, who had often rehearsed this nineteenth century relationship in his mind's eye, intuitively looked upon himself as Lawrence's Jewett. Just as Jewett had wanted something from his relationship with Vassar—the chance to be the creator of Vassar's college—so MacCracken saw an opportunity to do something important with Lawrence. He would persuade him of the benefits of starting a unique college in Bronxville, thus preserving his family name for posterity. That college would be Sarah Lawrence, a junior college for women who wanted the opportunity for experiential, self-directed education in a liberal arts setting. In guiding Lawrence towards the application for a charter, and in drafting it for him just as Jewett drafted parts of Vassar's application, MacCracken would have the chance to exploit his dream of an institution where the students came first, where the curriculum was built around the concept of their self-activation, and where they had the chance to translate experience of life into bona fide academic credit. This would make up for his rebuff over euthenics, and, who knows, perhaps even restore it to favor.

In the years between 1915, when MacCracken first started to think in broad terms about innovation and experimentation in women's education, and 1924, when he wrote Lawrence a solicitous letter feeling him out about his plans, MacCracken's special interest in euthenics and "socialization" of education had grown, but the Vassar faculty's interest in euthenics had so dwindled as to be almost non-existent. By 1924 it was clear that incorporating the philosophical bias of euthenics, as he and the Blodgett group conceived it, wholesale into the Vassar curriculum was not a real option for MacCracken. Too many on the Vassar faculty, especially in the sciences, were resistant to the whole idea. Frustrated and desirous of the opportunity to put his ideas into play, MacCracken quietly groped after the new opportunity afforded by Lawrence's desire to found an institution. Perhaps here was the chance to try his ideas in a special theatre. There were other considerations, also. Enrollment in women's liberal arts colleges had continuously increased since before the war, and the existent colleges did not have sufficient places to meet the demand.

As MacCracken said:

> At that time I was also very much worried by the huge advance registration at Vassar College. . . . In 1923, the year before I got into this with Mr. Lawrence's lawyer at his request, Vassar College had closed its registration for eight years ahead. And this means that the students who were to come to Vassar College were in their seventh grade in elementary school, and what could they know about college at all?
> . . . It had to be stopped.

The reform which helped stop "it" was, as we have already seen, the four-college admission plan by which the college was gradually put on a competitive basis. However, that conversion left many students out; there simply were not enough college places to go around. MacCracken noted to Constance Warren that in fact he had first felt the larger and pressing obligation to undertake responsibility for improving women's educational opportunities two years after he got to Vassar. He agreed at that time to work with a committee of the General Federation of Women's Clubs in New Jersey to assist in the organization of a woman's college, the New Jersey College for Women (which subsequently became known as Douglass College, part of Rutgers University). In fact, on February 12, 1918, the night a fire started in the dining hall at the back of Main Building at Vassar and quickly burned it down, MacCracken was summoned back to Pough-keepsie by phone from a dinner meeting in New Jersey where he was in the midst of formulating these plans.

By August 1924 MacCracken wrote Lawrence that he was working on his project. The next month Lawrence acknowledged receiving from MacCracken a draft of a constitution for their joint educational enterprise. But later that month (September 17) MacCracken wrote again about the difficulties entailed in getting a charter. New York State categorically refused to grant a junior college charter. (Franklin Roosevelt who was on the Vassar board by then was unfortunately not yet governor, although records of trustee deliberations suggest that he was already interested in the junior college movement.) MacCracken's proposal to Lawrence to solve the charter problem was that they apply for a four-year college charter, with a focus on the first two years:

> *Sometime in 1924, I think it was, I wrote this letter. I wrote Mr. Lawrence in March of 1925 and we exchanged letters for some time in which I tried to discourage his idea, first of a boy's school. And I remember writing him a letter in which I told him there were almost too many boys' boarding schools now, that they were competing heavily with each other, whereas women had no such opportunity and most of their schools were crowded. And I proposed the idea of a junior college, which might be attached to the school. I believed at that time that it was a way of reaching him in his [then] present stage of thinking. He liked that idea, and then as the correspondence went on I tried to wean him of the idea of having a school at all and going in wholeheartedly for the full two years of junior college. He was a complete novice in the knowledge of conditions in education at the time, and had to learn what a junior college was. . . .*
>
> *It was the first [junior college] to which the Regents gave a charter. Packer Institute [in Brooklyn, New York, presided over for a long time by Truman Backus, who from 1866 to 1883 taught English at Vassar] was in the nature of a junior college and had long existed, and there were other schools that gave courses to graduates, but if you think of a junior college as something actually legally chartered, this was, I believe, the first granted by the Regents . . .*
>
> *Progressive education was in the air. I don't remember just when progressive education was organized, but it was shortly after*

this, I think. But I was in touch with Mrs. Queene Ferry Coonley of Chicago, who I think was the first president of the Progressive Education Association. She was one of the givers of Alumnae House to Vassar College; I believe that the organizational meeting of the Progressive Education Association of America was held at Vassar College, which I attended. I was very much interested. I also was a reader of John Dewey and his philosophy. I attended his lectures and invited him to lecture at Vassar College . . . his beliefs were shared up here. Miss Wylie of the faculty was a very progressive woman. . . . She started an educational project. Miss Buck, her great friend, was one of the first to introduce participation by the students in the control of the classroom, and an experimental theatre . . .

I had been, I think, at this time a member of a conference on progressive education that was held at Bradford Academy, near Haverhill, Massachusetts. Miss [Marion] Coats [Vassar, 1907, who was to become the first president of Sarah Lawrence] was the head then. She was considering the establishment of a junior college; what we were discussing up there was what a junior college should consist of. My recollection is that I presented a fairly complete idea of its organization and studies, its aims and the method by which those aims could be to some extent obtained. And it interested Miss Coats and the others there.

MacCracken carefully explained to Miss Coats, in a letter of November 30, 1925, exactly what he had in mind in using the term "socializing the curriculum," the concept that he felt might particularize the character of a new junior college plan, at Bradford and elsewhere.

Socializing the curriculum means:

1. Recognition that it is possible within the undergraduate years to carry out certain application of theory in science applied to life.

2. That theory and practice should go hand in hand during the learning process.

3. That the isolation of the sciences from each other and from other ways of looking at the same data as in philosophy, aesthetics and ethics, while immensely valuable from the point of view of the development of the sciences, has been lacking from the point of view of education; and that this data must be recovered for the use of the entire curriculum. History, philosophy and art must all make use of data now restricted to the area of science, otherwise they will die of dry rot. The sciences, on the other hand, have been in equal need of aesthetic contribution.

4. That through the isolation of the sciences, certain gaps in knowledge have been created which can never be filled by cooperation among them. This is particularly true of the applications of science to human life in the field of Euthenics, Education, Religion, Citizenship, and so on.

As Constance Warren later pointed out, the conference which MacCracken participated in at Bradford led to the "reorganization, along progressive lines," of Bradford Junior College, and eventually to the recommendation that Coats be made the first president of Sarah Lawrence College, while MacCracken would become the chairman of the Sarah Lawrence board of trustees.

Dudley B. Lawrence, William and Sarah Lawrence's son, gave his version in a July 1958 memo, which he wrote to set the record straight, of how his father came to found Sarah Lawrence College. The memo stated:

The first suggestion of a women's college in Bronxville came in the early twenties at a time when ... my father had already passed his eightieth birthday. [Matthew Vassar was sixty-nine when he founded Vassar College.]

Mr. Lawrence was always a creator. He loved to personally plan and build important structures such as the Hotel Gramatan, the Lawrence Hospital, the Osceola Inn in Daytona Beach, and others. It was in this spirit that his home, Westlands, was built in 1914-16. ... At eighty-two he was confronted with the problem of a future for Westlands. He was determined that the property should serve some useful purpose and not become just another oversized house to be demolished or sold for taxes.

One suggestion was made that the Lawrence Hospital [a Bronxville hospital] should be removed to the Westlands site. This received serious consideration but was subsequently abandoned as not being a suitable location.

William Lawrence then turned his attention, according to his son, to the possibility of founding a women's college. His wife had always been "an enthusiastic advocate of higher education for women," and the Lawrences' daughter had gone to Vassar.

Dudley Lawrence's memorandum continued:

> *I remember Dr. James Taylor, then president of Vassar, visiting at our home and much later, I believe, President and Mrs. MacCracken were guests down in Florida. There can be no doubt that Dr. MacCracken's influence, advice, and later, his devoted service to the infant college were of the most paramount importance in its establishment.*
>
> *The original idea was that Sarah Lawrence should be a two-year junior college on the theory that many girls could accomplish more there than in four-year colleges, which they frequently left in the middle of their course. This, I believe, was Dr. MacCracken's first suggestion.*

According to the memo of the younger Lawrence, the rest of the Lawrence family did not go along with the college plan at first. They felt that "it was too late [at age eighty-two] for the elderly man to personally undertake the erection" of a college. But William Lawrence was stubborn, and had a "one-track mind." So before he died, he obtained a provisional charter from New York State with the help of MacCracken, made plans for the layout of the college campus and buildings, and even personally staked them out.

Early in 1925 MacCracken and Lawrence exchanged numerous letters in which they tackled the problems before them. Not the least of these was the question of who would run such an institution of learning. Lawrence promised from his winter home in Florida to take up landscaping the Westlands site of the planned college when he returned later that spring. He also outlined his thoughts about a preparatory school and a junior college, with the standards of Vassar and Smith; the preparatory school was to be established first. MacCracken wrote in favor of connecting the prep school and the junior college, and along the way recommended Miss Coats as head of the school. Furthermore, MacCracken and Lawrence discussed the selection of a board of trustees, with MacCracken as chairperson, and five invited trustees from the Vassar College board. (MacCracken probably thought up this arrangement. He would have remembered that when Vassar, who was on the board of trustees of Rochester University, gathered his initial trustees for the Vassar board, back in 1861, he invited six Rochester trustees, including Martin B. Anderson, the president of Rochester, and William Kelly, who was elected the first Vassar board chairman, to serve on the Vassar board and offer guidance through the slippery beginning channels.)

After Constance Warren retired in 1945, she wrote a memorandum including stories she had heard about the early power plays over the founding of Sarah Lawrence:

> ...As I have heard the story, when word leaked out in the newspapers that Mr. Lawrence intended to give his place, with money, for an educational institution, Nicholas Murray Butler boarded a train and came right up here to try to get it for Columbia. Mr. Lawrence was furious, and these two bull-headed old gentlemen met head-on. Mr. Lawrence was so mad that he immediately got in touch with MacCracken, Mr. Lawrence's daughter having attended Vassar, and asked MacCracken to consult with him as to what he could do with his money.

MacCracken put it this way when asked by Warren for his memories of the event:

> ...Oh, I know all about that. ...Mr. Butler threatened Mr. Lawrence about 1926. He said, in substance,"You can't start a college in the New York area unless it is with my consent, and I don't consent. And I can put an end to Sarah Lawrence College." It was already announced then, and that was the first that Mr. Butler had heard of it. He invited Mr. Lawrence to give the college to Columbia as a junior college of Columbia; and he told him he would give the new college the same relationship to Columbia that Barnard College enjoyed. ...And this disturbed Mr. Lawrence so much that it led to his request for an affiliation with Vassar College for his own protection.

Warren, eliciting more memories from MacCracken in the 1961 interview, asked him whether it was not true that Lawrence said at that point, "If this college fails, the money goes to Vassar." MacCracken claimed never to have heard that. Whereupon Warren reminded him of an agreement which was ratified by the boards of trustees of both colleges in 1927 which stated:

> At the end of such five year period, or when a permanent charter has been secured, and if the agreement has proved satisfactory to both parties, a transfer of Sarah Lawrence Junior

College with all of its property of every kind may be made over to the Vassar Corporation, and the Sarah Lawrence Corporation retire from business, with the proviso, however, that the Vassar Corporation shall forever keep the name and for ten years thereafter retain the present site—that is, the Westlands property, the founder's home and the junior college plan. If the arrangement has not proven satisfactory to both parties, the Board of Trustees of Sarah Lawrence College shall have entire discretion to determine the future of that institution.

MacCracken went on to tell Warren that not only Nicholas Murray Butler, but also Dean Virginia Gildersleeve of Barnard, tried to twist Lawrence's arm, and that Lawrence was "simply terrified," to which Warren replied, "Perhaps not so terrified as made...furious... because...he was a man of very strong independent principles. ..." MacCracken countered: "Yes, but he was an old man then; he was ailing. He was letting go of his money. As he says in one of the letters here to me [which MacCracken had brought to the interview], 'I feel like the captain that has launched a ship without either sails, mast, or rudder. Now you must provide these for me.'"

(The parallels between the Matthew Vassar-Milo Jewett relationship and William Lawrence-MacCracken relationship continue:

"I wish someone would tell me what to do with my money. It's the plague of my life—keeps me awake at nights—stocks going down, banks breaking, insurance companies failing," Vassar observed to Jewett, when his nephews, Matthew Vassar Jr. and John Guy Vassar Jr. were clamoring for him to put money into a local hospital which they wanted to endow.

"Well, Mr. Vassar," Jewett later recalled saying at the time, "for several years past, I have had a scheme in my mind which I am unable to carry out, but it is one which you are abundantly able to execute and which I think will meet all your wishes in the disposal of your property. ...It is to build and endow a College for Young Women which shall be to them what Yale and Harvard are to men. ...If you will establish a real College for girls and endow it, you will build a monument for yourself more lasting than the Pyramids; you will perpetuate your name to the latest generations; it will be the pride and glory of Po'keepsie, an honor to the State, and a blessing to the world.")

Sarah Bates Lawrence died on May 8, 1926, after which her husband wrote to Marion Coats on May 26, inviting her to head the college. In a June 4 letter to his son, he first mentioned adding "Sarah" to the name of the Lawrence College. Coats replied that she was considering accepting the invitation to assume the leadership of the school, but that she was duty-bound to put in two more years at Bradford Academy. She proposed, however, that they proceed with plans for the college and aim for an October 1927 opening. Prior to the opening, she suggested, she would be on a retainer for her consulting services. Subsequent letters exchanged between Coats and MacCracken indicated that she relied heavily on MacCracken for advice. During their correspondence, she proposed that Sarah Lawrence Junior College serve as an overflow college for Vassar freshmen and sophomores, making more intrinsic a previously conceived looser affiliation between the two, in which only the trustees and administration of the college were involved. On July 20, 1926, Marion Coats formally accepted the invitation to become the head of Sarah Lawrence College when it opened in 1928. Lawrence wrote her on August 20, 1926, that he "looked to her" to "steer this ship which is yet in the harbor, after it is out to sea." In September, she submitted "My Profession of Faith, Educationally, and a Letter of Introduction to the Board of Trustees of the Sarah Lawrence Junior College."

Meanwhile MacCracken had been assiduously pursuing the elusive charter. In April 1926 he submitted a statement to the New York State Board of Regents in defense of the junior college concept. The charter of the college would not be approved, however, until December 9, 1926, when the acceptance of such a charter by the state inevitably caused much publicity, some of it unwelcome. Later that month MacCracken wrote of his concern about the direction the press was taking. "A million dollar college for brides" became its easy handle for reporters. This was not exactly what MacCracken had in mind when he thought of a curriculum which applied itself to the subject matter of euthenics and an integration of the sciences with the arts. And the costly $1500 tuition at the time was a predictable hurdle and target. Nevertheless, in the face of these challenges, MacCracken made a statement to the Vassar board that Sarah Lawrence should be a project of cooperation between the two institutions. He proposed a formal five-year affiliation.

MacCracken remembered in his interview with Warren:

Two days before he died [on May 16, 1927], [Mr Lawrence] summoned his secretary to his bedside and dictated further thoughts and instructions about how to proceed with the College construction.

MacCracken and the Vassar trustees on the Sarah Lawrence board carried the plan to completion and the college opened in September 1928, but not without some financial problems. Half way into the very hectic period of construction, the college needed $250,000 to complete its buildings. It was clear that the Lawrence family was not interested in invading the family trust to further support the college. Dudley Lawrence, who had agreed to serve as a college trustee, vividly recalled an anxious afternoon in which MacCracken and Ray Morris (brother of Helen Morris Hadley), a Vassar trustee on the Sarah Lawrence board and a partner in Brown Brothers, "ventured into the depths of Wall Street to get money" from the Bankers Trust Company. Everyone left the interview pessimistically believing no money at all would be forthcoming, but "Dr. MacCracken's prestige and Mr. Morris' high reputation in Wall Street ... brought about (an) astonishing result." The operation was financed.

In June, invitations went to certain Vassar trustees to serve on the board of Sarah Lawrence College. Among those tapped, in addition to Ray Morris, were Stephen Duggan, Arthur Lesher, and J. Lionberger Davis. (Later, under Warren, another similar group of trustees from Vassar succeeded them.) Marion Coats, still finishing out her term at Bradford, prepared at long distance during this period to assume the presidency at the institution's opening, by then scheduled for the fall of 1928.

A first sign of incipient disagreement between MacCracken and Coats, however, came in February of 1928 when Coats addressed a group at Vassar's four-year-old-Alumnae House. Her speech caused MacCracken to write her a letter, criticizing her remarks that denigrated other four year colleges in contrast to Vassar. He wrote that other Vassar members shared his opinion. The dispute seems to have had its roots in an apparent misconception held by Coats that dated at least as far back as June 1926, when she lobbied for a strong "affiliation" between Vassar and Sarah Lawrence. She and her mentor clearly had differing ideas about what that meant.

In April of 1929, Vassar's admission of a student from Sarah Lawrence to its junior class appeared to set a precedent, but the Vassar faculty that year expressed opposition to Sarah Lawrence students having blanket permission to transfer to Vassar with advanced standing. Marion Coats issued what registered as an ultimatum regarding Vassar's mandatory acceptance of Sarah Lawrence students, and she went too far for MacCracken. He wrote that, considering her ultimatum, he could not continue both as president of Vassar College and chairman of the board of Sarah Lawrence, and he would therefore withdraw from his Sarah Lawrence commitment. Two days later, on May 8, she countered with an offer to resign herself, and suggested Constance Warren as her successor. It was not until July 17, 1929, that a press release announced the resignation of Marion Coats as president, effective at once.

With the resignation of Marion Coats and the arrival of Constance Warren, Sarah Lawrence, MacCracken, and Vassar entered a new era of friendship. From that point until he retired in 1936, as planned, from the Sarah Lawrence board after ten years of service, MacCracken served the role of trustee advisor to Warren's eminently successful presidency.

In March of 1931 Warren led the board in the college's application for a permanent charter. Although there was some debate as to whether they should file formally or continue under the provisional charter that had been granted in 1926, the permanent charter was pursued, and on September 10, 1931, a permanent "absolute" charter was granted, empowering Sarah Lawrence to confer a bachelor of arts degree.

At the time of Constance Warren's retirement in 1945, MacCracken had this to say about Warren and the college she masterminded:

> *The announcement of the founding of a college devoted primarily to experiment, with its own curriculum, its own professors, and its own students was, of course, greeted with derision twenty years ago. Today all over the land carefully planned experiments at the college level, and even at the university level, are going on.*

In Sarah Lawrence's case, MacCracken observed, the experimental college created a new trivium through the juxtaposition of science, social science, and art.

> *The physical laboratory stands in the modern college side by side in the same building with the studio of painting, to the mutual profit of both. No longer is science tucked away at the back of the college campus in utilitarian buildings while art occupies the foreground adorned in pseudo-Gothic. Art and science, in short, are but two words describing the same process, the search for knowledge and its expression by man's unconquerable mind.*

It was inevitable also that Sarah Lawrence should begin to experiment with the earlier years of college as the place for improvement. The unfortunate gap between school and college, both in matters of discipline and in organization of knowledge, had resulted in an immense mortality [the loss of students unprepared to bridge the gap].

Because of "inadequate teaching in the colleges," young women were not making progress towards planning their life goals. At Sarah Lawrence, under Constance Warren, "a group of young teachers fully trained in the social sciences" applied their theories "not to students in general but to their own students in particular." The result was, MacCracken concluded, that Sarah Lawrence exerted its very powerful force for change on national education by orienting its students to use their creative imaginations in entering life actively through their education; by enjoying its experiences; by solving presented problems; and, at the conclusion of their education, by engaging life in the larger world, as they had their education. The Sarah Lawrence attitude of preparing students to enter life as an interdisciplinary laboratory had been a real contribution to American education.

MacCracken asserted:

This implantation of strong purpose early in the college course is the secret of what may be called educational public health.

"Strong purpose" stood for the quintessence of modernism in education to MacCracken. He knew, however, that in the Vassar of his time some of the faculty had been similarly shaking their students up as hard as they could to accomplish the same worthy objectives and had succeeded. There was more than one road to reform. Yet he undoubtedly displaced his frustration over the plight of euthenics at Vassar through his accomplishments in Bronxville.

It was Harold Taylor, president of the Bronxville college from 1945 to 1959, who in a public statement at the time of MacCracken's retirement from Vassar, perhaps most accurately stated it. Sarah Lawrence, Taylor said, was the product of Dr. MacCracken's suppressed desires: "It was his dream child born out of wedlock."

CONSTANCE WARREN AND HENRY NOBLE MACCRACKEN,
WITH ELLIOT DUNLAP SMITH, A SARAH LAWRENCE TRUSTEE,
DECEMBER 9, 1936.

HALLIE FLANAGAN DAVIS,
VASSARION, 1941.

CHAPTER FIFTEEN

HALLIE FLANAGAN'S EXPERIMENTAL THEATRE: FILLING THE BILL EXACTLY

MACCRACKEN SPENT the first decade of his Vassar presidency chiseling away at the Victorian institution James Taylor had left him. By 1925, he could see a new form emerging. Self-governance was no longer just an outline on paper, but a living and viable part of the school. He had lost a battle on the euthenics front, but ever vigilant for ways to realize his visions, he had undertaken with William Lawrence to found an experiential college away from the campus, but linked in new ways with Vassar; and furthermore, the first Summer Institute of Euthenics and the Vassar Nursery School were on the horizon on the Vassar campus itself.

So the times were ready for MacCracken and the Vassar community to welcome a new character to the developing scene. Similar to the role MacCracken had set for himself at the helm of the college—that of captain with a vision and a mission to steer its course, ever mindful of its traditions, into a new century and new horizons— Hallie Flanagan was charged by MacCracken with the task of creating a new instrument, a new context, where a new kind of experiential learning could take place. A "character" she was, too, in many senses of the word. She was a heroine in the immediately unfolding saga of the Experimental Theatre at Vassar, and, indeed, beyond that, theatre in America, much as MacCracken was not only the force behind Vassar's educational transformation, but also a major figure in the evolution of a new movement in women's education in the twentieth century on national and international fronts.

MacCracken heard about Hallie Flanagan's theatrical successes at Grinnell College, Iowa, and as George Pierce Baker's assistant at his theatre *Workshop 47* at Harvard, and decided in the mid-twenties to see whether he could persuade her to come join the Vassar English department and develop a similar theatre program at Vassar. It was part of his curricular push into interdisciplinary work with a modern outlook. Hallie, on her part, must already have got wind of the favorable conditions for developing a theatre at Vassar under Mac-Cracken. She probably had found out from George Baker that Mac-Cracken also had studied the history of drama and dramatic criticism with him when he was at Harvard, before the workshop existed. In any case, she took the position MacCracken offered her in the English Department in 1925. It was a step that neither one regretted, although, like many of MacCracken's other joint ventures, it had critics as well as partisans. For MacCracken and Hallie Flanagan, it was at once a symbiotic relationship.

Organized under Hallie's brilliant direction over the next few years, the Experimental Theatre offered Vassar students (and others, like actors among male townsfolk and Vassar professors) the opportunity to participate in the creation of a new kind of art form. Education as a "d.p." (as the credited dramatic production major was nicknamed) provided, for the limited but dedicated numbers of students involved, the almost ideal kind of correlation and depth that MacCracken had hoped to achieve between the social sciences, the sciences, and the arts. This major, then, paralleled that of euthenics, for which he pushed at relatively the same time in a different direction. Unlike euthenics, however, which to many on the faculty seemed too "applied" for the liberal arts and—mistakenly—too threatening to women's gains in domestic emancipation, the Experimental Theatre's new program promised students the excitement of permanent liberation from old educational conventions. It gave them a chance to step actively into a new mode of creative study through the medium of the stage.

The stage had really been set for Hallie's coming to Vassar long before Rose Peebles, chairman of the English Department in 1925, at MacCracken's behest, wrote her at Grinnell, sounding her out as to whether she would think of accepting an appointment. Not only was MacCracken himself a leading authority on drama and interested in furthering its study at Vassar, but the Vassar English department had already developed a sub-specialty of teaching playwriting, and, through

Professor Gertrude Buck, had carried drama from a classroom in the department out to local neighborhoods through a community theatre.

With an early Ph.D. degree from the University of Chicago, Buck had joined the Vassar English department, under Professor Laura Wylie, who was chairperson at the beginning of the century. She and Wylie both had advanced ideas about the empowerment of the student and the useful and necessary role of observation, experience, and performance in teaching English in particular, and the arts in general. Buck believed that the only way for students of dramatic literature, which was her specialty, to develop a real understanding of their subject was by doing—creating and producing plays out of their own experiences of the world around them, as well as by studying the classic dramatic literature of the past.

Although under Taylor there surely was no chance of creating a drama concentration in which students would receive credit for performance, especially of their own plays, on the contrary, as soon as MacCracken came—actually in the interim period just before he came—Buck applied to George Pierce Baker's innovative program at Harvard for admission to his workshop. She was one of his first women students. Baker conducted his Harvard workshop from 1914 until 1924, when he moved to Yale on the Harkness Endowment, to start the first full-fledged School of Drama, which he headed from 1925 to 1933. After a year of stimulating study, Buck returned in 1916 to her teaching at Vassar, prepared to introduce into the English curriculum the principles of a playwriting workshop in which the limited number of students admitted to the course would write, and eventually stage, direct, and perform their own plays, not only for the Vassar community, but also for outside audiences.

Buck's career was cut short when she died prematurely in 1921. But she had lighted a flame of interest, and there were others, both in the department and outside, who did not want it extinguished. Professor Winifred Smith, a member of the department and specialist in the history of drama was one—a Vassar alumna with a Columbia University Ph.D. and a thesis on Pirandello and the modern drama. More important was that there were others in the department prepared to keep Buck's program alive after she died. Laura Wylie, the chairperson of the department from 1894 on, even in those earlier days, like her colleague in history, Lucy Salmon, had begun to cultivate anew the vigorous tradition of students' involvement in their own education; and the English department, like the history department, had encouraged its students to make use of observational sources in the laboratory of the world off-campus, to feed and shape their views and incorporate such materials in their discussion and writing. The English department itself was changing under the catalyst of these new attitudes, and so when Wylie, too, was no longer on the Vassar scene (after 1924), her successor Rose Peebles led forward with the same attitude.

In this context of "Gertrude Buck's tradition," MacCracken hoped and believed that Vassar would be able to continue to develop the new kind of teaching of drama that Buck had begun. Both as president and member of the department himself, he was conscious of the promise and innovation of the workshop method, the expanding curricular needs in drama of the department, and the Vassar student and faculty penchant for performance at the drop of a hat. Around the time of Buck's death, he established the Buck Fund with his own gift to the college in her honor. The fund was to be used to foster dramatic presentations and other enterprises between town and gown, relationships which Buck had done so much to cultivate.

Although there was no official theatre space in any building on campus, the Assembly Hall had a stage which was used for lectures and could lend itself to being remodeled for more sensitive dramatic enterprises. In addition, in 1915 just in time for the celebration of the college's fiftieth anniversary and MacCracken's inauguration, an outdoor theatre, designed by Loring Underwood, a Harvard University landscape architect, had been carved out of a sweep of hillside on campus. There occasional plays could be given, both as part of the regular academic program and of the extracurriculum.

Peebles' letter to Hallie on behalf of President MacCracken in 1925 cautioned that it was "all preliminary," and not an official offer, but she opened her letter with an assurance that President Mac-Cracken was "anxious" for Hallie's coming. She went on to discuss plans for a reconstruction of the group of courses in the speech subdivision of the English department, where an instructor had been trying to deal with regular courses in elocution, as well as to fill the void created by Gertrude Buck's death. She named the courses that Hallie would teach, including playwriting, play production, and possibly one section of freshman English or some other English course; and, finally, she "unofficially" assured the Grinnell College instructor of an associate professorship at $3000 a year, and help in finding living quarters for her and her young son Frederick. All of this, of course, was on the condition that Hallie would come for a visit and have personal interviews with the president and the general faculty appointment committee. A formal offer should come from the president in February, she wrote.

MacCracken apparently did not wait for the personal interview. Four days later Rose Peebles wrote to Hallie again, this time reporting results of the faculty advisory committee meeting that recommended hiring Hallie for a two-year term at $3000 for the first year, and $3100 for the second. The nagging question was raised as to whether Miss Gretchen Steiner, the teacher of speech, and a friend of Hallie's, would consent to stay under the reduced teaching assignments which would result from Hallie's appointment, or go to Yale, as had been foreshadowed in the earlier letter, but it was clear by the end of this letter that Hallie Flanagan, not Steiner, was crucial to the ultimate goal of the Vassar department of English and Speech, as outlined by the faculty advisory committee. That goal was "to establish the experimental theatre with friendly relations to community and town" and to continue the traditions of Gertrude Buck. On January 29, 1925, Rose Peebles wrote that Hallie Flanagan's acceptance had been received.

Hallie, as she was later called by almost everyone at Vassar, had an impressive *curriculum vitae.* Thirty-six when she came to Vassar, she had graduated with Phi Beta Kappa honors from Grinnell College where she taught drama and founded and directed the Experimental Theatre department. She had married, lost, and buried her college friend and first husband, Murray Flanagan. She had been a working mother and still had one young son to raise, although another son had tragically died. She had won a prize for a play she had written, *The Curtain,* and had been selected for Baker's prestigious Harvard English *Workshop 47* in drama. In 1924, she had received her master's degree in theatre from Radcliffe.

She was short, a petite 4' 8", but very long on opinions of how things should be done. Her first letters of an official capacity to Peebles in March of 1925 launched into disagreement over the flexibility of the department curriculum, the use of the word "scenario," and the necessity of play production as an incentive to playwriting students. At the end of the month of negotiation by mail, she sent her own outline for the curriculum. Her course description for playwriting called for each student's adapting a short story to the stage, as well as writing an original one-act play. The play production course was designed to instruct students in choosing plays with discretion, directing plays with intelligence, and staging them with taste. All of these lessons would be learned through participation in production of the playwriting students' one-act pieces.

Whether or not Peebles initially agreed with Hallie's approach is not on record, but a May 7 letter revealed that, in a conversation with President MacCracken, Peebles learned that *he* certainly did agree with Hallie's approach—with the slight modification that first semester play production would focus on presentation of a classical play and second semester class participants would produce works of the playwriting classes.

In his published annual report to the board of trustees in 1926, MacCracken expressed the buoyant optimism about his progress in changing the college that accompanied his hiring of Hallie:

> *There is a sense of freedom, particularly among the younger members of the staff, a feeling that their own initiative will meet with consideration, and a willingness to cooperate between departments that is most helpful for the future. There are, it is true, a few exceptions to this rule, most of which are due to educational differences upon the educational theory incorporated in our policy in the last few years. In a college so full of plans for the future, differences are inevitable and, indeed, helpful, in a sense of stabilizing the general direction of its work.*

During her first academic year as director of the Experimental Theatre, Hallie had her play production classes—true to her curriculum design—produce two original plays by students in the playwriting class, as well as the fourteenth century miracle play, *Guibour*. In her book *Dynamo* (1943) which recalls the various stages of development of the Vassar Experimental Theatre, Hallie wrote that the miracle play was chosen to celebrate Vassar's having a theatre. It did, in fact, seem a miracle that the multipurpose stage, used also several days a week for "freshman hygiene lectures" and addresses by visitors in other departments, could have been transformed late in the fall of 1926 into a fourteenth century scene of sacrifice, complete with Guibour burning at the stake—a strain on the lighting facilities, as noted by a watchman, according to Hallie. In *Dynamo* she wrote:

> *The Vassar Experimental Theatre emerged in its present form, not out of chaos, which is a valuable energizing agent*

accompanying all creation, but out of well-ordered quiet not so conducive to activity.

The student plays that year were *The King's Ward* and *She Canna Perish*—a year rounded out by miracle, romance, and realism. The year also culminated with Hallie's selection as the first female recipient of a Guggenheim Foundation grant for a year's study of the European theatre. Her mentor George Pierce Baker had written a letter of recommendation, and Hallie learned in April of 1926 that she had been selected. The warmth of MacCracken's April 19 letter of congratulations to Hallie was no less heartfelt for his expression of hope that she would postpone her sabbatical leave for a year, as she had only just begun her work at Vassar.

Hallie did not postpone her Guggenheim study, however. Indeed, in a letter to Mr. Henry Allen Moe, Secretary of the Guggenheim Foundation, she requested that she not be given additional funds from Vassar College for her grant, as it might "bind" her to the school. Clearly, Hallie valued her own role as a free agent, both in leaving and returning to Vassar.

Accommodating that role within the tight budget and tighter policies of the college couldn't have been easy for MacCracken. He had to fill somehow the gap when she was gone while maintaining a place in the faculty firmament for this already bright and still rising star when she returned.

Meanwhile, Hallie traveled throughout Europe and Russia, studying theatre in many forms and recording in her notebooks observations that would not only compose a book about these experiences, entitled *Shifting Scenes of the Modern European Theatre*, but would also inform production after production of the Vassar College Experimental Theatre. For both Hallie and MacCracken, reaching out to the global community was a vital part of localizing and particularizing experience. Whether the experience was MacCracken's work with the Kosciuszko Foundation or the World Youth Congress, or Flanagan's travels through the world's theatres, or her considerable contribution to the Federal Theatre Project, for both of them, all was brought full circle and back to the Vassar campus where the benefit was first generated and ultimately felt.

The theatre was the mutual ground and first love for Hallie and MacCracken—the theatre, that is, in the very largest sense of the word. For both of them, the power of the theatre was immense, representing power to communicate, to change, to do good, to create world peace, and to create.

Hallie returned from her Guggenheim travels with revolutionary ideas for theatre at Vassar. One result was the November 1927 production of Anton Chekhov's *Marriage Proposal* in realistic, expressionistic, and constructivist representations. Vassar was invited to bring the play (performed at Vassar November 12, 1927, and again on March 17, 1928) to the Yale University Theatre on March 3, 1928. Of that accomplishment—a Vassar play at a men's college theatre—*The New York Times Magazine* for May 20, 1928, said:

> *Vassar has perhaps advanced further towards the progressive theory of education than any other college. The final play to be given there this year is an example of the progressive group understanding. Musicians, historians, and writers receive academic credit for work. ...A leading part is taken by the President of the College, a first step perhaps towards an entirely new form of higher education.*

Of the more than 100 plays produced by the Experimental Theatre during Hallie's tenure at Vassar, half were original plays, translations, or adaptations by students or members of the faculty. MacCracken indicated that he performed in about thirty-five of the hundred productions. His roles ranged from Theseus in *Hippolytus* (performed in Greek), Enobarbus in *Anthony and Cleopatra*, the Stage Manager in *Our Town,* and Professor Borodin in the politically-charged production of the Russian play, *Fear.*

The audience many times reviewed him and the theater:

MARY McCARTHY, 1933:

> *MacCracken I remember very well as Theseus in* Hippolytus. *He was good. He was very good. I thought that was one of the highest moments in the theatre. [Hallie] put on a production of the* Hippolytus *in Greek and MacCracken played Theseus. I think Phil Davis [Professor of Greek, whom Hallie later married] played Hippolytus. And then a most extraordinary woman called Miss Tappan, in the Classics Department. Oh, she looked like some sort of berry fruit, a dark berry fruit. She had rather dark skin, quite nice looking, reserved, slender, and something nun-like about her. She became an Episcopal*

PRESIDENT MACCRACKEN AS THESEUS IN *HIPPOLYTUS*.
(Photograph by Margaret DeMuth Brown)

nun. My impression was that she was a very good scholar. There was something very nice and refined about her. I am not sure whether I had her in class or just somehow knew her. Miss Tappan. Anyway she played Phaedra, and she was wonderful. They were all [wonderful]. Probably Phil Davis was the weakest. And the girls in the class had made these giant papier-mache figures of Aphrodite and—it must have been—Artemis on either side of the stage. So that the devotees of the Goddess tended to play on her side of the stage, that is, Hippolytus . . . and Phaedra on Aphrodite's side. It was all in Greek. It was one of the best things I've ever seen.

But a funny thing happened in that Prexy forgot his lines. We didn't know that in the audience, because, according to the story—it sounds legendary—he ad-libbed "to be or not to be" in Greek and just slipped it in where he couldn't remember his lines. No one noticed except old Miss Macurdy [professor of Classics] with her ear trumpet. She realized what Prexy was up to, and that was all very amusing. He was very good at it and loved to clown.

(Mary McCarthy studied playwriting with Hallie.)

I came to quite like her. I had been very prejudiced against her. I tended not to like campus cult figures, which she was, definitely. In fact, she was quite a nice woman, I thought, and she was very bright and full of energy. Prexy always called her a "pocket Venus."

HULDA BRADBURY WALSH, 1932
chorus member of *Hippolytus*:

The four faculty members in the play knew Greek [Mac-Cracken, Tappan, Davis, and Margaret Washburn, who played the nurse]. Hallie herself didn't know Greek. She took Prexy's word for the Greek. She told him where to stand. He loved serious theatre. C. Mildred Thompson hated serious theatre, but loved amateur theatre. She had it in for drama students: was very rough on them. Possibly she was jealous of Hallie Flanagan. Hallie was very attractive and got around MacCracken.

ESTHER PORTER POWER
(Director of the Experimental Theatre while
Hallie was Director of the Federal Theatre Program)

Power said in "The Vassar Experimental Theatre" in *The Vassar Alumnae Magazine*, April 1939 :

> *In 1932 the* Hippolytus *of Euripides, though produced in Greek, held and interested its audiences as perhaps no production in this theatre has ever done. Scholars from all over the country who attended the production and discussed it with us, were amazed that in the twentieth century the play could evoke the same emotional reactions in a college audience that it must have had in Greek audiences of the fifth century B.C. ... A similar enterprise was carried through in 1934 when a modern production of* Anthony and Cleopatra *was closely related to the Shakespeare classes, where the text had been studied, so that students not in the Theatre came interested and prepared to see the material brought alive today.*

HELEN SANDISON, Professor of English
Miscellany News, December 1934,
Review of *Anthony and Cleopatra:*

> *Enobarbus' [played by MacCracken] clear and pointed utterance gave full meaning to his pivotal role, which combines far-seeing reason, censure, admiration, disillusion, loyalty that ebbs but returns . . .*

THE NEW YORK HERALD TRIBUNE
January 13, 1934:

"FEAR," SOVIET PLAY,
STAGED AT VASSAR COLLEGE
Dr. MacCracken, President,
Heads Cast in Drama
Put on by Prof. Flanagan
Has Its U.S. Premiere
Most popular play in Russia
of Last Two Years

by Denis Tilden Lynch

> *A little astonishment and unmeasured applause greeted the American premiere last night of that strangely moving drama, Fear, at first banned by the Russian Soviet as counter-revolutionary, but which has been playing to S.R.O. audiences throughout Russia for two years and is still the most popular play in the U.S.S.R. . . .*
>
> *. . . The hero of* Fear *played by Dr. MacCracken, president of Vassar, is the dramatic prototype of Professor Ivan Petrovich Pavlov, in his day the world's greatest physiologist, winner of the Nobel prize in 1904, who clashed with the proletarian dictatorship when it sought to make politics dominate his labors.*

MacCracken reviewed MacCracken in the Experimental Theatre in his 1939 graduation speech honoring Hallie:

> *To walk out on the stage knowing that no prompter is close to you in the wings, and that a critical audience is before you, and to attempt creatively to interpret Shakespeare and Euripides honestly and wholeheartedly, is a training not only in self-reliance, but in cultural ways of understanding. I shall not soon forget the evening of* The Holiday of the Elizabethan Shoemaker *when a student, taking for the nonce a minor part in the play, leaped into the breach caused by a miscued entrance and improvised an Elizabethan speech so readily that scarce one person in the audience observed the flaw. I see her here before me today. It is characteristic of our Vassar Theatre that our* Journal of Undergraduate Studies *contains her essay on trade unions in the theatre, a piece of original historical research.*

Hallie dedicated her book *Dynamo,* an account of her work at Vassar, "to President Henry Noble MacCracken who set the Vassar Experimental Theatre in motion and allowed it to utilize energy." Truly their mutual dynamic energies fed on each other. *Dynamo* was published after Hallie left Vassar on what started as a three-year leave (her fourth leave since joining the Vassar faculty) to teach at Smith, a leave from which she never returned to the Vassar theatre.

MacCracken fostered and actively supported Hallie's efforts, often demanding a balancing act between cost and benefit. Her productions were thought too expensive for the department budget. Many in the college thought she spent more time away from the campus than teaching there during her Vassar career. Indeed, her leaves did amount to almost half her years on the faculty, necessitating quite an administrative feat of juggling courses, requirements, and instructors. Dean Mildred Thompson, powerful force on campus that she was, was not a fan of Hallie and her chosen field. She thought that "Hallie's girls" spent too much time on their drama courses and too little on others. They stayed up until all hours of the night rehearsing and often missed other classes. Hallie took steps of various kinds to deal with that problem, and actually discovered through research with the recorder (registrar of grades) that her drama students did better than most students.

The drama students were apt to be in the forefront of left-wing causes during those Depression years and demonstrating for them in public places. The plays that they wrote chose themes that combined their surging interest in politics, freedom of speech, the labor movement, the battle against fascism, poverty, the bread line, the Federal Works program, and housing. They used new dramatic forms, such as the Living Newspaper, developed jointly by them and Hallie, to make their productions correspond with the changing words and ideas of the times. They often, however, had their eyes on tradition even as they worked in the present and faced the future. The theatre performance of Thornton Wilder's *Our Town*, for example, in December 1940, in which MacCracken starred as the Stage Manager, made use also, by special arrangement, of film sequences from Sol Lesser's motion picture adapted from Wilder's original play, to show pointedly the contrasts between the two media.

In 1935 when eighty Vassar students went to Albany to oppose the Nunan Bill, which would require oaths of allegiance from students entering colleges receiving public funds, the political activities of Vassar College students received scathing criticism in the press. Doris Yankauer, a drama student, and Herbert Mayer, a New Yorker, together wrote a play about this event which, directed by Hallie, was produced in the theatre on March 2, 1935: *Question Before the House*. The issue of the play was whether college students should take political actions, going beyond collegiate investigation and research.

The New York Herald Tribune reported:

> *The play closes on a note of defiance. Cries a young woman on the carpet to the president: "I must leave the college and give up my scholarship to one who is in accord with the spirit of the college. I disagree as to the functions of a college. I believe one of*

the prime functions of a college is to question the social order, and when it finds injustice as flagrant as that exhibited in the strike, to move actively to end such injustice."

MacCracken, with his comparative dramatic sense at work, himself tackled the Nunan episode separately. Following the Albany march in February, the college quickly got together a model assembly in which students from twenty-six colleges and universities participated to review problems. The president's statement on this occasion defended the student action as acceptable and understandable under Vassar's educational policy:

> *For many years American college students have been cen-*
> *sured for being wholly indifferent to the realities of the political*
> *world in which they live. They are often today represented in*
> *novels as mere children playing at life.*
>
> *The introduction of such studies as political science in the*
> *college course has changed the students' academic reading. It is*
> *inevitable that these academic interests should be reflected in the*
> *non-academic life.*
>
> *Every college with well-organized departments of economics,*
> *political science and history, must expect its students to take a*
> *real interest and even to participate in the political movements of*
> *their day, just as every college that teaches music must expect to*
> *have a glee club that amounts to something in the way of serious*
> *music.*

MacCracken's statement is testimony as to how far he thought post-war colleges and their students had come since he had begun to seek ways to implement experiential education at Vassar and among American students in general twenty years earlier. Certainly what was going on under Hallie in the Experimental Theatre exceeded anything he had been thinking of in connection with Mrs. Blodgett's euthenics. The dilemma of the Yankauer/Mayer play was one of modern society—a confrontation of the individual and the social system. Mac-Cracken was altogether proud that this kind of confrontation was taking place in the intellectual world of Vassar students.

Not only had the theatre curriculum grown during Hallie's time, but by 1938 it became its own department, finally independent of the English department. This separation dated at least to MacCracken's "Proposed Modification of the Organization of Instruction at Vassar

College," submitted to the faculty on January 15, 1934, and was based, in part, on Hallie's 1932 "Report on Correlation of Theatre Arts With Other Subjects in the College Curriculum."

Between MacCracken's recommendation to the faculty and the actual setting up of the separate theatre major came Hallie's years with the Works Progress Administration's Federal Theatre Project, including Vassar's hosting of the Summer Theatre Institutes of 1935 and 1937. Vassar College sponsored the institutes jointly with the W.P.A. and the Rockefeller Foundation. Those were years of art and moral causes coming together for Hallie and for MacCracken. When Hallie was put under gruelling interrogation by the Dies Committee hearing in 1938, she answered their accusations forthwith:

> MR. STARNES: *Do you believe that the theatre is a weapon?*
> MRS. FLANAGAN: *I believe that the theatre is a great educational force.*

Hallie and MacCracken both received more than their share of lambasting from the right wing. MacCracken's speech to the Vassar graduating class in 1939, one which honored Hallie after that interrogation by the Committee, addressed the "widespread charges of radicalism that are attacking the Federal Theatre."

> *The realistic portrayal of conditions in American life is, of course, a radical idea in the theatre, but that this radicalism is untrue to any real American tradition I have yet to learn. A congressional investigation has certainly not brought it out. Riots have not taken place at the door of Federal Theatres, such as accompanied the performance of Shakespeare's* Richard II *in Elizabethan times in England, and Victor Hugo's* Hernani *in Paris. A Federal Theatre is a social but not a political theatre, and has always discussed great issues.*

MacCracken himself was subsequently attacked by the Committee for his own work involving the World Youth Congress. Both managed to rise above the attacks, relatively unscathed, to higher planes than their attackers.

If Hallie's work with the Federal Theatre Project and her returning to direct the Experimental Theatre in a separate drama department could be called a climax, of sorts, to this drama of characters, then surely the falling away of action, the denouement, must follow quickly, with Hallie's departure to Smith College to become a dean, and her decision on February 10, 1945, not to return to Vassar. In 1945, the Parkinson's disease that would eventually cause her death was diagnosed. (A year later, MacCracken would retire, ending his thirty-one year career as Vassar president.)

MacCracken had not only passed to Hallie, but had joyfully helped her carry, the torch of Gertrude Buck's legacy to the school. On that tradition, they had created a new one to be honored, forwarded, and built upon successively by later students and faculty. Both strong characters, Hallie and Noble did not always see eye-to-eye on matters as mundane as budgets and buildings, as personal as salary increases and sabbatical leaves (Hallie's), or as lofty as how to achieve world peace. But, conflict (dramatic and otherwise) aside, MacCracken provided for Hallie a backdrop of unconditional support and, as president of the college in which she taught for fifteen years, he gave her the license and the props with which to excel. For him, she was the means of executing and further acting upon a major theme of his life, an integral part of his vision for Vassar and for himself: the theme of communication, of bringing together disparate worlds, of bringing the global perspective to the local level through words and actions. From the inception of the Experimental Theatre, to the work of the Federal Theatre Project, Hallie and Noble found in each other a partnership of kindred spirits and a genius that lighted the way of his and her own individual vision.

CHAPTER SIXTEEN

FRANKLIN AND ELEANOR ROOSEVELT: PRESIDENTIAL NEIGHBORS

FRANKLIN ROOSEVELT, LOCAL TRUSTEE: A COLLEGE/COMMUNITY COMMITMENT

My dear Dr. MacCracken,

Your letter of Feb 21st has finally found me down among the Florida keys, and though I have had no official communication from the secretary of the Board of Trustees I am more than pleased with the action of the Board of Trustees at their last meeting. It is going to be a great pleasure for me to come into closer association with Vassar College and I am particularly looking forward, also, to seeing you more frequently and more intimately.

Naturally, also, I am hopeful that I will be able to help in bringing the college into closer association with Dutchess County. Until you came to Vassar, we who had lived in the neighborhood for many years knew very little about the college or its work. In fact, for most of us Vassar might just as well have been a thousand miles away.

— Franklin Roosevelt
February 1923

THUS BEGAN AN ASSOCIATION between the Roosevelts and the college that lasted until the death of Eleanor Roosevelt in November 1962. While Franklin was a trustee for many years, active or honorary, from 1923 until his death, Eleanor was a friend and frequent visitor. In the first years of the association, Franklin had more to do with the college than Eleanor; after a while, and especially after he became President, it was the other way around. Many times when Eleanor was in Hyde Park she would send down her car to the campus to pick up some Vassar students to come for a visit, or she might drive down herself, popping up on the campus—the invited guest for a meal of the students in the cooperative house—or for a lecture, or to give a talk at the Vassar Summer Institute of Euthenics in the summertime.

As Roosevelt's gubernatorial and presidential jobs often caused him to be absent from Dutchess County, his visits to the college became less frequent, whereas Eleanor's kept up steadily over the years of her life. Occasionally the MacCrackens were invited to an event at the summer White House on the river at Hyde Park. During the World Youth Congress held at Vassar in the summer of 1938, Eleanor Roosevelt's presence at the conference, in which she was keenly interested, opened a new dimension in her relationship with Noble MacCracken. She came to his defense in the midst of many attacks from the right which alleged that Vassar was making itself available to house the congress of an imputed communist group.

As America debated intervention on behalf of England and the Allies in 1940, however, MacCracken and Roosevelt approached a parting of the ways. MacCracken thought America's entry into the war would resolve nothing, and he was opposed to Churchill's position and the joint agreement of Roosevelt and Churchill adopted as the Atlantic Charter. On the Vassar campus, MacCracken had very few supporters among the faculty for his anti-involvement position, although among the students there were some who strongly agreed. As campus wartime tensions and anxieties increased in 1939, and until America's entrance into the war in December 1941, MacCracken's position, especially among his fellow administrators, became rather isolated with respect to the war issues. His colleague C. Mildred Thompson, the dean, was very much a supporter of Churchill's position, and their relationship became noticeably strained when, in the spring of 1940, Thompson promoted a petition among the faculty urging the president of the United States to support England and the allies in their defense measures, short of war. When Roosevelt wrote a letter to Thompson thanking her for this effort, the silence towards MacCracken spoke for itself.

MacCracken was abroad on leave in Europe in the fall of 1922 when George Nettleton, the Yale English professor substituting for him as acting Vassar College president, went to Hyde Park and had, as he said, a "very pleasant talk" with Roosevelt, who had served as Woodrow Wilson's Assistant Secretary of the Navy. Nettleton carried a message from the Vassar board of trustees, asking Roosevelt to join the board as a local trustee. Roosevelt's only hesitation in accepting was whether he would be able to negotiate the board meetings with regularity because of his recently acquired polio, with which he was just learning how to deal. He agreed, nevertheless, to the proposal, and was elected to the board at the February 13, 1923, meeting. Roosevelt continued on the Vassar board through his New York gubernatorial tenure. In 1933, after he had become President, his ten-year trustee-ship was due to end in June. The board desired him to stay on as honorary trustee while he was in the White House, however, and extended him the invitation to do so, which he accepted. He was still an honorary trustee when he died at Warm Springs in 1945.

The Roosevelts were from old, conservative, Dutch stock in the Hudson Valley, but their politics were more liberal than most of their fellow residents of Dutchess County, who by and large voted Repub-lican. The future President did have a group of Democratic political associates in the neighborhood, such as Judge John Mack and other prominent local professionals, and later when he came back from Washington, he would count on these people, as well as his Wash-ington aides, to help him negotiate his public appearances in Dutchess County. Speaking from the porch of the president's house or the platform of the chapel, Roosevelt would sometimes use the Vassar campus as his stage.

Soon after FDR joined the board, MacCracken wrote him that he thought he would find the board of trustees "as active and as loyal as any board in the country." This was a big change, MacCracken offered, from the situation eight years before when he himself came in as Vassar president. Then some members of the board still treated the college as "an expensive plaything," he acknowledged. Now in the 1920s, MacCracken wrote, the trustees were a group of men and women characteristically eager to give time and thought to the development of the college. (In June 1923, as we have learned—a few months after Roosevelt came on the board—the trustees adopted the *Vassar College Statute of Instruction,* a new set of collegiate bylaws in which the college was conceived of as an organic institution and the duties and responsibilities of trustees, faculty, administration, and students were clearly set forth. Whereas under Taylor the trustees had engaged in many matters relating to the details of the academic side of the college, that was no longer the case by 1923. The *Vassar Governance*, as the new constitution was later called, soon became a model for government in academic institutions around the country, as well as defining MacCracken's goals for autonomy at Vassar itself.)

In MacCracken's first years, the local trustees, who, in practical terms, tied and untied the purse strings of the college, lived in Poughkeepsie or nearby—John Adriance, Daniel Smiley, H.V. Pelton—and had a free reign in settling the day-to-day matters of the business part of the college. But after 1923, the local trustees ceased operating in that practical role. What MacCracken wanted for the college at that point was the election to the board of someone new whose presence could bring distinction and prominence to the connection. Roosevelt was the choice. Having Roosevelt on the board would draw the college into the affairs of the county, the state, and the nation.

It is not too surprising that MacCracken gravitated towards Roosevelt; they had much in common. They were both Democrats, they were both very community conscious, and each participated in many civic and political activities. Harvard-educated men, they were both quick-witted and had golden tongues. At a deeper level, they were interested in social change, yet steeped in tradition. When they made each other's acquaintance, they must have seen how deeply they were both interested in the history of the county and their part of the country. Both of them early made the acquaintance of Helen Reynolds, a prominent local historian, who presided over the historical research of the Dutchess County Historical Society, of which they were simultaneously on the board. Both of them revelled also in digging up antiquities and connections with the earlier settlers of the past. Roosevelt was an inspired choice, all around, for local Vassar trustee, and in some respects, although not all, was MacCracken's ideological matchmate.

The first assignment given Roosevelt as trustee was an appointment as chairman of a county committee (the other members of which were the warden, the dean, and the president of the Vassar Students' Association), with the task of making plans for a Dutchess County Day at the college. This was a conscious step on the part of the college to become more visible and participatory in local Dutchess County affairs. Around the same time that Roosevelt was tapped as trustee in 1923, Laura Delano, his cousin, was invited to head a committee of

HENRY NOBLE MACCRACKEN AND FRANKLIN D. ROOSEVELT,
VASSAR COLLEGE COMMENCEMENT, JUNE 9, 1931.

local friends of the college "which," MacCracken said, "we desire to form here in the county in order to promote more pleasant social relations and to let our neighbors know more about the work this really unique institution is doing. It seems a great pity that we should go on living together without knowing more about each other."

"The index to Dr. Taylor's *Vassar* did not contain the word 'Poughkeepsie,'" MacCracken observed after retirement. "If I ever wrote a book about the college, it would be found."

The local newspaper account of the event reported that over two hundred residents of the county visited the college on the first county day in 1924 at the invitation of MacCracken and the trustees. The guests were ushered first into the parlors of Main Building, where they were received by President MacCracken, Dean Thompson, Warden Jean Palmer, and four trustees: Mrs. Minnie Cumnock Blodgett, Mrs. M. J. Allen, Mr. R. G. Guernsey, and Mr. H. V. Pelton. Student guides, acting as hostesses, took the visitors around the campus and to the various halls. At four o'clock, a play, *The Under of Wishes*, by Hallie Flanagan, soon-to-be Vassar's theatre professor, later to be tapped by Roosevelt for the leadership of the Federal Theatre Program, was given by the students at the outdoor theatre, and after the play, the faculty met the guests at tea in the gallery of Taylor Hall, the elegant new art building, built in 1914.

Because the campus urgently needed a new dormitory to accommodate the mounting numbers of students, the Committee on Buildings, of which Roosevelt was at once made a member, was considering the erection of a new structure in the center of the quadrangle of dormitories and one classroom building, which would be linked to all the existing quadrangle dormitories and would provide a common kitchen for all—an earlier version of the All Campus Dining Center, ACDC, which in 1972, replaced Students' Building, the early student center, built in 1913. One hundred and forty students lived off campus in 1923, and this plan would have improved dining facilities and freed rooms for dormitory space. The idea was scuttled when it was decided instead to develop Wing Farm, an area to the northeast end of the campus, and build Cushing House in 1928, along with Blodgett, Kendrick, and the Wimpfheimer Nursery School. During 1924 the Buildings committee voted "their moral obligation to erect Sanders Physics Building." Henry Sanders, chairman of the board earlier in the decade, had left money for that purpose, but the building had been much postponed when the Blodgetts loomed onto the scene with the promise of things to come in the way of an euthenics building. Roosevelt was very interested in these enterprises, and put forth his own ideas as plans were debated. When he couldn't make meetings because of government commitments, he sometimes sent memoranda about his thoughts.

In 1925 trustee Roosevelt was especially concerned that with a rise in tuition the children of professionals—middle class people—would still be able to afford a college education. In his capacity as chair of the Committee on Religious Life, also, he presided over deliberations which considered making attendance at Vassar chapel (non-denominational services) voluntary for the first time since the beginning of the college. The idea, promoted by MacCracken, was that the college president would invite the cooperation of faculty and students in planning for the "successful adoption, maintenance, and support of voluntary chapel service." Roosevelt stated that he would hesitate to vote for the abolition of required chapel on Sundays and expressed the view that it would be well to separate the weekday and Sunday questions. The plan which was finally adopted catered to his ideas. The trustee minutes specified :

> *On such Monday evenings as the President may deem advisable, he may summon in assembly the whole of the college, not to last over one-half hour, at the same hour and in the same place. With the exception of a single hymn, such a meeting would not be religious but would be devoted to the consolidation of the ideals of the college. The remaining four days of the week would carry a simple religious service, not differing greatly from the then current service, as conducted by the president.*

Those trustee deliberations preceded the acceptance of the idea of voluntary chapel services, and the institution of morning chapel talks given by MacCracken, a custom kept up for many years. (His notes for those talks, ranging in scope from recounting Chaucer's tales to addressing contemporary social activism, constitute one whole box of documents in the MacCracken Papers in Special Collections.) Matthew Vassar had decreed that all sectarian influences should be carefully excluded from his college, but that the "training of . . . students should never be intrusted to the sceptical, the irreligious, or the immoral." MacCracken's presidential predecessors, all Baptist clergymen stretching back to 1861, had presided over required daily and Sunday chapel services, which some students and faculty, including the astronomer Maria Mitchell, had continuously fretted against even back in the early days. The clergymen presidents had also successively offered a mandatory and solemn presidential course in moral ethics for seniors, a kind of exit-into-life course, pulling together issues of morality.

MacCracken was a man of deep religious convictions, but as soon as he became president, he requested from the trustees permission to abolish the ethics course and substitute instead a required course in the philosophy of the liberal arts education, to be offered to freshmen rather than seniors. Consistent with this resecularization of the Vassar educational environment, MacCracken was asked in 1929 to look into procuring a denominational pastor (chaplain) for affiliation with the college, to determine directions that might be followed in connection with campus religious life, but as there was no money in the budget for a new enterprise, he could not implement that idea at that time.

The general question, initiated by MacCracken, of Vassar's helping William Lawrence to found the experimental junior college Sarah Lawrence came up in 1926, early in Roosevelt's tenure. Certainly in 1926, it was helpful to MacCracken to have Roosevelt on the board as he heartily endorsed and supported the president's forward-looking interest in the Sarah Lawrence collaboration. Later on in 1932, with Roosevelt still active on the board, the Vassar trustees declared themselves as more than pleased with the initial five-year development of Sarah Lawrence and asked MacCracken to continue his relationship as *ex officio* member of the Sarah Lawrence board.

In 1929 Roosevelt, by then governor of the state of New York, was a member of the first trustee committee on undergraduate life that, among other questions, established permission for students to smoke in particular places on campus. (Later in November it was proposed by the newly formed household management committee of the trustees that the rooms thus set aside for smoking, should be known as "rooms in which students may smoke," not as "smoking rooms." That way, it would be clear that the rooms could be kept under the supervision of the wardens, and that smoking could be controlled.) The governor was also a member of the first trustee endowment committee, which established the need for an assistant to the president to work on money-raising, a move which in turn led to a separate development office in 1929.

On the tenth of June 1931, Roosevelt, then in his second term as governor, delivered the Vassar commencement address. Ahead of time

Roosevelt thought it was likely that he might have to miss the commencement, so Stephen Duggan, fellow trustee and head of the Institute of International Education, the I.I.E., agreed to stand in if necessary, in which case he would have given a specially prepared address on "America's Place in International Affairs," an appropriate topic for one who had done so much to promote international education at Vassar and elsewhere. But Roosevelt did turn up, the first governor of a state to deliver a commencement address at Vassar, and gave a short speech on the theme that study is like navigation, liberally illustrated with anecdotes to bring home his point. The speech conveyed the idea that "the crass ignorance of the educated classes about governmental matters [was] one of the most appalling things about the post-war years" and the students were exhorted to do better than the older generation had done to understand what was going on in governmental affairs around them.

Two years later on June 1, 1933, MacCracken proudly reported to the trustees:

> *For the first time in the history of Vassar a trustee of the Board has been elected to the highest office in the country. Franklin D. Roosevelt, whose term expires with this meeting, has maintained throughout his connection with the college undiminished interest in its work. While his administrative duties have prevented his attendance at recent meetings, he has been most faithful in personal conferences and in correspondence. The many contacts which the college enjoys both with the President and Mrs. Roosevelt must remain a treasured part of its history.*

MacCracken had determined a course of action to keep Roosevelt interested in remaining on the board as an honorary member, however, knowing that his affiliation would continue to lend distinction to the college even if the President didn't have time to do his trustee homework. Thus before Roosevelt's trustee term was up, in April of 1933, MacCracken sent a short but pithy progress report to the White House about how the town-gown projects were going: the students were making surveys for various local agencies and the college was opening its doors more widely to townspeople for concerts, lectures, and forums. Roosevelt was invited to attend commencement, to make his final appearance as active trustee, an invitation which he had to decline. At a board meeting near the time of commencement, however, the trustees unanimously voted to ask him to stay on as honorary trustee, which Roosevelt agreed to do. MacCracken put it this way in his letter of invitation: "Your post was described as carrying with it all the authority you would like to exercise, and none of the responsibility."

After Roosevelt had agreed to stay on the Vassar board, the Mac-Crackens gave an August reception for him, to which residents of the county were invited. MacCracken went to Hyde Park to escort Roosevelt to the campus, and joined Roosevelt in his open and specially-equipped car for the ride back. During the ride, Roosevelt gave him a lesson in how to pose for photographs, first greeting people standing on one side of the road as the car went through, and then on the other. Roosevelt said to MacCracken, "You'll learn," the *Poughkeepsie Evening News* dutifully reported on August 26, 1933. Mac-Cracken and Roosevelt were having a wonderful time, each associating with the other, fellow masters of histrionics.

Roosevelt delivered his speech from the MacCracken's front porch, after an introductory greeting by MacCracken who said:

> *Mr. President: The people of Dutchess County bid you welcome. You have graciously fulfilled your promise in coming from your vacation days, days that for anyone else would be called hard work, to speak again to your neighbors. A year ago when you spoke to us at Washington Hollow [nearby township], there were whispers in the air, whispers about somebody that was a stranger to us of Dutchess County. He was whispered to be vague. He was thought to be timid. He was rumored to be weak. Worst of all, we heard he was aristocratic. We had never known such a man, and we wondered whom they had considered. Now the rumors and whispers have died away, and a great chorus of praise and pride has filled our ears. A man stands out whom everybody knows. The portrait is more familiar but not even his neighbors knew him last year as the world knows him now. He has taught us to be strong. He has kindled his courage in our own hearts. He has drawn for us a clear and definite plan by which through sacrifice and cooperation, American democracy may survive. And best of all, he has placed human values first, and has affirmed that the state exists for the welfare of all, and not least for the common men and women like his neighbors.*

During these Depression years, MacCracken advised Roosevelt from time to time what people in the Vassar community were thinking; he believed that the college might represent a kind of listening post. One sign of recovery from the Depression, for example, he pointed out to Roosevelt by letter in 1934: advance registration for future classes at Vassar from January to July in 1934 was the largest in over ten years, and in 1934 fewer students needed special aid. (The college during the Depression had gone on to a semi-self-help regimen, designed to cut down on college and student expenditures. Some students maintained their own quarters and did their own house-keeping, and a cooperative house was established, at first in euthenics quarters in Blodgett Hall, in which students also did their own purchasing and cooking.)

In 1935 when Harry Hopkins, the old childhood and Grinnell College friend of Hallie Flanagan, drew Roosevelt's attention to her as a promising candidate for the directorship of the Federal Theatre program (part of the Federal Emergency Relief program), MacCracken lost, at least temporarily, an outstandingly innovative faculty member and one who had already brought great liveliness to the Vassar community as director of the Vassar Experimental Theatre. By that time the Vassar theatre had come into national prominence. Eleanor Roosevelt had attended some of Hallie's lively interdisciplinary Living Newspaper plays which explored serious contemporary issues and experienced their excitement. When Hallie travelled to Washington at Hopkins's invitation to consider heading the program, Eleanor supported her for the position.

When Roosevelt was reelected in 1936, MacCracken sent him a telegram saying: "Our cup runneth over," to which Roosevelt replied: "Dear Henry: That is a mighty sweet note of yours."

Yet, as indicated above, everything was not entirely harmonious between MacCracken and FDR, as World War II approached. In May 1940 seventy-five Vassar College students signed a letter to FDR protesting that they did not agree with him on the war-peace question with regard to the United States's role in the European conflict. MacCracken's own stand on American involvement in World War II was in direct conflict with FDR's foreign policy—which he often explicitly criticized. Although in February 1941, and again in April of the same year, he declined to join the American First organization (with which he was flirting because its philosophy of non-intervention approached his own), MacCracken gave several speeches and made many public statements that year in keeping with his pacifism, endorsing a non-interventionist policy.

In August 1941 MacCracken gave such a speech at Carnegie Hall, after which FDR made it immediately clear that he disapproved strongly of American isolationists, pacifists, and non-interventionists. After FDR announced in September 1941 that United States ships would fire upon threatening Axis ships, MacCracken appeared before the Senate Foreign Relations Committee to testify against the proposed changes to the 1939 Neutrality Act, which would allow American ships to be armed. Pearl Harbor sharply ended Mac-Cracken's involvement in the anti-war movement, but Roosevelt and MacCracken did not thereafter resume their former cordial relationship.

Dean C. Mildred Thompson, on the other hand, was very openly in favor of Roosevelt's policies during the same period. The two administrators had to agree to disagree over this issue, which provoked some strain between them. When one hundred and twenty-five faculty members wrote a letter to Roosevelt in October 1941 pledging their support of his foreign policy, Mildred Thompson sought to soothe MacCracken's anguish by sending a formal note to her colleague, of whom she was genuinely fond, in advance:

> *My dear President MacCracken,*
>
> *With a sense of courtesy and respect for you, and in understanding of your genuine belief in the right of free expression, both within the college and without, we wish you to have a copy of our statement of public policy before it goes to the President of the United States, and before it may appear in the press.*
>
> *We feel sure you will receive this statement in the spirit of tolerance for different opinions which you have long shown and which we greatly value. . . .*

ELEANOR ROOSEVELT:
CORDIAL FRIEND AND COLLABORATOR

ELEANOR ROOSEVELT'S TIES to Vassar students, faculty, and administration were many over those same years. She sometimes invited Vassar students to be her guests at Hyde Park, Val-Kill, and even Washington, and from time to time shared her own celebrated guests with Vassar students. She came to the Poughkeepsie campus for lectures, conferences, and institutes—most notably the week-long meeting of the Second World Youth Congress in 1939—and seemed to enjoy them and learn from them.

Knowing what students were thinking during the Depression and World War II years was of great importance to the President. Eleanor was keenly interested in these issues in her own right and ready to become his ears and eyes and report to him her reading and assessment of current student opinion and dialectic. The Vassar campus and its community interest in airing issues in conferences, afforded her a neighborly sounding board both during the undergraduate school year, and also in the summer at the sessions of the Summer Institute of Euthenics, which she attended at least once every summer between 1926 and 1958, the lifetime of the institute, and at other summer conferences, such as the Second World Youth Congress. Eleanor wrote in "My Day" in 1949 and 1958, that her speaking at the Summer Institute was an annual event, but she wrote specifically about doing so only in 1942, 1944, 1948, 1949, and 1958.

It would be unfair to assert that Eleanor just came to campus to keep her finger on the student pulse for Franklin. Her visits to the campus always promoted her own causes. She had her own agenda. Susan Ware points out in her essay, "ER and Democratic Politics," that Eleanor Roosevelt typified the "vanguard of women who entered political life after 1920 in the wake of the 19th amendment." She shared their "issue orientation." In November 1937, for example, the Vassar Political Association was holding a conference on housing. Secretary of the Interior Harold Ickes was to be the keynote speaker, but Eleanor Roosevelt preceded him on the platform on this subject. For the occasion, the new experimental visual arts Social Museum displayed a housing exhibit, constructed by the Works Progress Administration and loaned to the college by the New York City Housing Authority. It showed the growth of sanitation, public health administration, and slum clearance over a period of two hundred years, according to the *Miscellany News* (October 10, 1937) and was Vassar's first attempt, in the earliest days of the Social Museum, to put on a workshop "in the methods of displaying results of study other than the printed word."

MacCracken and Eleanor Roosevelt hit it off in particular ways. In 1936 at the height of the Depression, MacCracken and a Poughkeepsie business executive, Ernest Doolittle, organized the Temporary Emergency Relief Association of Dutchess County (TERA), which after two years was replaced by the program of FERA (Federal

Emergency Relief Association). There were two other members of the organization, but MacCracken, as the executive secretary of the committee, took several hours a week from the campus during lunch hours for two years to handle most of the work. TERA organized public works during these Depression years and established a fixed minimum wage in Dutchess County of twenty-five cents an hour. MacCracken oversaw the organization of relief stations, which received and distributed food on a ticket and stamp basis, similar to that of food stamps in the 1990s. There were some forty stations around the county, mostly in grocery stores. At one point the project was handling $25,000 a week, with no theft and no graft, at least as far as MacCracken knew.

In connection with this assignment on TERA, MacCracken uncovered a very serious social condition in Dutchess Junction, a river neighborhood of shacks, formerly dwellings of black workers in brickyards in southern Dutchess County, New York. The local banks had foreclosed on the brickyards, but did nothing to alleviate the problems of former workers, displaced and unemployed as a result of the bankruptcy. The city of Beacon, New York, from which Dutchess Junction was outlying, failed to take any responsibility in the matter. MacCracken tried to get some responses started, but in the end didn't succeed. He at length decided to write a letter to his friend Eleanor Roosevelt pointing out that sooner or later this situation would be discovered by the press, and laid at Roosevelt's door. Eleanor Roosevelt replied immediately, asking MacCracken to take her on a tour of inspection. This MacCracken did, and he described the day's tour in one of his unpublished autobiographical fragments:

> *I had at this time a little Chevrolet coupe in which I took her from Hyde Park. On the way I laid the whole situation before her, saying that doctors, nurses, and postmen refused to enter the huts. I showed her the letters I had received from the state officials, who had put the whole thing off. The light of battle came into her eyes. We went through perhaps a dozen of the huts, where she met and talked with the inmates. She then asked me to issue a call for all the residents to meet her. It was a warm summer day, and we sat on the gray tufts in a brickyard excavation. She talked chiefly to the women, telling them that they were responsible and must . . . get their children clothed, food in their houses, and wood for the winter. If they would act,*

the men would fall in. She told them to divide the work; one squad for washing and cleaning the houses, another to run a vegetable garden of corn and cabbage, chiefly; and another to take care of the sick. Fortunately we found one man, a Syrian, who had a small liquor and cigaret store. He agreed to receive the food and prepare reports for the committee.

I remember that on the way back in the late afternoon (we had had no lunch) I stopped at a Beacon filling station, and Eleanor hopped out to get the local opinion. It confirmed everything we had told her. Beacon was in a bad condition with much unemployment of its own.

Two days after the visit I received a call from two negro social workers attached to the state department of welfare. In the meantime, supplies had been sent in. There was reemployment of many of the men in other places and within two years most of the shacks were deserted.

This led to the [founding of the] Poughkeepsie Community Chest . . .

MacCRACKEN, ER, AND THE
SECOND WORLD YOUTH CONGRESS

MacCRACKEN'S MOST IMPORTANT collaboration with Eleanor Roosevelt, and one that involved both Vassar students and visiting students from many foreign countries, took place two years later, in the summer of 1938 during the Second World Youth Congress held on the Vassar campus. That spring after consulting with his trustees, MacCracken decided to invite the student leaders of the Second World Youth Congress to hold their projected meeting at Vassar in August. This was the most radical conference that MacCracken had backed to date on the campus, and he issued the invitation, knowing full well that it would antagonize as many alumnae, students, faculty members, and townspeople as it would please, but he was prepared for that and had the full support of the trustees, headed by Helen Kenyon, 1904.

The Second World Youth Congress followed on the heels of a series of previous conventions held between 1934 and 1938 at New York University, Detroit, Washington, and a contentious previous one at Vassar itself, in December of 1937. "The World Youth Congress to Prevent War and Organize Peace" was announced as a conference to

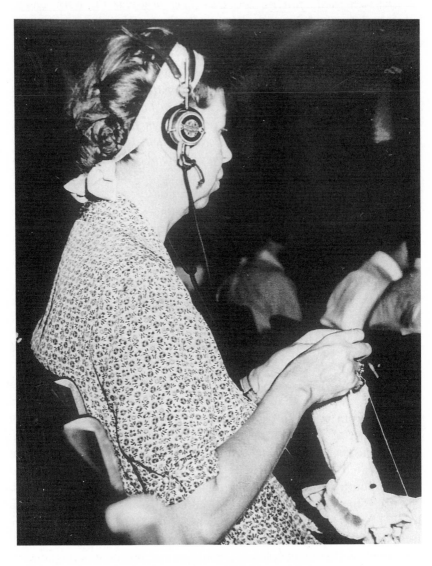

ELEANOR ROOSEVELT AT THE
SECOND WORLD YOUTH CONGRESS,
AUGUST 21, 1938.
(Photograph by Jason Albertson)

be held at Vassar from August 16 to August 23, 1938. (The first World Youth Congress had been held in Geneva in 1936, when, according to *The New York Times,* anti-Hitlerian sentiments were expressed by the delegates.) Elizabeth Shield-Collens, the English director of the congress, said in advance that she expected 500 delegates—fifty each from the U.S. and the U.K., but none from Germany, Japan, or Italy, despite her cordial invitation. About forty-two countries would be represented, she said, and the organizers were prepared for the fact that some delegates would be communists.

This news elicited hostility, antagonism, and threats to withdraw support from the college, among Vassar alumnae of a more conservative bent than MacCracken, and certainly among the by-and-large Republican and conservative Poughkeepsie community. Telegrams and cablegrams flew back and forth in the early summer, and Kenyon issued a public statement to the press, indicating that the Vassar board of trustees supported the president and his project. MacCracken paid dearly for the conference, receiving heavy criticism in spite of his optimistic remarks. A group of conservative alumnae circulated a petition to the trustees in advance of the conference, protesting and denouncing his project:

> *Whereas in the name of liberalism and free speech, Henry Noble MacCracken has opened the doors of Vassar College to Communist speakers and Communist-controlled organizations, and*
>
> *Whereas, Communism is scientifically organized propaganda with the open purpose of world revolution, and the avowed enemy of Christian government, and*
>
> *Whereas the columns of the Alumnae Magazine are closed to any one who dares raise her voice against present college policies, and*
>
> *Whereas the campus last summer was the home of W.P.A. theatre cohorts, about whose radical and revolutionary purpose there is no question, and*
>
> *Whereas the Alumnae House welcomed the Peace Conference last Thanksgiving, whose avowed purpose of propaganda was definitely stated by Lenin years ago, and*
>
> *Whereas President MacCracken welcomed the American Student Union during the Christmas holidays, an organization the Communist nucleus of which is pledged to work for the*

overthrow of the United States Government and the setting up of a new social order, and

Whereas, this American Student Union includes in its plat-form that its members pledge to support their government in no war it may be involved in but leaves them free to fight for Communism, and

Whereas, the said union came into being through the machi-nations, not of bona-fide students, and is officered by non-students, and

Whereas, said organizers of the union and officers thereof are members or agents of groups having international affiliations as well as being disloyal in acts and teachings, and

Whereas, Henry Noble MacCracken has given open and offi-cial sanction to these activities by welcoming this group with its executive secretary, Joseph P. Lash, who since 1934 has been active in the ranks of the radical Marxians and now covers his true purpose under the camouflage of the American Labor Party, and

Whereas, Gil Green of the Young Communist International of Moscow and former head of the American branch of the movement has announced that the Second World Youth Congress will be held in the United States in 1938, and

Whereas, the published Resolutions from the Ninth Congress of the Communist Party of the U.S.A. say: "Among the youth the struggle for the united front has made great advances... The utmost concentration is required for the building of the American Youth Congress and to organize mass struggles,"

and...

Whereas, as a result of this publicity the good name of the College has been irreparably hurt—

Therefore, for the above reasons we, a group of interested citizens, wish to register an emphatic protest against the present policies of Vassar College.

(Signature)

Neither trustees nor MacCracken caved in to this barrage of conservative criticism, and the congress took place on schedule. MacCracken was determined to make it an exemplary educational experience for the participants. Just before the congress he wrote an article for *The Alumnae Magazine* entitled "The Principle of Conference," which outlined the four types of conferences that he considered to be useful. As an illustration of the "principle of conference" in general, he mentioned the fact that in October that year a joint meeting of two national associations, the Association of American Colleges and the American Association of University Professors, had taken place in the newly remodeled "Aula" on the Vassar campus, a space created for just such discussions, to iron out differences and settle on agreements. Bringing together two organizations whose points of view on particular issues were sometimes in conflict went to the heart of MacCracken's notion of what a conference was all about. But that was a fairly simple conference compared to the complicated congress that was about to take place.

The delegates came to discuss a complex series of issues about peace. The discussion revolved around how to move towards peaceful means of settling issues in an ideologically conflicted world, whose currents of nationalism, colonialism, and democracy were rapidly moving towards a military clash. The World Youth Congress agenda committee had established four commissions, each one to study a series of complex questions around a given topic, and then report back to the whole group in general sessions. The subjects to be examined were: "political and economic organization for peace," "economic and cultural status of youth and its relation to peace," "religious and philosophical bases of peace," and "the international role of youth in seeking peace."

MacCracken's greeting to the delegates on August 16, 1938, set the tone of the meeting:

> *... May I wish the World Youth Congress all success, as you members begin the task of thinking together about peace. In spite of all that has been said and done about peace, peace still remains the most radical, the most revolutionary idea in the world.*
>
> *It runs directly counter to the physical nature of man which, at least in anthropological eras, is predatory and combative. It conflicts with the organization of all civilized governments which have Departments of War but no Departments of Peace. It cuts directly across those divisions of society—language, color, race, religion—which man feels most deeply and is prepared most*

courageously to defend. Most of all it is opposed to the economic struggle for materials and markets which is a continuous war without weapons from day to day.

Nevertheless and in spite of all these paradoxes the idea of peace survives. . . .

Peace can be destroyed by intimidation. Organized society, by organized abuse can talk the idea of peace out of the minds of a whole people and set those same minds towards war, which were once set towards peace. Just as the radio message can be distorted by the static electricity of the air, artificial or natural, so the idea of peace can be destroyed by untruth, by provocation, by circumlocution, until its image disappears amid the clamour of the world's fears and hatreds.

. . . the greatest danger to peace is not government or political creed or color or religion. The greatest danger to peace comes from two great rival ideas, for each of which we have profound respect. Your commissions will undoubtedly deal with these conflicts. The first idea with which peace must come to grips is the idea of justice. This may be expressed in the English proverb "nothing is settled until it is settled right." Shall we put peace or justice higher in our scale of values? If we wait until all injustices have been settled, what shall become of peace?

The second great conflict in ideas which peace must meet is the idea of honor—national honor, class honor, personal honor. All of these come into direct conflict with the idea of peace. War is not only a trade and an art, it is a profession. The soldier who wears his country's uniform is taught that everything that is high and noble and courageous is embodied in that uniform under the flag. Not until the world's leaders are willing to sacrifice the idea of honor to the idea of peace will there be peace in the world.

It is well for us to remember that we are meeting at a college. Two great forces which exist here at Vassar as at every university are on the side of peace rather than against it. They are history and science. That which restrains the nations of the world today from plunging our many countries into war, is memory. History has recorded the cost of war in human society and the cost, history tells us, is too great.

In the same way science, through its two great divisions— social science and natural science—has solved many questions which it thought could only be solved by war. For the products of the earth which have caused most of the wars, science produces substitutes. For overpopulation, science produces occupation and intensive agriculture. For the hatreds engendered by myth and legend, tradition and prejudice, for the fatal pretense of race superiority, science with cold analysis disposes of these claims and puts the weapon of reason in the hand of peace.

I know that many of you will say, "history records war and inculcates hero-worship." Science places at the disposal of war its most fatal implements. I admit these arguments. Again I affirm that no forces have worked and are working so mightily for peace as history and science. I sometimes think these are the only forces that will ever bring peace on earth. But there is one more friend of peace among ideas, the greatest argument. It is what we call in English and in other languages "common sense." Some languages call it "good sense." Peace is common sense and peace, in spite of its paradoxical nature, appeals to our inmost belief as good in itself. That part of our nature, the common experience and the deep desire, which demands poetry as its expression, has always sung of peace. And so to the historian and to the scientist I add the poet as a friend of peace.

What could be more natural then, than that a college such as Vassar, fostering history, science and poetry, should open its doors to a group of representatives of the youth of the world who wish to talk about peace?

. . . I have always believed in youth. I have always found in youth the justification of my confidence. For this I am sometimes called gentle, or credulous, or sentimental. Call it what you please, it abides with me as a cardinal principle of my policy in education. With the greatest interest I shall follow the sessions of this congress of youth as it charts the currents of ideas, and marks the shoals or reefs, the hidden dangers of the shore; and as it tries once again to outline the safe, though tortuous, channel, that will lead us all to the desired haven of peace.

MacCracken had invited Eleanor Roosevelt, who shared his concerns for student discussions of peace and conflict resolution, to give the opening address to the delegates of the congress, and to attend all of its sessions, which she agreed to do. She anticipated good results from the meetings, and in her opening remarks, hailed the world's youth as "the best agents for peace." After that, she attended the rest of the sessions, sitting in the back of the room and knitting, watching the folk dances, listening to student analysis and argumentation. She was pleased with the results, had several sessions with individual groups of representatives, and publicly defended herself and MacCracken against accusations of being dupes of the communist party. MacCracken, for his part, said over and over again that even if there were members of the communist front who had come to the conference, democratic procedures called for exchange of all points of view.

There were six days of hearty engagement in discussion and debate, after which a Vassar Peace Pact was adopted and published by the representatives of youth of forty-nine countries. Although there had been tense, difficult, and embarrassing moments, MacCracken was gratified at the results of this congress. At the end, the students gave him a ten-minute standing ovation. It was one of his personal satisfactions in an anxiety-ridden decade. Later he asked several college community members who had attended the sessions as observers to write down their appraisals of the congress and send their responses to him. The responses were favorable. He also received many unsolicited letters, both negative and positive. An alumna of the class of 1896 wrote that she had discovered at the Vassar reunion a couple of months before that a dangerous gathering of youth was going to take place on the campus, and she decided to come and hear for herself.

> So far as I could discover, the ideas expressed were not new. But the sincerity and earnestness of the delegates is beyond question, and one may hope that after every free exchange of views, such an opportunity for getting acquainted with representatives from the ends of the earth, after working together so hard and so seriously—one may hope that these young people will indeed be combining forces for the peace of the world. Their tolerance, their success in ironing out such difficulties as arose from clashing opinions, their fine spirit of brotherhood and the wiping out of racial and class distinctions give promise for the future. These things are even more significant than what was said, than resolutions and plans.

Eleanor Roosevelt's presence and personal interactions in informal ways before, during, and after the regular sessions of the Congress enhanced the experience for the delegates from home and abroad, and made it an event of national importance. Subsequently at a banquet

ELEANOR ROOSEVELT AT THE VASSAR
SUMMER INSTITUTE OF EUTHENICS.
(Photograph by Howard Green)

in New York in February 1939, according to Winifred Wandersee in her essay "ER and American Youth," ER maintained that the Congress had not been dominated by communists. At the Sixth American Youth Congress in Lake Geneva, Wisconsin in 1940, however, the first lady was among the missing, by then "worried" by the group's isolationist stance. FDR had announced on June 10 that year that the U.S. had changed its policy from "neutrality" to "non-belligerency."

ELEANOR ROOSEVELT
AND MILDRED THOMPSON

ELEANOR ROOSEVELT was an even closer friend of Mildred Thompson than of MacCracken, and as time went along, Thompson, in her capacity as dean, arranged many small and informal meetings for her with Vassar students and faculty members. It was Eleanor who intervened to get Thompson elected as the "feminine afterthought" to the Allied Education Conference in London in April 1944.

ER returned to the United States from the Caribbean at the end of March that spring to discover that an all-male delegation was being sent to London by the State Department. She held a press conference almost immediately and proclaimed, "Women should be represented at the peace table and at every international conference now held dealing with any subject laying the foundations for future peace." Two days later the State Department announced that Dean C. Mildred Thompson of Vassar College was being added to the American delegation, chaired by Senator J.W. Fulbright of Arkansas, bringing the delegation to six. The other members were Archibald MacLeish, poet laureate; Dr. John W. Studebaker, U.S. commissioner of education; Dr. Grayson Kefauver, dean of Stanford University; and Dr. Ralph Turner, State Department observer.

"If I hadn't been sitting down at the time, I would have fallen down," Thompson said to her history class. She had only a matter of hours after the phone call from the State Department in Washington to teach her class, make out an exam for History 360, finish her income tax returns due on April 15, appear on Janet Flanner's talk show called "Listen, The Women" (a prior commitment that she honored even in her hurry), and fly to Washington to confer with officials there. Shortly after that, she went to England, where she immediately entered into the preliminary discussions with delegates, already assembled, from the United States and elsewhere. She was the only woman who was a functioning delegate; the alternate from Australia, a woman, was not called upon officially to participate.

The chief purpose of the conference was to make plans for winning the peace by rebuilding the educational systems of the conquered countries in Europe, once the war was won. A document was drawn up during the conference and endorsed by the participating nations. Thompson played a very substantial part in the conference, and sent reports back to her women friends in Poughkeepsie of the opportunities to get to know some of the world's diplomats and what was on their minds.

Thompson returned from this stint exhilarated by her experience. ER, in a "My Day" column, publicly congratulated her on her role and invited her to Hyde Park to talk about the conference and plans for the future. For the next year or so, although she resumed her duties at Vassar with all the stressful problems of an acrimonious faculty debate having to do with shortening the degree-requirement during the war, and the other anxieties of running a college while the nation was at war, Thompson enjoyed national publicity. The year 1944 could justly be described as the high-point of her career. She was much in demand on the lecture circuit, not only before Vassar clubs, but also as a soldier in ER's campaign to get more capable women into the limelight and into public policy positions working for peace. The first lady had endorsed Queen Elizabeth, Mrs. Winston Churchill, Queen Wilhelmina, and Madame Chiang Kai-shek for posts at peace tables, "thus standing for a feminine emphasis in the shaping of the peace."

Thompson addressed a conference in Boston in June 1944, at which two hundred women from seventy-five organizations gathered to "plan a list from which more women [could] be chosen by government officials for both national and international service." ER said she was turning the leadership of the future over to these women, and asked them to bring forward the names of other qualified women for future engagement in the affairs of peacekeeping. Thompson told the delegates to this conference that "nobody noticed that she was a woman after the meetings [in London] began."

In the fall of 1944, speaking to the *Miscellany News* reporter about her summer, Thompson said: "My summer reads like the short annals of the poor—and busy." She wrote a report for the Foreign Policy Association on the London education conference, performed on a radio program entitled "Beyond Victory," and wrote an article

"Education and the Woman" for *Good Housekeeping* magazine, in which she urged women to get more education and to put it to work for civic purposes.

The Roosevelts' easy interaction on many occasions with individuals and groups of people in MacCracken's and Thompson's Vassar, especially in the thirties and forties, awakened many students, and even faculty members, trustees, and parents, to politics and national affairs, to taking sides and thinking for themselves on issues of war and peace, and the unsolved Depression problems of hunger, homelessness, and unemployment. Eleanor, especially, was seen by students and faculty (at least some of them) as a role model, involving herself in significant political and community action, effectively moving causes, showing what women could do. She was also very helpful to individual students and to the Vassar political organization, making arrangements for officers to attend a conference in Campobello, and even inviting students to the White House.

MacCracken's arm, reaching out into the community to bring outsiders in, and his knack for encouraging students, both inside and outside classrooms, to become engaged with the developments of their own times, were nowhere more observable than in the college's give-and-take relationship with the Roosevelts. For some students, indeed, the opportunity to meet, or just hear from a local platform, Eleanor and Franklin Roosevelt, and discover how they thought, presented themselves, listened, and got things done, constituted the essence of experiential learning, which was the fulcrum of MacCracken's theory of education. For at least one student who grew up during the Depression years, subjected to conservative parental fulminations against the "country squire in the White House," the chance to get an entirely different slant on the Roosevelts, showing their sides as concerned educators, county citizens and neighbors, proved MacCracken's point.

CHAPTER SEVENTEEN

FROM SWORD TO PLOUGHSHARE: MacCRACKEN'S QUEST FOR PEACE

T HERE NEVER SEEMS TO HAVE BEEN any question in MacCracken's adult mind that war was not the way to solve problems. Even though he had roamed around lower Manhattan with the Gramercy Park gang and, if his tales can be believed, picked boyhood fights with other gangs, one aspect of his youthful experiences that he remembered most clearly revolved around his father's interest in the peace movement. It certainly seems possible to attribute many of Noble MacCracken's adult methods of working for peace, and his dedication to developing a liberal arts curriculum in which international understanding and problem solving would be of primary importance, to the prior interests and efforts of his educator father.

These two MacCracken men shared many of the same convictions and ways of looking at the responsibilities of those in charge of educational institutions in a democracy. Both believed that the educational community should not be falsely isolated from the flow of real-life issues, but rather, be immersed in them and offer enlightenment about them. Chancellor MacCracken had been the original vice-president of the Peace Society of the City of New York, which he helped to organize in 1907, and the president of its College Committee on Peace Propaganda. The membership of the committee, which also included Andrew Carnegie, Oscar Villard, Lyman Abbott, and Truman Backus, worked out a model curriculum for "peace propaganda" to be instituted wherever possible in colleges and universities. Curricular reforms were to include instituting programs in the study of international law, the history of arbitration, the introduction of the study of the "spirit of peace" in the teaching of literature, and the placing of far less emphasis on war in the study of history.

The elder MacCracken also was a moving spirit in various groups advocating international cooperation, such as the international peace conference in Lucerne in 1905, and a similar conference in Milan in 1906. These conferences endorsed, and began planning for, the exchange of students and faculty between American and European universities, as well as the establishment of an international university in Europe. At about the same time, George Kirchwey, Dean of the Columbia University Law School, undertook to chair what was called the second Hague Conference at Lake Mohonk, New York in late May and early June 1906, the first conference having been held at the Hague in 1899. At both of these conferences, resolutions were passed asserting that the peace of the world is affected by disruptions in any of its parts, and that the nations of the world must become part of one comprehensive union. (Mary Wooley, president of Mt. Holyoke College, was very involved in this aspect of the peace movement and concerned, as the younger MacCracken became, to make the role of women in the movement prominent.) The two Hague conferences led to the formation of a subsequent group, first called the League for Peace and Freedom, and then, simply, the League to Enforce Peace.

✻   ✻   ✻

IT WAS NO WONDER, then, that the younger MacCracken began to participate in the peace movement when he got back from his frantic scholarly year in England in 1909 and began his professional career as teacher. Soon after he took up his responsibilities as English instructor at the Yale Sheffield Scientific School, he began to broaden his activities away from his books, and to move into the enlarged framework of social concerns that were to dominate his interests both as prominent educator and public citizen. Almost immediately after his arrival in New Haven, he became chairman of a commission on the Davenport Chapel at Yale, a deacon of the New Haven Center Church, and a worker/teacher in the (New Haven) Italian Mission, where he conducted classes. In addition, he organized the Byers Hall "Fireside Talks" for students. His announced subject was simple—

starting one's own library, but the hidden subject was more complex—taking charge of oneself.

These particular commitments were the first of literally hundreds of committees, conferences, organizations and gatherings that Mac-Cracken formed, or took part in, over the years (inside academia and outside). His aim, like his father's before him, was to resolve questions among people and groups through discourse, and to encourage participatory education at all levels, especially among adults. His developing moral ethic, placing the responsibility for social action in a democracy squarely on the individual, was the basis of his own behavior, and he saw it as the foundation of any effective system of modern education. He believed each student had a dual responsibility, as learner from the past, but also as trustee of the future.

His challenge to himself as college president was to provide an environment where learning for participatory citizenship, as well as personal fulfillment, could take place. He believed that properly educated citizens working together could make society function coherently. The place to initiate taking hold of one's social and civic responsibilities was where one was at the time because the principles of trusteeship were universally applicable.

He regarded himself as a constructive peacemaker, and called himself a Christian pacifist, although he was not aligned with a religious group that particularly advocated pacifism, such as the Quakers. He believed that one's country should be able to defend itself from foreign aggression on its own shores. Yet, because he did not see war as solving national or international problems, he was personally against America's entry into both World War I and World War II, although in each case he quickly rallied, once war was declared, as the person in the institution charged with mustering institutional resources for the wartime requirements.

He never relinquished the notions that in the future affairs might be settled by reasonableness, that knowledge and science might be applied to the roots of problems, or that the world could eventually become a league of nations—one world. Later, during the period between the two wars, he did everything he could to wage peace, especially in his college, but also in his community, his nation, and, one is tempted to say, his globe. He created an ambience at Vassar that fostered awareness of the social and political questions that would take group effort and action, as well as individual initiative, to address. He wanted to create an atmosphere for self-education that would

enable the students to undertake civic, cultural, and political responsibilities of adulthood in an enlightened fashion, as well as pursuing
their own more private ends. Both the curriculum and the extra-
curriculum, he believed, should provide opportunities for students to
understand the new and the old.

*   *   *

THE LEAGUE TO ENFORCE PEACE

TOWARDS THE END of 1914 when he was still employed at Smith
College, MacCracken joined a group of "serious thinkers, under the
leadership of G. Lowes Dickinson, an English essayist, to consider the
question of how to bring about permanent peace after the war."
There is nothing left in MacCracken's papers to show exactly how he
became involved with this group, but he was on the roster of the
Peace Society of New York (in New York City) as participating in a
discussion on October 7, 1914, in which Hamilton Holt, then leader
of the Peace Society and editor of the *Independent*, presented his ideas
about a possible structure for a League to Enforce Peace, the committee which ultimately brought the League of Nations' idea into
being in America. This was the group that his father had started
seven years earlier.

A committee of the group was charged at that meeting to consider
what the Society could do to promote its cause. Among the participants were MacCracken, professors John Bates Clark and Frederick
Lynch, and Robert Underwood Johnson, as well as Holt. "This was the
initial action out of which the League to Enforce Peace began,"
according to Ruhl Bartlett in his study of the genesis of the idea. That
original meeting was followed by a meeting of the Plan of Action
Committee on October 28, 1914, presided over by Professor George
Kirchwey, to which twenty-eight people were invited, but of those
invited, only seven attended. There were two more such meetings in
November and December that year, and a dinner at the Hotel Astor in
New York City in January 1915.

Between January and April at the Century Club in New York City,
four meetings about the same general subject took place under the
auspices of an independent larger group, separate from the Peace
Society, although some of the same people were involved. These four

dinner meetings were held for private discussion by invited guests pondering the subject of how to bring about permanent peace after the war. The fourth meeting on April 4 was presided over by A. Lawrence Lowell, president of Harvard University, with William Howard Taft, ex-President of the United States, as the guest speaker. At this meeting it was resolved that the country should work to "form a League of all the great nations in which all justiciable questions between them would be submitted to a judicial tribunal." It was further agreed that the national members of the league would "use their military force" to prevent any of their members from going to war before "the question at issue" had been put before a tribunal, or Council of Conciliation, for adjudication. The people at this meeting then made the decision to plan for a conference to be held in Philadelphia at Independence Hall, to initiate a national movement for a league of nations.

MacCracken did not mention being present at these meetings, or at other similar ones, including the Lake Mohonk Arbitration Conference, arranged by Albert K. Smiley, a Hudson Valley neighbor. Most likely, he could not take in too many of them as he was undoubtedly much preoccupied with his pre-inaugural preliminary activities at Vassar in the spring of 1915. But he did continue to be extremely interested in this step towards the peace movement, and to be involved in its committee work, and he gave it much thought. He was wholeheartedly in favor of the idea of the formation of a league of nations after the war was over.

Even though he was busy with end of the academic year activities at Vassar, however, he did go to the Philadelphia meeting. On Bunker Hill Day, June 17, 1915, MacCracken took the train to Philadelphia and joined the assembly of about 300 people, in the building where the Constitution had been signed. In this symbolic place, the League to Enforce Peace was officially founded by the members of this group. In his (unpublished) recollections of this event, MacCracken said that he was made a member of its national committee and was one of the original signers of their charter document. He wrote:

> ... *The day was boiling hot and Mr. Taft drank at least two gallons. We adjourned shortly before 7 o'clock and I recall running all the way to Penn Station with Lowell setting the pace.*

...In May of the following year, 1916, at the League dinner President Wilson first announced his adhesion to a league of force. Marjorie and I were present and sat at table directly opposite the president. We thought it the most historic moment of our lives. As a member of the national committee I worked in 1918-19 to secure the votes of Senators to the League of Nations. I recall one day reading of the defeat of Wilson by Lodge and others when I sat on a log and wept with disappointment...

Between its founding in 1915 and America's entry into the war in April 1917, the League promoted its views as widely as it could. At Vassar, for example, MacCracken invited the former U.S. president, William Howard Taft, to give a speech on "Our World Relationships" on January 21, 1916. The First National Assembly of the League was held in Washington on May 26 and 27, 1916, and MacCracken and Marjorie, as he mentioned in his comment, were there for the thrilling event. Wilson virtually endorsed the League to Enforce Peace proposals and suggested that America's isolation from world affairs was a "figment of the imagination." Thereafter he was to work for the ideals embodied in these proposals until he was incapacitated.

The Democratic platform that year incorporated the League issues from Wilson's May speech. After Wilson won the election on a platform of "He Kept Us Out of War," the League's membership grew, and there was general support for the idea, although it was not uncontested. (It should be noted that the League to Enforce Peace did not oppose the war; the members simply hoped to prevent another one.)

After the U.S. Congress declared war against Germany on April 6, 1917 ("to make the world safe for democracy," Wilson declared), various branches of the League wasted no time in cooperating with the war effort, but especially in promoting discussion of the objectives for the peace settlement which would come after the war was over. At this point MacCracken himself plunged into the national effort in several directions, all of which were related to his interest in keeping alive the objectives of the League to Enforce Peace.

In the fall of 1917 MacCracken took on the job of organizing and directing the American Junior Red Cross as an outcome of his War Aims appointment. MacCracken conceived of and formulated plans for the American Junior Red Cross, which was to be an organization to create peace and to deal with the damage of war, by educating children about the issues and assisting them in participating in the war emergency, but more than that, by helping them to learn about peace and about other children in other parts of the world. He proposed his plan to the officers of the national Red Cross in Washington during the summer. He said that after "three refusals" his plan was accepted, when he won over to his project Samuel Greer, the director of the Atlantic Division, and Eliot Wadsworth of Boston, the vice-chairman. The national War Council approved the plan in September on condition that he would head the enterprise and take on full responsibility for its educational program. This resulted in his request to the Vassar board for a two-thirds release time leave from his job as president during February through June (the second semester of the academic year) in the winter and spring of 1918. He would be given two-thirds of his Vassar salary during that period, with no salary at all from the Red Cross, except for the payment of his expenses of commuting from New York State to Washington, D.C.

The success of his initial efforts for the Red Cross in the four weeks of September led to an additional commitment—his "being burdened" with the first Christmas membership campaign, from October to December 1917 for the regular (senior) Red Cross. This enterprise he apparently ran out of his Vassar office, with what must have been frequent intervals in Washington, but the secretarial work was carried on in Washington, fortunately for the Poughkeepsie post-office. In spite of "a blizzard blanketing the country with snow" during Christmas week, twenty-one million adult citizens joined the Red Cross that fall and early winter, by paying a membership fee of one dollar to national headquarters.

On January 8, 1918, Wilson endorsed the idea of a League of Nations in his "Fourteen Point" speech to Congress. That same month at Vassar the alumnae of the college voted to send a relief unit to France. A great many Vassar people were involved in the enterprise, both recruits from among the alumnae and fund-givers from the college community at large. Eight Red Cross Recreation Huts were operated for convalescent soldiers at the American Base Hospital Center in Savenay, France. After the war this unit did relief work for the French government. In March 1919 it established a *Goutte de Lait* (milk station) and dispensary for those in need at Verdun. Financed through September 1920 by Vassar alumnae, it was taken over by

Verdun residents, with the help of Luxembourg and the Netherlands, and continued until World War II.

After the armistice (which, as we have learned, coincided with MacCracken's return to Vassar full time from "sick leave"), the Red Cross requested the college to permit him to accompany Mr. H. P. Davison, head of the organization, to the Peace Conference tables at Versailles, to which President Wilson had gone with his League of Nations idea, to help draw up plans for an International League of Red Cross Societies for peacetime cooperation. The request, perhaps not unexpectedly after what had transpired between him and the trustees, was denied. MacCracken nevertheless for two future summers spent time in Europe working on Red Cross projects, chiefly the Junior Red Cross in France, Switzerland, Italy, Czechoslovakia, and Austria, as the American organization expanded to become worldwide, local to global.

His active work towards the idea of the League of Nations continued for the next decades. He worked as a member of the League to Enforce Peace to secure the votes of senators for American ratification of the League provisions in the Versailles treaty, but the Senate went along with Republican Henry Cabot Lodge and others, and the provisions of the treaty were rejected.

MacCracken wrote of these times:

> ...My interest in the League of Nations continued when in 1922 I attended meetings of its Committee on Intellectual Cooperation, of which Bergson was chairman. Curie, two American astronomers [were members] and Oscar Halecki was Secretary. I also attended League meetings in 1925. Later in 1948-49 I was chr. of the Dutchess County Chapter of the American Association of the United Nations. Public meetings were held but the lack of interest was discouraging.

OVERTURES FOR PEACE

DURING THE twenties, thirties, and forties, MacCracken either himself organized, or in some cases accepted positions of primary responsibility in administering, new organizations created to promote understanding among variant groups. His efforts reached out in many directions and took countless hours of administrative time devoted to policy-making, committee organization, speechwriting and speech-making, travelling and conferring.

The groups widely differed, exposing him to fresh needs and new problems on an almost daily basis—activities that had nothing specific to do with the running of his college, and yet, looked at from an overall point of view, had everything to do with it, since it constituted the raw stuff of human experience with which he was trying to imbue the education of Vassar undergraduates, as well as the continuing education of the alumnae. There were periods when he belonged to over thirty such organizations simultaneously, managing to climb down from one board committee chairmanship, only to agree to take on another. Some of them he continued with for the years of his presidency, putting extraordinary effort into making them produce results. The benefits to the college were often indirect, rather than direct—in the case of the mechanism for admitting foreign professors and students to American colleges in general, and Vassar in particular, the results were sometimes minimal. Yet taken together, they represented a step forward in the internationalization of the American undergraduate student consciousness. MacCracken worked very hard for at least two decades on two such seminal institutions—the Kosciuszko Foundation, and the National Conference of Christians and Jews

On May 2, 1923, MacCracken received a letter from a Polish immigrant, then a professor at Drake University, named Stephen Mizwa, stating that Mizwa had enjoyed MacCracken's recent article in *Current History,* a magazine of *The New York Times,* on "Beacon Lights of Civilization in Central Europe." This was an article about MacCracken's experiences visiting eastern European universities. Mizwa wrote MacCracken that he had come to the United States in 1910, graduated from Amherst, gone on to Harvard, and had recently been working to enable other students from Poland to receive their education in the United States. In the article he had read that MacCracken had brought to Vassar a handful of foreign students in the previous couple of years, and was going to employ an exchange professor, Dr. Sudlecki, as a teacher in 1924. Would MacCracken be interested in furthering such arrangements at other institutions, Mizwa wanted to know. If so, he would be glad to join forces with him and take some of the responsibility for developing an exchange program. MacCracken responded on May 8:

I know of no other institution in America that has taken
steps along lines of exchange of professors and students from
Poland, but feel sure that such a matter could be arranged if
there were a Polish-American Committee to promote it.

A friendship over this mutual interest and desire promptly grew up between MacCracken and Mizwa, and they started an enterprise, called the Polish-American Scholarship Group, in September 1924 to undertake the project. The Honorable Lasislaus Wroblewski, Polish Consul General in New York at the time, was made president, and MacCracken, vice president. Nine scholarships were given by the organization in 1924-25. Then, in October 1925, that group was dissolved, and the Kosciuszko Foundation subsequently organized, occupying a suite of rooms at the Consul General's office. An effective student exchange plan was put in operation by the organization by September 1926. MacCracken worked hard to raise money for the foundation, and he remained its president until April 1956, when he made his valedictory address at a testimonial dinner at the Plaza Hotel in New York ten years after he had completed his Vassar presidency. Through the exchanges, a better understanding of Polish culture and history, as well as language, were gradually introduced to American educational institutions, with reciprocal arrangements abroad.

MacCracken's membership in the National Conference of Christians and Jews began shortly after its organization in 1935. He recalled later attending for several summers its Institute on Human Relations. In 1938 he became chairperson of its educational division, working closely with President Constance Morrow of Smith College, determining how to assist displaced Jewish persons from Eastern European countries who were encountering problems of anti-Semitism as they settled in America. During the summer of 1938 MacCracken helped implement an attitude-building conference at Williams College in Williamstown, Massachusetts, seeking to eliminate prejudice and "attain amity, understanding, and cooperation among Protestants, Catholics, and Jews." Between 1939 and 1946 MacCracken spoke at many meetings under the auspices of this organization, always seeking, as he put it, to create good will among all faiths. In the summers of 1944 and 1945, while still committee president, he attended summer staff meetings.

When he retired from the Vassar presidency in 1946, he served the organization full time as a consultant on education. In a comment about this assignment, he noted that he travelled 25,000 miles during two years, addressing audiences in temples, churches, and elsewhere. By 1947 he agreed to serve as general secretary to the organization, taking the place of Everett Clinchy, the organizational director, when he was away from his office. Each summer between 1946 and 1948 MacCracken was chairperson of a world conference on human relations—held abroad at Lady Margaret Hall in Oxford in 1946, and Fribourg in 1947 and 1948, in the monastery of the Silesian order. There the tension became so great that MacCracken was forced to retire from his position.

Other peace efforts centered around the Vassar campus itself. In the fall of 1931, MacCracken received word that the college would that year receive the *Federation Interalliée des Anciens Combattants'* Educational Prize for Peace. Every year a medal was given to three institutions which took exemplary positions in working for the causes of peace. Vassar was the first woman's college to receive this coveted prize.

In September 1933 the Women's International League for Peace and Freedom, invited by MacCracken to hold their three-day session at the college, gathered at the Vassar Alumnae House. Some of the members were Vassar-connected people. Many were not. The subject of the conference was "International Problems and World Peace." MacCracken spoke on "This Interdependent World," and was in general agreement with the principal speaker—Eleanor Roosevelt's friend, Caroline O'Day—who spoke about the rapidly changing postwar role of women and their opportunities to bring about peace. Women's earlier "duties"—before the war and before the battle for suffrage had been fought and gains consolidated—had been circumscribed by their responsibilities towards men, and their welfare was measured by men's standards. Now, after increased political and social emancipation, their prerogatives were no longer restricted "duties." The particular import of O'Day's discussion was that women, in their newly won access to the world of politics formerly dominated by men, might begin to have some impact on the issues of war and peace. MacCracken agreed with that wholeheartedly, and his own speech was in that vein also. In addition, he emphasized a pet idea of his about the need for the government to put educational attachees in every foreign legation to integrate and interpret the

United States' attitudes towards the rest of the world, including those that were being remolded, as American interests became more international. Whereas during the nineteenth century, the United States had still been taking its educational lead from Europe, now as the twentieth century progressed, the U.S. had something to teach Europe about education and about democracy. MacCracken said that when he had suggested the attachee idea to Franklin Roosevelt, it had been rejected, but he persisted in thinking it was a good one.

The audience of women at this short, but intense, conference was trying to examine ways in which peace could be pursued. Its members felt that international understanding, which was necessary to world peace, could only be brought about if the current generation of women transferred their ideas about peace to the next generation, and the transference embraced the idea of actively waging peace. The subject of the failed League of Nations weighed heavily on the conference. But there was a general optimism among the delegates that peace could be won in their time by their actions. They agreed that it was up to women to abolish war and press for disarmament.

Scheduling this conference to be held at Vassar was but one of many moves on MacCracken's part during the years after the first world war to encourage a variety of paths towards peace. He was completely open to speakers of various convictions coming and expressing their ideas to Vassar audiences. Following soon after the league conference, socialist Norman Thomas made a speech at Vassar on the subject of the failed Treaty of Versailles, suggesting that it had "invited" Hitlerism. Mary Wooley, president of Mt. Holyoke, who was a delegate to the ongoing Geneva Disarmament conferences, spoke about their progress. To celebrate Armistice Day that year—1933— MacCracken arranged for a performance at Vassar of Millay's *Aria de Capo*, a play about the futility of war.

On April 13, 1934, a day dedicated on many campuses to keeping the peace, thirteen bulletin boards at Vassar were lined with peace propaganda. MacCracken and Eleanor Dodge, warden, donned academic garb, and followed by faculty members and students choosing to join them, marched away from the campus, two miles down the Main Street of Poughkeepsie, across Market Street, back towards the college on Cannon Street, singing the medieval students' song "Gaudeamus Igitur," alternating with "Baa, Baa Bombshell," written by one of the student protesters:

CHORUS
Baa, Baa, bombshell, have you any will?
No sir, no sir, I'm just here to kill.
Little bomb, who made thee, who gave thee thy mission?
A money-grabbing crook and a dirty politician.

A year later, a similar celebration prompted an article in the April 10 *Poughkeepsie Star*:

International peace strike call at eleven o'clock to celebrate peace day, now an annual event on college campuses, issued by youth section of American League Against War and Fascism, American Youth Congress, International Seminary Congress, Student League for Industrial Democracy, National Council of Methodist Youth. Instead of marching downtown as they had the previous year, nine hundred [student] strikers, accompanied by a few faculty members, Eleanor Dodge the warden, MacCracken, and three local clergymen, marched around the Vassar campus, carrying anti-war, pro-peace posters. Quoting Ephesians 6:12: "For we wrestle not against flesh and blood, but against principalities, against powers, against the rulers of the darkness of this world, against spiritual wickedness in high places," MacCracken gave an off-the-cuff speech admonishing super-patriots like the American Legion and D.A.R, that their actions encouraged war rather than peace. His main emphasis was on the need to imagine that peace could be successful.

The next day the vice-chairman of the Ninth District of the American Legion opined that some of Dr. MacCracken's ideas were ridiculous (April 12, 1935, *Poughkeepsie Star*). On April 13 the *Poughkeepsie Eagle News* criticized MacCracken:

Dr. Henry Noble MacCracken's inferential arraignment, in his speech at the anti-war day exercises at Vassar College yesterday, of the Ladies Auxiliary of the American Legion and of the Daughters of the American Revolution as organizations which somehow are working against the cause of peace seems to us to have been based on false impressions. ... Peace advocates in general can do few things more likely to injure their cause than to

create the suspicion that somehow or other an enlightened desire
to avoid war is incompatible with what the country knows as
patriotism.

A COURSE ON PEACE?
(There had been one in his father's institution
twenty-five years earlier: why not Vassar?)

ON SEPTEMBER 1, 1939, Germany declared war on Poland. As
tension over the war was running high on the Vassar campus, students
seeking an outlet petitioned the faculty to teach a course on peace.
There was, however, no mechanism for introducing a spur-of-the
moment new course, without going through regularized channels of
curricular change, which typically took a year to process new courses
(suggested by departmental faculty, not students.) The students' idea,
although enthusiastically supported by MacCracken, nevertheless
ended up stalemated in faculty committee, without ever being transformed into a course. The carefully guarded departmental territorial
jealousies still protected the curriculum from what was regarded as
disciplinary invasion rather than multidisciplinary cooperation. Mac-
Cracken, very disappointed, thought that a multidisciplinary course on
the subject of peace should and could take its place in the curriculum
as a central theme of human experience, and be treated in a complex
way on the basis of observation, information, and theory drawn from
historical and modern sources in many fields and disciplines.

He described the situation in an article "A Course on Peace?" for
The Alumnae Magazine in April 1939 as "the dilemma in which higher
education finds itself." The failure of the faculty to be able to, or even
want to, act on this strongly felt, immediate desire on the part of students for a course on peace was symptomatic as MacCracken saw it
of a real dichotomy in higher education. MacCracken's vision of education, especially in the social sciences and arts, continued to dwell
on the immediacy and efficacy of students' motivation to understand
the issues of their own world, with relation to their own frames of
reference. He remained somewhat disappointed that many of the
others in the college were not in accord with him, and that progress
in making the Vassar education relevant to contemporary issues was
slow and indirect. College was theoretically provided for the benefit
of the student, whose needs for particular areas of knowledge and
information did not necessarily break down into neat and well

separated categories, the subject matter of particular disciplines. MacCracken, in fact, believed that disciplinary education in certain respects served as a restraint. The narrowness and inflexibility of disparate disciplines seemed inadequate for providing opportunities to meet modern and practical educational needs about problems of the world with which Vassar students were already confronted and with which, as far as he was concerned, they ought to be grappling. In MacCracken's experiential world, in which he was trying to redefine some aspects of liberal education, they seemed both appropriate and necessary. He wrote:

> *The imminence of war, and the consequences to the world of war in [the students'] youth, are so terrifying in their possible effects as to make the subject one of immediate urgency. If the disciplines are insufficiently developed to handle such a vast problem, so much the worse for the disciplines. Let interests displace disciplines. In doing so, the curriculum may be revolutionized , since a subject so absorbing in its immediate relations cannot but be one to which students will give all their efforts.*

VASSAR CATALOGUE [1993/94]

Multidisciplinary Programs

> *Each multidisciplinary program concentrates on a single problem or series of problems that cannot be approached by one discipline alone. The integration and coherence of the program are achieved through work of ascending levels of complexity.*

*　　*　　*

MacCRACKEN'S POSITION
ON THE WAR AS IT APPROACHED

SINCE HIS POSITION before the United States entered the war seemed to others most nearly to approach that held by the America First party, MacCracken was pressed as the nation moved to enter the war to become an officer of that organization. That he refused to do, preferring to maintain his independence: he felt clear differences between his position and that of America First ideologists, chiefly his strong and compelling belief in internationalist pursuits. He believed that Americans should be citizens of the world. In no way did he want this country to be separated from the main movements of the rest of the global world—and the many ties that bound it to various European and eastern European countries. But what he couldn't accept was the impurity, as he saw them, of both England's and Germany's motives in the prelude to war. He concentrated on the complete futility of war. His speech to an America First Group in the summer of 1940 was typical of his many public statements:

THE AMERICAN WAY

I thought a long while before accepting your invitation: I speak as an individual, as a member of no committee or group. My views are uncensored. They are offered in no spirit of bitterness or opposition, but solely in the hope of clarifying the American way over the dark road ahead. The greater the dangers there are along that road, the more need there is for enlightenment. As a member of the Democratic party, I have supported our President in his social policies, and in his position in international affairs which he took during his candidacy for the third term. I believe in his declared intention to keep us out of war. I hold it therefore in no sense obstructive to examine the eight points of the recent parley at sea [between Churchill and Roosevelt], from the position of a citizen who wants the United States to adhere to its true course. The real obstructionists are those who want to block the true road, and want to force us off the road into a detour by way of Suez, Singapore, and Vladivostock before we get back to the true road, which is the American road, the Washington-Jefferson road, of honest friendship with all nations, entangling alliances with none. Why quit our own, to stand on foreign shores? That is the American question.

I was, as I said, an ardent advocate of the League [of Nations] in 1918, but after twenty-five years, as I look back upon that time, it seems to me that I was mistaken, and that those who opposed our entrance into the League were right. They analyzed more truly than I did the motives of the ruling nations that entered the League after the World War. The League was the instrument for bickering and not of justice.

But I believe today as strongly as I believed in 1918 in Woodrow Wilson's idea of a true League of Nations based upon three great principles: first, acceptance of membership in the league as a most solemn covenant and obligation for the surrender of sovereignty to the extent that member nations accepted the decisions of its World Court as binding, and supported the decisions of the League by force of arms at the League's call; second, an acceptance that all international questions were open and subject to legal review; third, that the only force to be left in the world was to be that of the League, executing its covenants and mandates, and fulfilling the decrees of its court. Woodrow Wilson in an address at that time spoke of the League as extending the principles of the Monroe Doctrine to the rest of the world, and to me the idea of the League went far beyond this statement. What Woodrow Wilson meant by this was that the weaker nations of the world were no longer to be subject to the fear of territorial seizure, no longer to be open for colonization or forceful exploitation.

But to me the League had a far higher obligation. It had the obligation of reviewing the existing condition of the world, the status of subject peoples everywhere, not merely in the mandated territories wrested from Germany or Turkey, and of revising the conditions of their subjection to the ruling powers in justice to the interests of the common man. This, you see, is an extension not merely of the Monroe Doctrine but of the Declaration of Independence to the whole world, and affirming the principle that I profoundly believe to be true, that every man has inherited from his Creator the inalienable rights, among others, "of life, liberty and the pursuit of happiness." The Declaration of Independence was unequivocal and universal in its affirmation.

MacCracken did not agree that "once Hitler [was] destroyed, everything [would] be all right." He believed that the treatment of Germany and Russia, Japan and Italy, new centers of population growth and industrial expansion, in the peace treaties after World War 1 made "a new contest inevitable," and that Hitler became the "instrument of this conflict."

Hitler to me is a mere incident in a long history, a chain of events whose links are forged too strongly to be broken by any such general decision. We are living in the twentieth century in the late afternoon of a long day of colonial conquest, in which the leading nations have been a western fringe of maritime nations of Europe, with England at their head.

In his speech he asserted that the United States should:

... aid [Britain, but] refuse to enter into an alliance with [it]. ... And the grounds of my belief are the same as Wilson's: that we cannot sanction or endorse the policy of colonial expansion, which is the chief factor that has endangered the peace of the world for three hundred years. ... If we enter the war all out as allies of Britain, we are committed to the status quo of colonial empire. If we enter the war now, we shall be unprovoked, unprepared, and uninformed. We shall inevitably be drawn into the stream of colonial conquest, and there is a great danger lest our economic defense of Central and South America become in turn an economic mastery of the destiny of this portion of the world. ... The acceptance of such a League [as the League of Nations] carries with it, no doubt, the extension of the principle of mandates, no longer national but upon an international basis. ... Only by this means can the world escape the inevitable conflicts which must occur again and again in history, until an end has been put to the injustice of the subjection of man by his fellows by means of national force.

As war approached, not many on the Vassar campus shared Mac-Cracken's "stay-out-of-the-war" position. It seemed an ambiguous finale to his career-long quest for peace. He found himself increasingly isolated from the faculty, the alumnae (who wrote him constantly about his lack of patriotism), and many students.

In retrospect, his comment in this speech on Hitler seems unfathomable, untrue to his own observations. He had spoken time and time again of his worries about anti-Semitism, beginning in 1923 with his article on the Eastern European universities, and continued in his reiterations of the need for understanding among races. He had spoken out for internationalism and against both fascism and communism at the Second World Youth Congress. How did he reconcile his strongly-felt and enunciated repugnance for fascism with his comments in this speech about non-intervention against Hitler? A search, as far as it can go fifty years later into evidence of Mac-

Cracken's thinking, fails to clarify what seem to be mutually exclusive positions. None of MacCracken's answers to his critics seemed to address the issue for which he was being taken to task.

CHAPTER EIGHTEEN

WINDING DOWN DURING THE WAR

IN THE FACE OF THE ENCROACHING WAR, MacCracken led the college's celebration of its Seventy-Fifth Anniversary in June 1940, as he had led the Fiftieth, in October 1915. The format of the gathering was much the same. Instead of a *Pageant of Athena* unfolding Vassar history, there was an Experimental Theatre play called *Vassar's Folly: A Chronicle*, doing the same. Instead of Lillian Wald, Julia Lathrop, Emily Putnam, and Ellen Semple sharply urging graduates to prepare for active lives of civic, professional, and social service after college, Helen Lockwood, 1912; Marjorie Schauffler, 1919; Edith Clarke, 1908; and Ethel Phillips, 1930 were giving similar advice in a symposium entitled "What Should a Woman's College Do Today?"

Roosevelt had offered a proclamation from the White House to honor the occasion:

THE WHITE HOUSE

During my ten-year term as a Trustee of Vassar, I came to value certain definite contributions to education made by the college. The social equality that prevails in all plans for student life, and its system of student self-government, are in themselves fundamental courses in democracy. The free play of ideas between scholar and teacher, an institutional tradition, is the achievement in academic practice of the principles of democracy. The nation-wide scope of student enrollment at Vassar is a potent corrective for the few ills of sectionalism that remain to us. I can testify that there are few communities in our country that are not graced by at least one Vassar alumna communicating to her fellow citizens something of the democratic spirit and progressive ideals of her college. The seventy-five years we commemorate are half the life-span of our nation. Not often in our history have we faced a period so threatening to our peace and to our ideals as now. Vassar women are counted among our national leaders in education, business, science, and the arts. They are equipped for leadership in their communities. This leadership will be needed in the years before us as never in the long and impressive history of Vassar.

Although MacCracken had yet to live through the contentious culminating years of his presidency, he must have been heartened by Roosevelt's remarks, especially the passages toward the end citing the graduates' preparation for a life of leadership. In his twenty-five years as president he had worked unceasingly to enhance the set of conditions and relationships in the college that promoted active student engagement.

The months before America's entry into the war and the wartime years—MacCracken's last years in office—were times of unusual stress on the campus. Like many others around the country, most members of the Vassar community were upset by the worsening events of the war, the images in the news of the deepening horrors of the march of fascism, personal family anxieties and the plights of relatives, the interruption of personal plans, and coping with realities.

Elizabeth Moffatt Drouilhet, 1930, who was warden at Vassar (dean of residence) during this period, and very close to the daily life of the college, reviewed some of her memories of those darkening days in a taped interview in 1982. She observed:

One of the really difficult problems during the fall of '40 was the absolute conflict between Prexy [MacCracken] and the dean [Thompson]. The dean headed the all-out-aid-for-Britain [movement] and Prexy headed the America First [movement]. ...I had to work with both, but the feeling was so bitter that there was not terribly much communication between either side. And this continued right up until December 7, 1941.

One of the really significant moments that I recall [however] was...an assembly for late morning of December 8, when Prexy stood up and talked for about fifteen minutes...saying that he opposed the war, he opposed the U.S. involvement in European affairs, as everybody knew; BUT he was above all a Constitutionalist, and [since] the U.S. was now at war...all his energies would be devoted to the war effort. For anybody who had been right between the two things, it still was an awfully impressive speech, for which I had tremendous admiration for Prexy. I think this was the final straw, though, in wearing him down to . . . a feeling of bitterness . . .

[A] tremendous change came with the impact of the war on the college and the necessity for a more liberal approach to many areas, and then the post-war years represented, in my opinion, the greatest change [of all] in the college.

As Drouilhet indicated, during that period late in his administration, MacCracken had to preside once again over a college overcast by a war of which he did not approve. This time it must have been much harder for him. His stands on the issues of war and peace were criticized both inside the campus and outside, where by now, he was conspicuous on the national scene.

Head air raid warden for the college community, Drouilhet spoke about her ultimate responsibility for the college's safety in MacCracken's wartime Vassar:

As I think back on it, nothing much occurred during December [1941]. Everybody was in a state of shock following Pearl Harbor. Shortly after the new year began, along with the rest of the country, we went through organizing for blackouts, for air raids—and in general making the civilian preparation [for a possible air raid attack]. We designated the air raid shelters for every building on campus.

Emergency plans called for the corridors of the basement of the library, the campus's most important center of learning, to be turned into a shelter in the event of total war. No doubt the irony of this alternate use of the library was not lost on MacCracken as the campus mobilized for preparedness.

Drouilhet continued:

We had the emergency blackout light. A footnote—probably one way that I got to know the campus as well as I did was that I . . . learned to walk the campus in total darkness. . . . [I had to learn] where all the manhole covers were, and where there was the slightest curve, to avoid falling flat on my face.

We did have air raid drills. We were notified on the various alerts—the yellow, and then finally the red, which [would mean] the raid was on us. Fortunately, we never heard the red. . . . Everybody had to go to the air raid shelter [during an air raid], and the shelter was in the inside corridors where things were blacked out.

As the semester wore on [in spring 1942] there were all the drives for war relief—everyone was knitting, making packages . . . and there was the general disruption as friends of students either enlisted or were drafted. There was a general lightening of leave regulations, because many students had to leave during the week and couldn't confine absences just to weekends, as that didn't meet the schedules of brothers, fiancés, and close friends who were leaving for service.

[Vassar, like the other women's colleges before the war, still had a modicum of parietal rules controlling students comings-and-goings on the campus.]

The biggest thing that we noticed was that all student activity was centered on the war effort. There was very little other activity. During '42 the students organized to entertain the British soldiers who had a rest camp in Peekskill [N.Y.]

The faculty started entertaining [too]. . . providing dinner for the British men, who came up because there was no money to pay for their dinners. I remember Jo Gleason [entertained] four soldiers one night, and there were two of us out there to help her. She saved up all her [rationing] coupons to get perfectly gorgeous steaks. . . . After cocktail hour, the steaks were cooked and brought out to serve, and suddenly we were aware that not one of the men was eating , and I said "I bet they want their meat well done." So we asked them: "Oh, yes." So these two inch steaks were put back and browned to shoe leather and they ate every bit. . . and enjoyed them.

Prompted by the trustees to consider what measures, if any, should be taken by the college administration and faculty to assist in the war effort, the president and the dean took before the faculty in 1942 the question of whether the degree requirement of the college should be compacted into a shorter time span. This was a response to the growing manpower shortage and would enable undergraduates to complete their education and get on with their lives. Although the number of credits required for the bachelors' degree was fixed, the college could, if it wished, shorten the four-year degree span by offering optional degree work in a summer term. (Other than housing the uncredited summer institutes of euthenics, which had no direct connection with the regular degree program, Vassar's campus usually lay idle during the summer.)

In the spring of 1943, half way through the war and after a fraying debate, the faculty voted by a small margin to recommend to the trustees that the college offer a three-year degree program, which would include work in two summer sessions, for the duration of the wartime emergency.

> Then increasingly in the winter of 1942-43, there was discussion that we had to do something to shorten the period of time to get a degree. All the men's colleges were going into a three-year, around-the-clock operation, and the faculty began to talk of what came to be known as the three-year plan. There was quite a bit of disagreement among the faculty as to how this should be organized. The State of New York granted us permission to divide up the 120 weeks for a degree in any way that we met the same requirements. . . . The plan as a matter of record became two fifteen-week terms and a ten-week term. To try to meet everybody's needs, a student could elect to go on the three-year plan, namely three years of forty weeks, or could remain on the four-year plan, four years of thirty weeks. . . . One thing that always interested me in our three-year plan, as opposed to similar plans in effect at other universities—ours was thought of as preparing a student to cover the same amount of work and continue for the fourth year for specialized training. This to me had a great advantage, as it did not prolong for quite so many years the time a student had to devote to getting ready for what she wanted to do.

As a result of the change in legislation, there were students graduating for the first time in the middle of the year, as well as in June, during the remaining war years. Although involved in a traditional system which provoked and involved strong ties to class, many of the students liked the idea of the shortened period for pursuing the degree requirement. Furthermore, the ten-week summer session gave a handful of faculty the opportunity to invent and teach innovative courses appropriate to the credit and the time span. Thus at last several multidisciplinary courses were offered, although still not one called "Peace." "Today's Cities," taught by several faculty members, breathed new life into the curriculum. MacCracken and Thompson were gratified, and it was clear that they would like to see these changes adopted permanently. But it was not up to them: it was the faculty's call to send a recommendation to the trustees.

When the war was over, the faculty had to decide whether or not to revert to a traditional four-year program. It became clear as time went along that about a third of the faculty wanted to make the three-year program a permanent feature of the curriculum. A vocal two-thirds wanted to return to the earlier status-quo.

Drouilhet spoke later of her memories of this debate:

> *As I think you can tell from my comments, I was very much in favor of it. I regret that we did this experiment at that time when most of the other colleges were doing just a straight accelerated plan, because I think that too many people thought of ours as just rushing through, rather than a thought-out arrangement to shorten the period of preparation before a young woman was ready to take on whatever her chosen career turned out to be.*
>
> *For all the philosophical reasonings and practical details of working out [the program], one thing was quite evident: the faculty split right down the middle. I have seen bitter disputes; one I recall is when the Latin requirement was dropped for admission [in the thirties] and Elizabeth Hazelton Haight [professor of Classics] spoke for forty minutes in a faculty meeting without ever stopping to draw a breath, saying this was the end of Vassar College and the proper education of young women. But nothing equalled the bitterness that the three year plan evoked. Friends stopped talking to each other—many people looked the other way when they saw an opponent on campus. There were secret caucuses—people arrived with their notes in their pockets—it's hard to describe the atmosphere of that period of bitterness.*
>
> *The bitterness grew and grew and grew until the final vote and continued afterwards. I think that the opposition—(as I said I was pro the three year plan)—thought that it took students longer to mature, thought that the periods were too rushed. Some of them did not like the thought of such short vacation periods—It would seriously handicap their research.*

It was financial planning in some ways that defeated the success of the plan—as well as theory. The faculty were given no extra compensation in the beginning for the extra term, and whether they took summer jobs, or took the time to do their own research, their time was shortened and they were teaching more hours for less pay. Had the college been able to hire extra people, or to give the added compensation in three years, some might have been happier with it.

But for whatever reasons, the fact remains that it divided the college, and for many years; in fact almost to the present [1981], for anybody who lived through it, there is that deep suspicion. Feelings ran so high that the show of hands—the customary way to vote if the voice vote was not conclusive, resulted in department chairmen and senior faculty checking on how everybody was voting, and, following meetings, expressing their displeasure in no uncertain terms, particularly with young members of the faculty who had not voted the party line. Eventually this resulted in a request for written ballots.

MacCracken, as president, was, as usual, chairperson of the faculty during the year of special meetings that preceded the decision as to whether the college would permanently convert to the shortened schedule. His heart did not seem to be in the issue of the debate, and he did not get deeply involved, except to the extent that he had to chair the meetings and act as go-between with the trustees, led by Kathryn Starbuck, president of Skidmore, who was chairperson of the board during this period.

The trustees, who did not want to make up their minds in a hurry, seemed much more interested in the idea of a permanent three-year program, followed by a fourth year of preprofessional work, than were the faculty. MacCracken, interviewed in the spring of 1946 before his retirement, said of Vassar's post-war plans: "We'll probably come out by the same door we went in." He continued, "The real problem is not how to regulate the student some more, but how to set him free, how to give him the four freedoms of college: freedom from family, freedom from faculty, freedom from administration, and freedom from himself." So there he was, essentially correct in his prediction, and still at odds with others over putting the student's independence and initiative first over faculty red tape, after thirty-one years. He called the vote correctly. The vote over whether to keep the three-year plan, or return to the four-year one, took place in February 1946. The conservatives won. It was the last issue but one taken up by the faculty before he retired. The last was a "related studies plan," freeing the student to design her own program with faculty advice. The pendulum thus kept swinging as MacCracken left the college.

* * *

A YEAR AFTER THE WAR'S END, MacCracken finished his duties as Vassar's president on June 30, 1946, and the trustees established the Henry Noble MacCracken Foreign Scholarship Fund in his honor. Before the summer was over, he went to England for the first summer conference of the National Conference of Christians and Jews on "Human Relations," and his twenty-three year recycling phase called "retirement" had begun.

HENRY NOBLE MACCRACKEN
AT HIS DESK IN RETIREMENT.

CHAPTER NINETEEN

SUMMING UP

F ROM THE TIME HE HAD LAUNCHED his academic career at Yale, MacCracken took stands about things that he considered important in life, and then, as often as not, he joined with others who shared his views to try to bring about changes favorable to his objectives. His attempts to try to change the world by reasonable persuasion and through art and organization, especially drama, were characteristic of his behavior both on the college campus and off, on the lecture circuit and over the radio airwaves, to formal audiences and to individual students, faculty members, neighborhood gatherings, politicians, distinguished administrative peers, and simply his friends.

Basically, he was a master-communicator/teacher who knew how to engage the interest of his audience and tried to teach others to do so also through example.

Buried somewhere in his miscellaneous uncatalogued papers is a fragment about engaging interest. There he told the story on himself of the midnight boredom known so well to English teachers wrestling with uninspired student compositions. Soon after he arrived at Vassar, he had asked his students in one class to write about why they chose to come to Vassar. As he told the story, he sat up late into the night reading the papers, most of which were very dull, but seemed to be trying to please the president as English teacher. They contained such observations as "I came to Vassar because I knew it had the best reputation and I would get the best education possible." "I came to Vassar because I wanted to have an education as good as my brother's" or "I came to Vassar because seventeen of my relatives, including a grandmother, two great-aunts, and fourteen cousins came before me." MacCracken was fighting sleep as the hour was late, and the papers were wordy, misspelled, and uninspired. Finally, he read, "I came to Vassar because although I applied to Bryn Mawr, Wellesley, and Smith, Vassar was the only college that would not refund the deposit if I didn't accept admission. And my father didn't want to lose his ten dollars." "At last," said MacCracken, "an honest woman!" (A piece of writing that rang true and at that moment caught attention!) He gave the student author a good mark. (An alumna from Wisconsin—interviewed almost seventy years later in a New Mexican retirement center—mentioned that identical memory about why she chose Vassar and confessed that she was the student who got the good mark.)

As a scholarly graduate student, MacCracken had explored the canon of Middle English and Elizabethan texts and familiarized himself with the language of the scribes, the scholars, the pedants, the poets, the historians, the chroniclers, and the playwrights. He spoke the many voices of Chaucer's pilgrims and followed their storytelling devices with delight. He had attended to the verse stories of Occleve and Lydgate and Gower. The literature of the Bible resounded in his mind's eye in Hebrew, Latin, and Greek. He knew his Aristotle, Livy, Plutarch, and Aristophanes, as well as his Horace and Thucydides. He often recited or sang ballads, some of them of his own invention, some of them collected by his Harvard predecessor, Francis J. Childs.

When he taught in Beirut at the Syrian Protestant College (in its modern transformation, the hard-pressed American University of Beirut) right after graduating from college (at which time he was debating between becoming a missionary or an explorer), he examined the problems of communicating with the Middle Eastern students whom he was trying to teach. There were students who spoke as many as eleven different languages, but not English, and none in common. His letters home were filled with the perplexities of cultural and linguistic encounters. He began to work on the problem and spent the summers of 1902 and 1903, between Syrian terms, in Europe developing his pedagogical skills. What he came up with was indeed unique. He wrote an imaginative textbook called *First Year in English* which was published in 1903, and subsequently went through several more editions, used as it was in fifty or more academies in the Middle East. In the book, he said, he introduced an "altogether new method of teaching [language], that of using gestures in connection with the actual word expressions." He taught the first six lessons with the help of bodily motions.

The teacher . . . joins voice and gesture, saying, "Stand up," *(at the same time motioning the student to rise.) The student* *rises. Then the teacher by placing his hand to his ear and* *seeming to question the student gets him to repeat the words,* *"Stand up." Thus the teacher proceeds getting the student to* *repeat each time the words which describe what he does.*

Lesson One.

"STAND UP."
"SIT DOWN."
"GO TO THE DOOR."
"GO TO THE SEAT."
"COME TO THE TABLE."
"TURN TO THE DOOR."
"TURN TO THE TABLE."
"GO TO THE SEAT AND SIT DOWN."
"BRING THE BOOK TO THE TABLE."
"GO OUT."
"COME AND SIT DOWN."

In 1953, after he had retired, MacCracken learned that the book, which had become a staple of English as a Second Language education in the Middle East, was still in use in Near Eastern countries, when he had a letter from a headmaster of a school in Mecca, Saudi Arabia. Typewritten, the letter said:

Dear Dr. Henry. We have been favored with your address, *from your edition of* First Year in English *and have the honour* *to inform you that we are pleased with the volume as we have* *read it a great many times.*

We are therefore asking your kindness for informing us *about its present method of teaching or learning it so that we* *may correspond according to your new method.*

Permit us to offer you our desire, that is about the verbs *contained at its back have not been conjugated in a full list, so* *we hope that you will be pleased to conjugate them and make in* *a special list.*

MacCracken said that in 1949 he and "a number of noted personages" presented a petition to the Economic and Social Council of the United Nations on the subject of genocide. The petition was given to the president of the council, Dr. Charles Malik, of Lebanon. After the business was over, Dr. MacCracken greeted the Council president in Arabic, and received a like courtesy.

> "Don't tell me," Dr. Malik said, "that there's someone in America who speaks Arabic."
> Then he said, "Let me see. MacCracken. Why of course. I learned English from your book many years ago."

(MacCracken might have heard after his retirement that in the meeting place on the Vassar campus that he named the Aula, some years later a Dartmouth professor, John A. Rassias, incurred great praise and some scepticism in demonstrating the effectiveness of a similar method to an audience ready for cutting-edge ideas in the teaching of language at a Vassar conference.)

Early in his presidency at Vassar, apparently without quite enough to do, he wrote A Manual of English with his colleague in English, Helen Sandison. He began that book by quoting Robert Louis Stevenson:

> The difficulty of literature is not to write but to write what you mean; not to affect your reader, but to affect him precisely as you wish. This is commonly understood in the case of books or set orations; even in making your will, or writing an explicit letter, some difficulty is admitted by the world. But one thing you can never make Philistine natures understand ... namely, that the business of life is mainly carried on by means of this difficult art of literature, and according to a man's proficiency in that art shall be the freedom and fulness of his intercourse with other men.

So was it with MacCracken.

Language, words, explanations of names, greetings, a quirky idiom, oral speech, formal speech, mannerisms, accents, silences, substitutions and mistakes, ditties, folklore, argumentation, questions and answers, humorous repetition, "peavining" out in a farmer's field, "high-falutin"-put-ons, punctuation...they all fascinated him. His "word hoard" was enormous; his range of ready examples for stunning juxtaposition and illumination, wide. He loved to think about, repeat, and mimic the words people used as they talked with him all day long, and from the airwaves of the past.

He loved to write down what he heard people say, twist it a little, cull it, and come out with the drama of human speech. Through the drama of speech, he caught life in the act.

Day after day as MacCracken travelled around the country for Vassar he talked with people and told them stories. He gave license to his considerable talents in narrative and dramatic writing by setting up dramatic scenes before his audiences. For example, he gave a talk to alumnae in New York in which he replicated a congressional un-American activities investigation. He posited himself, MacCracken, as the witness for democracy and drew up a cast of inquisitors who demonstrated many stereotypes of bigoted and semi-literate legislators, and the complete ignorance that they displayed about the meaning of democracy. He lectured the Jewish people in their synagogues and the Christians in their churches on the need for tolerance and human understanding.

He wrote his own speeches, often perfecting and refining them through several drafts until he achieved the exact nuances that he wanted. More often, he just let them flow, or wrote himself prompting notes. He indexed his speeches, although no two were ever alike, for he often departed from his text. He had the gift of the power of suggestion. In a few concrete images, he evoked just the precise detail from the past that would correspond to the particular observation of the present.

It is hard to imagine when as college administrator he found all the time that this writing must have consumed. He wrote prolific articles for newspapers, magazines, periodicals, and direct delivery, all of which linked the present with the past and the future.

✳   ✳   ✳

A MAN OF PRINCIPLE, firm convictions, and often high seriousness, MacCracken also enjoyed low seriousness. Few subjects, especially human nature, and including his own, escaped MacCracken's ironic eye, his witty pen, or his penchant for histrionics.

Life in the act at Vassar (taken from *The Hickory Limb*):

> *One of my first sights was a scene at the door of Main. Out from its portal came Miss Macurdy, [professor of Greek], dressed for a suffrage parade in Poughkeepsie, and proudly wearing a silk banner across her bosom, emblazoning the awful suffrage colors, and Votes for Women shamelessly displayed.*

Mr. Shattuck [professor of geology] met her. "I implore you, Miss Macurdy," he cried, "Don't go down there among that rough crowd. It isn't safe. You will be assaulted. You don't know what may happen." "Out of my way, Mr. Shattuck," cried the embattled Amazon, and off she marched . . .

Sometimes the unexpected self-assertion of women professors came from the same dynamic that makes professors' absent-minded devotion to one's special field. [That was the case with two women professors who went to a vaudeville show in Poughkeepsie in the 1920s.] Among my best friends on the faculty was Miss Martha Beckwith, who held at Vassar the Chair of Folklore. . . . In her researches she had lived with Hawaiians of the older stock, Negroes in Jamaican highlands, and reservation Indians. "Come, Miss Monnier [professor of French]," she said one day. "The paper advertises a genuine Hawaiian hula at the theatre. I want to see it. A car just went by with a big poster, too. Genuine hula, think of it!"

Miss Monnier's protests were of no avail. Off they went to the theatre on Main Street. At the door the usher asked for tickets. "Nonsense," said Miss Beckwith, "I am an authority." Awed and puzzled, the doorman let them through. They marched down to a central seat. The vaudeville was on, and the "hula girls," from West Forty-Second Street of course, capered on. "This is unscholarly," said Miss Beckwith. "I must protest."

"Please, Martha, don't make a scene. What is the use?"

Martha Beckwith rose and addressed the audience. "In the interest of truth," she said, "I must denounce this performance. It has nothing in any way that represents the true hula except the skirt, and even that is artificial. You are being taken in."

The theatre was in an uproar. "Go ahead, old lady. Speak your mind. Tell us about the hula. Sit down!" Miss Monnier did not sit down. She told them what the true hula was, until the petrified manager came to life and started off the "hula" once more.

"Come, Mathilde," said the scholar. "We will not stay for such an unscholarly performance." Miss Monnier followed Miss Beckwith's stately withdrawal while the customers cheered.

✳   ✳   ✳

IF MACCRACKEN WAS SEEN as a headstrong Hotspur by M. Carey Thomas, his lighter and more playful side was apparent to almost everybody else. To the ubiquitous Jack Hennessy, the singular original campus security officer, "making rounds day and night by bicycle looking for other stolen or misplaced bicycles," (stealing bicycles was the most serious campus crime in the thirties and forties), MacCracken frequently played the role of a Prince Hal, resourcefully reproved and parried in the act by Hennessy's down-to-earth genius. William Murphy, later first head of Vassar's employees' union, but a groundsman when MacCracken came to the college, illustrated the relationship between MacCracken and Hennessy in repeating in an interview a story that circulated among the employees in his time. Soon after MacCracken's arrival, the new president was wandering around the alleyways in the service area of the college behind Main Building one night after dark. Hennessy saw him. Not recognizing him, or pretending not to recognize him, he grabbed him by the collar and asked him who he was and what he was doing there. MacCracken said he was the new president, out for a walk. Hennessy said he'd see about that. Holding on to him, he guided him over to the president's house and rang the doorbell. Marjorie MacCracken answered the door. Whereupon Hennessy said,"Do you know this fellow?" "Why yes," said Marjorie, "this is President MacCracken." "Well, I'm glad to hear it, but you'd better tell him not to go wandering around like that on this campus at night," said Hennessy. The next day, MacCracken gave Hennessy a raise. So was formed a special friendship, which lasted throughout MacCracken's time at Vassar.

MacCracken amused himself with his own ironical juxtapositions and played ordinary scenes for their comic overtones. He told stories belittling himself. He set actions into play, guessing how they would unroll.

He met Vassar alumnae everywhere he travelled. "Last summer," he confessed, when putting together some memoirs—never published—"I was beguiled into attendance at a Paris Music Hall not noted for its prudery. My host, like the true American clergyman he was, wanted to see just how bad Paris could be, and therefore urged me to accompany him. At the end of one of the most revealing scenes, a soft voice at my side said, 'I suppose you are planning to introduce this art into dramatic production at Vassar, Dr. MacCracken.' My neighbor was a Vassar woman of not less than seventy, whose motives in attending the show I did not seek to learn."

He met students in odd places and didn't tell on them. Professor Scott Warthin had this story to tell about a walk with MacCracken:

At dusk one evening I was walking with Prexy and we were approaching Josselyn Hall. The French Tank, as it was properly called, hove into sight, and as we passed it, MacCracken told me how the students found an imaginative use for it in the first years after it was unloaded from a truck to be placed in a semi-permanent position on the field near the tennis courts. [In 1920 the French government had shipped the tank to Vassar in gratitude for Vassar women's war service and Vassar College's support. It came by steamship, riverboat, and finally truck to Vassar. Some bibulous Josselyn dwellers, ever resourceful during Prohibition and certainly not timid, did not treat it as a memorial.] MacCracken told me, "I was walking here at dusk one night. A window in the west wing of the dormitory opened. A female figure hopped out in a bathrobe. She darted stealthily to the tank, climbed up to the turret, which she opened, took out her bootleg liquor, and ran back to the open window. There she had trouble managing reentry with the height and the burden. I stepped out of the shadows and gave her a hoist. In she went."

(A variant of that story was told to Smith students during Prohibition by William Allan Neilson who claimed to have had a similar thing happen. Who cut the campus caper first or made up the lore is no longer clear.)

MacCracken said he committed a fraud the first year he arrived. The women professors had their annual play for the students, an affair from which men were excluded. In came MacCracken dressed as an old woman to interrupt the show, for which he happily suffered verbal abuse before reconciliation.

Vernon Venable, around 1930, at the time a young writer without a job, met someone on a path in the Swiss alps who knew Mac-Cracken. One thing led to another, and MacCracken hired Venable to teach philosophy at Vassar. The problem was, before he was hired, there were only two members of the department and they hadn't spoken to each other for twenty years or so. It was up to Venable to manage somehow. It seemed to Venable in retrospect a maneuver quietly savored by MacCracken, with predictable side effects. The scene was set, and the action unrolled to a denouement.

When it was MacCracken's turn to read a paper which should have been written down and solemnly delivered to an elite local group of twelve men of which he was a member (the club had been started by the much more formal Taylor), MacCracken ad-libbed. Even though his talk was good, and he had by then given at least 5000 other such talks, his informality was considered unsuitable and undignified for the occasion by the other members.

Mr. George Polk was Vassar's comptroller when MacCracken arrived, but unfortunately, as we have learned, there was no budget in place. Mr. Polk kept personal accounts with all the students who banked with him (rather like the United States Congressional bank in 1991). These transactions grew too large and risky for the college to continue. MacCracken wrote:

> *George Polk's beautiful copper plate script fills many books of accounts but his airy estimates of income and outgo used sometime to give me heart failure. He would come to my office one morning and say, "Doctor, it looks like we are going to have a surplus of $50,000." The cheering news would buoy me for twenty-four hours, when the comptroller would put in a second appearance and say, "Doctor, we made a leetle mistake yesterday; we are going to have a deficit of $50,000 instead of a surplus" and I would go home with a sick headache!*

In these veins, MacCracken poked fun on all sides, especially at himself. Often he seemed to promote a bit of teasing trouble or comic embarrassment and enjoy it at someone's expense before pulling the other person out, or maybe that was just the way he spoke of what he used to do.

FINALE:
MacCRACKEN ON MacCRACKEN

MacCRACKEN LOOKED BACK over his own lifetime in the decade before he died in 1970 and located for himself, as a way of reviewing events and their impact, a series of "honorable stations" that he had held at various stages in his career.

From his perspective in the 1960s, nearing age ninety, he could count the many organizations that he either had started singlehandedly, played a role in starting, joined with others to start, or floated ideas for someone else to actualize (not many of these since he initiated most organizations himself). He continued such activities because he believed that human beings could organize themselves to effect good in their various communities. Coordinating themselves into action groups, they could bring about change. Much of his philosophy stemmed from his conviction that broad-ranging literacy and education for individual human beings spelled empowerment at any level. He recognized the very strong importance of communication in a democracy, enabling individuals to put their ideas into motion at appropriate levels and in systematic ways. And he understood that people speak and are heard in many voices. He was fascinated with the possibility that through all these mechanisms and correlating links, the world could draw together peacefully and become one world. However this did not happen in his lifetime.

In his black notebook listing the "Honorable Stations," Mac-Cracken wrote of his retirement:

> *Mentioning one day my discontent about the lack of forward-looking policy in the (Dutchess County) Historical Society to our learned County Clerk, Mr. Fred'k Smith, he expressed agreement and regretted that many documents of the early period were still uncatalogued in his office. He asked me if I would catalogue them. I accepted and was paid at the minimum rate as a worker in his office, so as to comply with the state requirements of employment. The catalogue of more than 15,000 documents was completed in 1954. The documents cleaned, packed in airtight fireproof drawers, and preserved in a large 2 vol. catalogue in the County Clerk's office.*
>
> *The documents had so much history in them that I gave an interview to the press. ... With this as a motive I undertook to write a little history of the county, which I completed in 1956. Marjorie and I organized the Casperkill Press to publish the volume. We got some favorable terms from Hadon Craftsmen, and a New York publisher with a Vassar wife assumed the official title of publisher and sold the book outside the county.*
>
> *The book was so well received that I was spurred to write a second book covering the history from 1812 to date on the same terms. Lacking the spice of brand new source materials like that in my first volume, it has sold more slowly, but both books are still selling in 1964. ... To push the sales of the volumes, I accepted many invitations to speak. ... In all I suppose at least 100 appearances. They led, in turn, to an invitation to give five minute talks over radio WEOK, Pk. I gave 335 such talks*

recorded on tape and these were twice repeated. . . . In all more than 1000 appearances on this radio alone.

I was chm. of the 150th anniversary of Poughkeepsie as a city, and general chr. of the 175th anniversary of the Federal Constitutional Convention in the city in 1788.

I presided also at the dedication of the [Poughkeepsie] postoffice and had the pleasure of introducing President Roosevelt. He talked to me personally at length of the difficulties he had in driving the Post Office through to completion. At the very last minute the architects had moved the site so as to be off the axis of the civic center which he envisioned. In the course of this study I came across the personality of James Alexander and continued this study until in 1964 I have a MS completed and ready for publication . . .

I am at present, in 1964, giving a series of a dozen talks of 30 minutes each in the form of dialogue with a good friend, Evangeline Darrow, now crippled and confined to her chair.

✳ ✳ ✳

CODA

IN HIS COMMENCEMENT ADDRESS of June 10, 1925, Henry Noble MacCracken, celebrating his tenth year in the presidency, said:

If I were the founder of a new college, I would begin not with a program of arts and sciences, but with the student and his desire, his "studium." If he had no desire, I would exclude him. The student would be allowed to begin with his own interests.

"And when you have done this," a voice behind me from the faculty will say, "you will have just the same curriculum you have now. The student who wishes to know what is just cannot avoid Plato. . . . "

Oh, not quite right, good friend. Everything is the same, and yet everything is changed, because desire is there . . . because the student is beginning college in the spirit of research itself.

Twenty-one years later, interviewed on May 25, 1946, just before retirement, MacCracken told Millicent Taylor, a reporter for the *Christian Science Monitor,* that the "Ivory Tower heritage" had been replaced for good on the Vassar campus during his administration. She wrote about their conversation:

The absent-minded professor, and the college faculty so absorbed in research that everyday campus life of their students might well be on another planet, are both out of date as far as Henry Noble MacCracken is concerned. Both are signs of another and less worthy era of American education. The professor today, instead, is responsible for creating an environment of education, a moral atmosphere, for his students. This is as much a part of his teaching duties as research or class lecturing, according to Dr. MacCracken.

In a leisurely after-breakfast talk with me the other morning, Dr. MacCracken named as "separatism" a false and harmful condition still to be found in American colleges.

"Separatism," as he defines it, is where a Faculty group and a Student group, all on one campus, have interests entirely separate. Except for meeting in the lecture hall, the two groups do nothing together. Campus life for the students is an absorbing round of athletic events, student clubs, and social doings. The professors do their lecturing and then disappear. They feel under no obligation to influence the students in daily growth, intellectual or moral, beyond the lecture hall. At Vassar, they have got rid of this unfortunate condition. . . . [T]he vital outside interests of youth are harnessed to academic purpose, to the benefit of both. Educational subject matter is living material. Students and professors, in connection with courses, together do community service off campus. A survey of the town of Poughkeepsie conducted by the students cut across departmental lines . . .

. . . Students who deal with living material in their college studies—whose college experience is growth under professor-leadership—are going to go right on growing when they leave college. We who went to universities in the old "separatist" era know all too many students who upon graduation sloughed off every vestige of intellectual interest. Except for friendships and other social influences, college might never have happened to them.

Not so today. "[Our students] keep right on taking part in community affairs," Dr. MacCracken said. "They are active in local government." What they studied in college remains alive to them, because real, and takes form in action that becomes a natural and continuous expression.

This is higher education the modern way.

Henry Noble MacCracken at Founder's Day, 1946.

SELECT BIBLIOGRAPHY

Adams, Elizabeth Kemper. *Women Professional Workers: A Study for the Women's Educational and Industrial Union*. New York: The MacMillan Company, 1921.

Addams, Jane. *My Friend, Julia Lathrop*. New York: The MacMillan Company, 1935.

Bartlett, Ruhl J. *League to Enforce Peace*. Chapel Hill: University of North Carolina, 1944.

Bentley, Joanne. *Hallie Flanagan, A Life in the American Theatre*. New York: Alfred A. Knopf, 1988.

Bernard, Jessie. *Academic Women*. University Park: Pennsylvania State University Press, 1964.

Bordin, Ruth. *Alice Freeman Palmer: The Evolution of a New Woman*. Ann Arbor: University of Michigan Press, 1993.

Brown, Louise Fargo. *Apostle of Democracy, The Life of Lucy Maynard Salmon*. New York: Harper and Brothers, 1943.

Clarke, Edward H. *Sex in Education; Or, a Fair Chance for the Girls*. Boston: Osgood, 1873.

Cole, Arthur. *A Hundred Years of Mount Holyoke College: The Evolution of an Educational Ideal*. New Haven: Yale University Press, 1990.

Cook, Blanche Wiesen. *Eleanor Roosevelt. Volume One, 1884-1933*. New York: Viking/Penguin, 1992.

Dobkin, Marjorie H., ed. *The Making of a Feminist: Early Journals and Letters of M. Carey Thomas*. Kent, Ohio: Kent State University Press, 1979.

Flanagan, Hallie. *Dynamo.* New York: Duell, Sloan, and Pearce, 1943.

Haight, Elizabeth Hazelton, ed. *The Autobiography and Letters of Matthew Vassar.* New York: Oxford Press, 1916.

Herman, Debra. "College and After: The Vassar Experiment in Women's Education, 1861-1924." Ph.D. Dissertation, Stanford University, 1979.

Hoff-Wilson, Joan and Lightman, Marjorie, eds. *Without Precedent. The Life and Career of Eleanor Roosevelt.* Bloomington, Indiana: Indiana University Press, 1984.

Horowitz, Helen Lefkowitz. *Alma Mater, Design and Experience in the Women's Colleges from their Nineteenth Century Beginnings to the 1930's.* New York: Alfred Knopf, 1984.

Jordan, W.K. *General Education at Radcliffe College.* Cambridge, Mass.: The Harvard University Press, 1945.

Kendall, Elaine. *"Peculiar Institutions": An Informal History of the Seven Sister Colleges.* New York: Putnam, 1976.

Kendall, Phebe Mitchell, ed. *Maria Mitchell: Life, Letters, and Journals.* Boston: Lee and Shepard, 1896.

Lash, Joseph. *Franklin and Eleanor.* New York: W.W. Norton, 1971.

Linner, Edward R. *Vassar: The Remarkable Growth of a Man and His College, 1855-1865.* Elizabeth A. Daniels, ed. Poughkeepsie, N.Y.: Vassar College, 1984.

MacCracken, Henry Noble. *The Hickory Limb.* New York: Charles Scribner's Sons, 1950.

——————. *The Family on Gramercy Park.* New York: Charles Scribner's Sons, 1979.

——————. *Old Dutchess Forever, The Story of an American County.* New York: Hastings House, 1956.

McCarthy, Mary. *The Group.* New York: Avon, 1954.

Marburg, Theodore. *League of Nations, A Chapter in the History of the Movement.* 2 vols, New York: The MacMillan Company, 1918.

Newcomer, Mabel. *A Century of Higher Education for Women.* New York: Harper, 1959.

Papousek, Jaroslav. *The Czechoslovak Nation's Struggle for Independence.* Prague: Orbis Library, 1928.

Plum, Dorothy and Dowell, George. *The Great Experiment, A Chronicle of Vassar.* Poughkeepsie, N.Y.: Vassar College, 1961.

[Raymond, Harriet] "His eldest daughter," ed. *Life and Letters of John Henry Raymond.* New York: Fords, Howard, & Hulbert, 1881.

Richards, Ellen Swallow. *Euthenics, The Science of Controllable Environment: A Plea for Better Living Conditions as a First Stop Toward Higher Human Efficiency.* Boston: M. Barrows & Co., 1910.

Rosenberg, Rosalind. *Beyond Separate Spheres: Intellectual Roots of Modern Feminism.* New Haven: Yale University Press, 1982.

Rossi, Alice S. and Calderwood, Ann. eds. *Academic Women on the Move.* New York: Russell Sage Foundation, 1973.

Rourke, Constance, ed. *The Fiftieth Anniversary of the Opening of Vassar College. October 10 to 13, 1915. "A Record."* Poughkeepsie, N.Y.: Vassar College, 1916.

Rudolph, Frederick. *The American College and University, A History.* New York: Knopf, 1962.

——————————. *Curriculum: A History of the American Undergraduate Course of Study Since 1631.* San Francisco: Jossey-Bass, 1977.

Solomon Barbara. *In the Company of Educated Women: A History of Women and Higher Education in America.* New Haven: Yale University Press, 1985.

Synnott, Marcia Graham. *The Half-Opened Door. Discrimination and Admissions at Harvard, Yale, and Princeton, 1900-1970.* Westport, Conn.: The Greenwood Press, 1974.

Taylor, James Monroe. *Before Vassar Opened.* Boston and New York: Houghton Mifflin Company, 1914.

Taylor, James Monroe and Haight, Elizabeth Hazelton. *Vassar.* New York: Oxford University Press, 1915.

Ware, Susan. *Beyond Suffrage: Women in the New Deal.* (Contributions in American History, Number 80.) Cambridge, Mass.: Harvard University Press, 1981.

NOTES

I n the notes, the papers of Henry Noble MacCracken in Special Collections, Vassar College Libraries are referred to as HNMP; the papers of Lucy Maynard Salmon, as LMSP; the papers of James Monroe Taylor, as JMTP; the papers of John Raymond, as JRP; the papers of Hallie Flanagan Davis, as HFDP. All references to papers in Vassar College Libraries (VCL) are to papers in Special Collections.

CHAPTER ONE:
A DOUBLE ARMISTICE, NOVEMBER 1918.

8 "It had had no budget": "Statement of the president," Oct. 18, 1918, HNMP, box 120.

8 "trustee George Dimock": "Statement."

8-9 "understood perfectly": "Statement."

9 "a fire had occurred": Poughkeepsie newspaper clippings, Feb. 23, 1918, HNMP, box 120.

10 "In 1918, in the wartime economy": "Statement."

10-13 "It came from Frank Chambers": The Chambers's episode is related by MacCracken, "Statement."

13 "Mills seemed stunned": "Statement."

13 "he [should] consider it futile": "Statement."

13 "after October first": "Statement."

14 "no one was to know": "Statement."

15 "Pratt later wrote": "Statement."

15 Many letters of support of MacCracken are included in this box.

15 "which proved to be very telling": fragment, undated letter of C. Mildred Thompson to MacCracken, HNMP, box 120.

18 "In May 1914": LMSP, series 1, box 3, folder 28.

18 "Salmon, a superb goader": Lucy Maynard Salmon, two letters to MacCracken: Sept. 23, 1918, and Oct. 1, 1918, HNMP, box 120.

19 "wrecking crew": Letter of Louise Fargo Brown to Mac-Cracken, Sept. 13, 1918, HNMP, box 120.

19 "One of them, Henry Cobb": Letters from trustees, HNMP, box 120.

19 "ratify its action": Helen Hadley to Pelton, Oct. 15, 1918, HNMP, box 120.

20 "Within the circle": Elizabeth Kemper Adams to George Perkins, Sept. 23, 1918, HNMP, box 120.

20-21 Helen Kenyon to Hadley, Sept. 12, 1918, HNMP, box 120.

21 "Her report stated": Kenyon to Alumnae, Nov. 18, 1918, HNMP, box 120.

22 "This is mob rule.": Mary Morris Pratt, Oct. 18, 1918, HNMP, box 120.

23 Prof. Woodbridge Riley to MacCracken, Oct. 18, 1918, HNMP, box 120.

23-24 Prof. Frederick Saunders to Florence Cushing, HNMP, box 120.

24 C. Mildred Thompson to Mae Reynolds, Sept. 18, 1918, HNMP, box 120.

24-25 MacCracken letter, 39 pages, HNMP, box 120.

26-27 *Poughkeepsie Eagle News,* Nov. 13, 1918.

CHAPTER TWO:
MacCRACKEN BEFORE VASSAR

28 Information about John Henry MacCracken, *Leadership: The Magazine of Western College,* Spring 1990, p. 22.

28 "letter to the Vassar search committee": Henry Noble MacCracken, *The Hickory Limb* (New York: Charles Scribner's Sons, 1950), p. 9.

29 Henry Noble MacCracken, *The Family on Gramercy Park* (New York: Charles Scribner's Sons, 1949). His family all knew that he was given to embellishing the truth, especially perhaps in this book, in which he adopted the narrative voice of a youngster given to 19th century slang. Nevertheless, the book presents the best understanding we have of his childhood in his academic family.

30 Noble and the theatre, *Family*, p. 126.

30 MacCracken's studies at NYU, letter written to his mother from Beirut, HNMP, uncatalogued box.

31 "gold rush," Bert Burns interview with MacCracken, *Poughkeepsie Sunday New Yorker*, April 12, 1953.

32 Marjorie Dodd MacCracken in her daybook of youthful recollections, lent to the author by the MacCracken family, describes her family's house with vivid detail, inside and outside, and its situation:

> *[When she looked west from her front porch] ... all was respectable, even elegant. Our neighbours were solid and intelligent all the way to Madison Avenue; beyond that came the Rock of Gibraltar of the worthwhile, the house of the President of Columbia. From that point opulence set in until at Fifth Avenue pale palaces arose, on the ashes, it is true, of squatter beer saloons. My glance to the east immediately showed narrower brownstone fronts, then a series of little stores to the corner. ... The tiny stores crept up and down Park Avenue, neat, tidy, good friends of mine, displaying their wares. Beyond the crossing the slums began. ...*

32 Dodd: Standard Oil solicitor. Ralph and Jean Connor recounted in 1980 in an oral history interview with the author that Jean's grandfather, Luke McKinney, was the largest independent oil operator in western Pennsylvania and joined the Rockefeller group at the time of the formation of the trust. He was present in S.C.T. Dodd's office in Franklin, Pennsylvania, at the signing of the one-page document in question, and apparently thought Dodd had missed the boat in not taking shares.

34 MacCracken wrote to his mother in England about his father's astonishing energy in Denmark. HNMP, uncatalogued.

35 "Back in London": Henry Noble MacCracken, *The Hickory Limb* (New York: Charles Scribner's Sons, 1950), p. 2.

36 "No one worries about nepotism in England": The correspondence in this paragraph is based on letters exchanged between MacCracken and his father and mother from England, HNMP, uncatalogued.

36 "the more we see how corrupt and inefficient": HNM letter to parents, 1911, HNMP, uncatalogued.

37   Reference to Simmons College, *HL*, p. 3.
37   "as part of his job": *HL*, p. 3.
38   "Might not a man": *HL*, pp. 1-3.
38   "listening to Uncle Toby...": *HL*, p. 5.
39   Letter from MacCracken to Marjorie MacCracken, July 3, 1909. Marjorie MacCracken Papers, VCL, box 1.
39   In addition to Noble Jr., Maisry, and Joy, the MacCrackens had a second son, Calvin Dodd MacCracken, born in November 1919. The family later adopted a son, James.
39   Betts correspondence, Smith College archives, letter home from Agnes Betts, Smith 1916, to her parents, Dec. 17, 1914.
40   Jordan account. See Mary Augusta Jordan, Professor of English at Smith College, 1884-1921: "The Teaching of English at Smith College from President and Professor Seelye to President and Professor Neilson." Ms., Smith College archives.
40-41 The information about the Vassar English department in the 19th century is from Elizabeth A. Daniels, "History of the Vassar English Department," an unpublished paper delivered at the Evalyn Clark Conference on Excellence in Teaching, April 1991. The paper was based on archival records pertaining to English Department, VCL.
42   "two Vassar alumnae": *HL*, p. 7.
42   "Smith was going through rather sweeping changes in 1913 under Burton." Sources of information were President's "Annual Reports," 1910-1917; *Smith Alumnae Quarterly,* 1914-1917, *passim*; Jordan history of English department; papers relating to inauguration of President Burton, 1910; correspondence of M.L. Burton, 1910-1914, *passim*; Smith College Archives, General 32; Thomas C. Mendenhall (president of Smith College, 1959-1975), "Chance and Change in Smith's First Century," (The Katherine Asher Lecture of 1974), Smith College, 1976. His experience at Smith proved to be a wonderful training ground for MacCracken. Both President Burton and Dean Ada Comstock had advanced ideas about women's education and were beginning to face problems of growth and modernization.
43   "By 1910, according to Thomas Mendenhall": "Chance and Change," p. 8.
43   "MacCracken later recalled": *HL*, p. 11.
44   "According to MacCracken's account": *HL*, p. 11.

45   "Professor Stoddard": *HL*, p. 13.
46   "Wilbur Cross wrote": *HL*, p. 13.
46   "Not long after": *HL*, p. 14.
46   acceptance of job: *HL*, p. 14.
47   "visit to Vassar": *HL*, p. 14.
48-50 "Meeting the Press, 1914 Style": These newspaper clippings
       were in HNMP, box 120.

CHAPTER THREE:
VASSAR BEFORE MacCRACKEN

51   "courtesy call" on Taylors: *HL*, p. 20.
51   Taylor's resignation, February 1914, JMTP, box 17; Vassar
      College Trustee Minutes, vol 2. See also: letter, Taylor to
      Marion Burton, president of Smith, declaring intention to
      retire, Smith College archives, General 32.
52-54 The material on early Vassar students is based on the author's
       scrutiny of the certificates and testimonials of early Vassar
       students recently unearthed by the author and student assis-
       tants from the bowels of Main Building, Vassar College, where
       they have been accumulating since 1867. These materials are
       currently being systematically microfilmed, and some are
       already available in the series "Vassar College Admission
       Records" in VCL. Other materials are separately available in
       VCL.
53   "Autobiography", Laura Collier Brownell, VCL, uncatalogued.
52ff. Raymond administration, JRP; also "By his eldest daughter"
       [Harriet R. Lloyd], *Life and Letters of John Howard Raymond*
       (New York: Fords, Howard, and Hulbert, 1881), *passim;* also,
       annual reports of department chairmen, especially report of
       chairman of department of Belles Lettres, Rhetoric, and the
       English Language, Sept. 1866, VCL.
53   Autograph ms., Mary Whitney, Maria Mitchell Collection,
      VCL.
53   Caldwell, misc. papers, biographical folders, various newspaper
      articles, VCL.
54-55 Circular letter from alumnae to trustees: April 1884 (letter to
       John Guy Vassar), VCL.
56   "At that juncture, the Rev. J. Ryland Kendrick": Kendrick
      biographical folders, VCL.

56   "The successor was Taylor": The sources of information about Taylor are biographical folders, VCL and JMTP.

57   "The educational world is in ferment": Taylor, "Annual report to trustees," June 12, 1888, VCL.

57   References to Rockefeller and Harper: "[Rockefeller] seemed to have nothing to do in Poughkeepsie except talk to me." Thomas W. Goodspeed, *William Riley Harper, President of the University of Chicago* (Chicago: U. of Chicago Press, 1928), pp. 83-84.

58   "One of those was Laura Johnson Wylie": Elizabeth A. Daniels, "The Vassar English Department," Also, Laura Johnson Wylie collection, VCL.

58-59 "Margaret Floy Washburn, 1891, in psychology": bio. folders, VCL. Also oral history interview, Professor Jean Rowley, 1980.

59   "Her book, *The Animal Mind*": (New York: The MacMillan Company, 1908).

59   "Nowhere were these developing limitations": LMSP, *passim.* Also, various mentions of Salmon in assorted oral histories, esp. of Sarah Morris, 1980.

59   "Benson Lossing, the historian trustee of the college": Letters about teaching history, Benson Lossing Collection, VCL.

59   "Herbert Mills": Bio. folders, VCL; also, papers respecting history of economics department, VCL.

59   James Baldwin: Bio. folder, VCL.

59-60 Augustus Strong: Bio. folder, VCL. Also correspondence between Strong and Taylor, JMTP, VCL.

60   "In 1905": Trustee minutes: 2, 248.

60   "Behind the scenes": This incident is documented in the letters exchanged between Lucy Salmon and Helen Hadley in the Helen Hadley collection, folder 14, VCL.

64   Taylor's plan for a new college: Trustee Minutes for 1913, p. 12; also, *Outlook,* July 1, 1911.

64   "one administration building": The college built a new power house in 1912. Apparently Taylor put a small amount of his dream about management into reality.

65   "If I were": June 1911 issue of *Educational Review,* as quoted from *Poughkeepsie Eagle,* June 15, 1911, "Vassar College Scrapbook," 4, p. 72.

65ff. The suffrage portion of this chapter makes use of material researched with Professor Barbara Page and delivered in another form as "Suffrage as a Lever for Change," a joint paper at the Berkshire Conference on Women's History, Vassar College, 1982, and published in *VQ, 79*, no. 4, pp. 32-36. JMTP, box 1, is a source for suffrage.

66 "In 1907 Mary Whitney": JMTP, box 1, folder 15.

66 "President Taylor always insisted in public": JMTP, box 1, folders 8 and 15.

66 Vassar alumna doctor, Charlotte Baker, M.D., letter to Taylor, Feb. 5, 1908, JMTP, box 1, folder 15.

67 Inez Milholland, "Vassar Meets in Graveyard," *New York Sun*, June 9, 1908; "To Punish Girl Suffragists," *New York Herald*, June 10, 1908. For an interview with Rose Schneiderman about the graveyard rally, see "Vassar Girls Ready for the Ballot, Declares Leader of the Suffragettes," *New York Evening World*, June 11, 1908. All of these clippings are in JMTP, box 1, folder 15.

67 "stormy faculty meeting": Minutes of the Vassar Faculty, V, p. 69, March 22, 1909, VCL.

67 "I am afraid": JMTP, box 17.

67-68 Faculty discussions of freedom, etc., apropos of suffrage: Taylor's report of the faculty meeting on March 22, 1909; letter, Dr. Elizabeth B. Thelberg to J.M. Taylor, April 7, 1909; letter, Mary W. Whitney to J.M. Taylor, April 7, 1909: all in JMTP, box 2, folder 16.

68 "Taylor...methods...'impeached'": letter, Taylor to trustees, Feb. 13, 1913, JMTP, box 2, folder 16.

TAYLOR IN RETROSPECT

70-74 These oral histories were all conducted by the author between 1980 and 1990. Many of the individuals graciously agreed to talk with me for several hours, and followed up their formal interviews with more information communicated to me later. Some of the alumnae I interviewed were at Vassar only while Taylor was president; some were there under both presidents; some were there just under MacCracken. These alumnae had an astonishing ability to recall minutiae, important to them, about their college experience. Several of the interviews were conducted in lounges of nursing centers. Everyone was eager to cooperate to get the record straight. These tapes will be placed in the Vassar College library for use by researchers in the future. There are over a hundred of them. They are currently in the collection of Elizabeth A. Daniels, the interviewer and author.

73 Forbush, through Louis Howe, had a position answering correspondence for Governor Franklin Roosevelt. Later on she worked for the Treasury Department in Roosevelt's administration.

MacCRACKEN IN PROSPECT

74 Trustee memorial for Taylor: B. of T. Minutes, 3, 379-80.
74 Items in MacCracken's worldscape: He lists them and write summaries of them in "My Honorable Stations," an unpublished diary, ms., HNMP, box 120.
75 "MacCracken . . . to Josephine Gleason": HNMP, box 37.

CHAPTER FOUR:
"CIRCLE '80" AND "THE RAYMOND CONTROVERSY"

76 MacCracken's drama: HNMP, uncatalogued.
77 "the American George Sand": HNMP, uncatalogued.
79 "Soon after Marjorie MacCracken arrived": *HL*, p. 66.
80 "Student government changes": "Twenty-Five Years of Student Government at Vassar," *Vassar Alumnae Magazine*, 25, no. 4, pp. 7-8.

CHAPTER FIVE:
THE INAUGURATION: RINGING IN THE NEW VASSAR

83 "MacCracken's inauguration": Constance Rourke, ed., *Fiftieth Anniversary of the Opening of Vassar College* (Poughkeepsie, New York, 1915), *passim*. This book contains the anniversary and inaugural addresses. Constance Rourke, 1907, distinguished teacher and writer on American culture, was then a member of the Vassar English department. The anniversary addresses were as follows: James Monroe Taylor, "Vassar's Contribution

to Educational Theory and Practice;" Mary Augusta Jordan, 1876, "Spacious Days at Vassar;" Ellen Churchill Semple, 1882, "Geographical Research as a Field for Women;" Julia Clifford Lathrop, 1880, "The Highest Education for Women;" Lillian D. Wald, "New Aspects of Old Social Responsibilities;" Emily James Putnam, "Women and Democracy." The inaugural addresses were: John H. Finley, "The Mystery of the Mind's Desire;" George Lyman Kittredge, "The Scholar and the Pedant;" Henry Noble MacCracken, "In the Cause of Learning."

84 "Franklin oil wells": a reference to John D. Rockefeller's oil enterprise. Franklin, Pa., was where the Standard Oil Company was formed. Rourke, p. 140.

86 "He had already served notice": *HL*, p. 36.

86 "Vassar woman, a citizen of the world": *HL*, p. 43.

CHAPTER SIX:
BEGINNING FROM THE EGG

87 "Heat as well as light": *HL*, p. 34.

MEMORANDA EXCHANGED BETWEEN
MacCRACKEN AND SALMON: YESTERDAY'S E-MAIL

89 LMS to HNM, Feb.19, 1915, HNMP, box 20.

91-97 The remaining letters are to be found in LMSP, box 7.

CHAPTER SEVEN:
ADMITTING THE NEW STUDENT

98 Interview EAD and Vera B. Thomson, 1980, shortly before VBT died.

98 The founder's affiliation was Baptist, but he insisted that his college be secular. There is in fact no evidence that he was a "baptized" Baptist although he gave money to build two Baptist churches. Nevertheless, the college was advertised in Baptist magazines and presided over by Baptist clergymen for its first four presidencies. The Board of Trustees until 1888

was one-half, or fourteen, Baptist clergymen, and one-half, businessmen. MacCracken and others have believed that the early trustees and presidents made it more strict and pious than the founder would have liked.

99 The author received a letter from Quintard Joyner, Sewanee, Tenn., Feb. 11, 1992. Joyner is a descendent of Bessie Joyner, 1891. The letter indicated that Bessie Joyner, presumably having prepared herself to meet the Vassar entrance requirement in Greek, then prepared her brother for admission to a southern university by "tutoring him through two years of Greek in six months." (Bessie Joyner went on to be the principal of a school in the South.)

99 For the first two years of the college, the administration had difficulty classifying the students, so disparate and uneven were the preparations of most of them. President Raymond estimated that only approximately one third of the first group of students were adequately prepared; the rest had deficient credentials. A good source of information about the general chaos of early admissions credentials at Vassar and the problems of classification and preparation is found in John Raymond, *Life and Letters,* esp. Chapter 12, pp. 595-633. My own information about Vassar admission credentials comes from the study already mentioned of the original admission records which are now in the process of being microfilmed. The group includes records from 1867 to the present.

100 "Instead following the trustee restriction": Entrance credentials show clearly that many of the early applicants registered several years in advance of their year of putative entrance. By 1910 those would be the ones that received preferential treatment even though others in the pool who registered latter were better qualified.

96 "For entrance": C. Mildred Thompson, "Natural and Artificial Selection in Admission to College," *VQ,* 1921, p. 117.

102 "Thomson": Oral History, *op. cit.*

104 "Ella McCaleb": Letter, Jan. 7, 1916, McCaleb to MacCracken: "A student's work and problems before coming to college are so related to problems here that I think it would be a great waste of effort to separate them too widely." Letter, Jan. 24, 1916, McCaleb to MacCracken: "The plan of separating anything relating to entrance is such a radical, intimate

sort of change that, as I have said before, it should be put into execution gradually. If there must be a secretary on admissions next year, could she not be appointed at least for the year, as responsible to the Dean?" Letter, Jan. 25, 1916, McCaleb to MacCracken: "Let me say first that I wish above all things to have this matter settled pleasantly, and am most anxious to work to that end. I appreciate and share your wish to have my work lessened. So far (and please smile) you have stated that you thought best to take away 1 assistant, 1 stenographer and 1 office, and to introduce an element that must be difficult for awhile. You have not as yet told me what work Miss Thompson would do next year, though you probably think you have. It is really not the amount of work that bothers me as the feeling that I am most of the time uncertain of my ground. For two years I have been trying so hard to adapt myself to numerous new conditions that I have lost all elasticity." HNMP, box 2.

CHAPTER EIGHT:
DECENTRALIZING THE GOVERNANCE

105-106   See JMTP, boxes 1 and 16, for correspondence relating to governance, including "Papers bearing on the 'petition of 13'" [faculty members]: letters exchanged between Laura Wylie, Gertrude Buck, Margaret Washburn, Elizabeth Hazelton Haight and Taylor; and between various college presidents and Taylor in 1913.

106   Annotated [by Taylor] copy of "Laws and Regulations of Vassar College" in JMTP, box 16.

106-107   Material concerning faculty club study during interim period: James F. Baldwin, Emilie Louise Wells, Lucy Davis (the Committee); "Report of the Committee on Relations of Faculty and Trustees" [a paper read at a meeting in February, 1915 at which MacCracken was present.] HNMP, box 20.

107   Caroline G. Mercer, Professor of English, wrote "The Governance of Vassar College" ["A sketch of the history of the governance"] in March 1970. (Ms. VCL) The study details the steps by which the governance was drawn up.

107   As Professor Mercer shows, the governance was called "The Statute of Instruction." The trustees adopted a set of "Bylaws

of the Board of Trustees" in June, 1922 and accepted the "Statute of Instruction" on June 11, 1923.

108   "Indeed most of the colleges": See M. Carey Thomas papers at Bryn Mawr College Library, LeBaron B. Briggs papers in Briggs Collection at Radcliffe College, and Ada Comstock Collection of Elizabeth Schlesinger Library, as well as Smith College papers already mentioned.

108-111   "The policy and record of my administration, 1915-18," HNMP, box 120.

111   "At a later time": MacCracken statement in HNMP, uncatalogued.

112   "four colleges": It is interesting to observe that the modern descendents of this informal liaison, which started its life as a kind of self-help organization, are being attacked almost seventy years later as this book is being written (1993) as involved through their cooperation in violations of the anti-trust laws. In the earlier case, the need for uniformity in admission procedures was the precipitating cause for cooperation; now the issue is financial aid. Now procedures to standardize and equalize financial aid for the students are being treated as inimical to student welfare whereas they started out just the opposite, as measures to improve student welfare.

CHAPTER NINE:
MacCRACKEN's "VIOLENT CHANGE IN ATTITUDE":
THE ORGANIC INSTITUTION

114   "At the entrance of America into World War I": HNMP, box 92.

115   "Arlington": The name of that part of Poughkeepsie where Vassar College is located.

115-117   "Downtown Work": EAD interview with Josephine Voorhees.

117   "one of his most distinguished alumnae": The name of the alumna is Ruth Mitchell, 1912.

118   "In June 1919": Trustee Minutes, 2, 281.

120   Elizabeth Kemper Adams, *Women Professional Workers: A Study for the Women's Educational and Industrial Union* (New York, The MacMillan Co., 1921).

121-122   "Salmon speech": Fiftieth Anniversary of AAVC: June 15-21, 1921, transcript, VCL.

INTERNATIONAL OUTREACH:
GLOBAL AS WELL AS LOCAL CONCERNS

123   "Masaryk": Jaroslav Papousek, *The Czechoslovak Nation's Struggle for Independence* (Prague: Orbis Library, 1928), p. 78.

123   "Czech women": Mrs. Willard Straight. The students were Marie Podzimkova, 1922, who went on from Vassar to hold a Vassar fellowship at the University of Chicago and who returned to Czechoslovakia to work on child welfare; Vlasta D. Stepanova, 1922, who was national secretary of the Junior Red Cross of Czechoslovakia; Julia Matouskova, 1922, "secretary of the Students' Home in Prague, the only place in the country where twenty-five thousand Prague students from many races can meet on common ground;" Marie Doskova, 1922, who subsequently took her doctor's degree at the University in Anthropology, and began the organization of social work in Prague; and Marie Novakova, 1922, who became a teacher. MacCracken,"Education in Balkanized Europe," *VQ*, 111, 3, pp. 81-82.

123   "ready for holiday": Mss. about trip in HNMP, uncatalogued.

124   MacCracken wrote about this trip in "Education in Balkanized Europe."

125   "MacCracken returned to the States": "Studensia," HNMP, uncatalogued.

CHAPTER TEN:
THE DISAPPOINTING FIRST THRUST OF EUTHENICS

128   "Renwick and sewage": *Historical Sketch of Vassar College* (New York: S.W. Green and Co., 1876), p. 34.

129   "Her plan": Ellen S. Richards and Charles W. Moulton, "Ten Years Experience with Broad Irrigation at Vassar College," (Reprinted from the *Journal of the Association of Engineering Societies*, 36, no. 4).

130-131   "Euthenics": Ellen Swallow Richards, *Euthenics, the Science of Controllable Environment: A Plea for Better Living Conditions as a First Step Toward Higher Human Efficiency* (Boston: M. Barrows & Co. 1929), p. vii.

131   "her broad conception": Marcia Yudkin, "Earth, Air, Water, Hearth: The Woman Who Founded Ecology," *VQ,* 78, no. 3, pp. 32-34, 35.

131   Louise Fargo Brown, *Apostle of Democracy* (New York: Harper Bros., 1893), pp. 132-133.

132   "sound of a trumpet": *HL,* p. 27.

132-134 "Julia Lathrop": Blodgett dinner, in Jane Addams, *My Friend Julia Lathrop* (New York: The MacMillan Co., 1935), p. 39. Addams was mistaken in saying the meeting place was the Alumnae House, which was not built until 1924.

133   "Blodgett...first baby": Bio. file, alumnae records, Vassar Alumnae Association files.

134   Henry Mitchell MacCracken speech, "Relation of Metropolis and University," 1884, and related materials; Henry Mitchell MacCracken Papers, Archives, New York University.

136   Minutes of special meetings of Curriculum Committee (May 1922, April 1923), Faculty Minutes, 7, VCL.

137   Trustees and euthenics, Trustee Minutes, 1923, 3.

138   "Euthenics squeaked through": Faculty Minutes, 1924, box 2.

138   Margaret Washburn, *HL,* p. 37.

139   Report on Vassar Summer Institute, prepared by Mary Fisher Langmuir for meeting of Vassar faculty, Jan. 10, 1949, VCL. As Vassar developed its summer institute, Smith College started a school of social work, and Bryn Mawr, a summer school for workers. It was the beginning of an era which promised a new kind of adult education.

140   Joseph Folsom's program: "Field Work in the Social Sciences," Supplement to the President's report, Oct. 1936, pp. 10-17.

CHAPTER ELEVEN:
"THE OPEN ROAD TO THE FUTURE"

144   MacCracken speech to students, "The Students' Part in Education," December, 1926: Pamphlet of National Student Federation of America, 1926. Also in HNMP, box 124.

146   Evalyn Clark, "History of the Vassar Curriculum, 1915-1946," [n.d.], ms, VCL.

148   Changes to Vassar Curriculum between 1923-1927: Minutes of Vassar Faculty, 7-8.

CHAPTER TWELVE: VIGNETTES

C. MILDRED THOMPSON, 1903, MacCRACKEN'S DEAN

150 James Baldwin, "Vassar College, 1915-1946" (unpub. mss.), VCL. He mentioned neither the roles of Thompson nor Salmon in the progress of MacCracken's administration.

151ff. Thompson biographical folders, VCL.

151 "What she had done": *HL*, p 43.

152 *Atlanta Constitution*, Jan. 4, 1923.

153 "We present ... the Dean": *VQ*, 11, 1926.

154 "By seven, when we should have been": *HL*, p. 146.

VERA B. THOMSON, ADMINISTRATOR

154-156 Interview with Vera B. Thomson. EAD, Sept. 29, 1980.

JULIA COBURN ANTOLINI, 1918

156 Oral history interview, Julia Coburn Antolini, 1980.

CAROLINE WARE, 1920

156-157 Follow-up letter to oral history interview. EAD and Caroline Ware, letter, Feb. 16, 1981.

RUTH DILLARD VENABLE, 1924

157-159 Interview with Ruth Dillard Venable, Professor Emerita of French, January 1981.

EDNA ST. VINCENT MILLAY, 1917

159 Millay's tuition was paid by Charles Pratt.

160 "Oh, our poet!": Millay papers, VCL, box 2.

160 "Drama 220": Muriel Crane, *Miscellany News*, Nov. 19, 1952.

161 Jerome Beatty, *American Magazine*, January 1932 (clipping in Millay file).

CALVIN COOLIDGE

162-163 *The Delineator*, XCVIII (June 1921), pp. 4-5.

CHAPTER THIRTEEN:
MacCRACKEN'S VASSAR,
MARCHING TO A DIFFERENT
DRUMMER FROM THE OTHER SISTERS?

167   "Seven Sisters": HNMP, box 90.

168   "dowries," "checkbooks": One alumna told the author that
       when her brother went to college, he was given a bank account
       by his father; she, on the other hand, was doled out an allow-
       ance. One should remember here that MacCracken started a
       bank for his women students.

168-169 Lamont speech: HNMP, box 90.

169   "$6 million": Of course, Taylor had solicited money from
       Rockefeller, Pratt, and others on an individual basis.

169-170 James Monroe Taylor to John D. Rockefeller, 26 December,
       1888, folder 342, box 45, series III.1. CO, record group 1. 2,
       Rockefeller Family Archives, Rockefeller Archive Center,
       North Tarrytown, N.Y.

170   "In conversation": HNMP, box 17.

171   Publication: HNMP, box 90.

172   "Hughes speaker": Marion E. Park (Bryn Mawr), Mary
       Wooley (Mt. Holyoke), Ellen Pendleton (Wellesley), Ada
       Comstock (Radcliffe), Virginia Gildersleeve (Barnard),
       William Allan Neilson (Smith), and Henry Noble MacCracken
       (Vassar).

172   "MacCracken's unique theme": Unfortunately after 1929 the
       Depression probably cut down on the number of Vassar grad-
       uates seeking paid jobs, at least until after World War II.

173   "Manning, Comstock, Thomas, etc." Interview with Helen
       Taft Manning, Bryn Mawr, Pa., May 27, 1981.

174   MacCracken annual report to trustees, 1921, pp. 5-6.

174-175 "Fiftieth Anniversary": June 15-21, 1921, transcript, p. 12.,
       VCL.

175-176 Lockwood quotation: Lockwood Papers, Box 4, folder 63,
       SC.

CHAPTER FOURTEEN:
MacCRACKEN'S "DREAM CHILD":
SARAH LAWRENCE COLLEGE

177   At the beginning of this series of footnote annotations and commentary, I wish especially to acknowledge the help of Roberta Cashwell, who did the fundamental research on this chapter in the Sarah Lawrence College archives before the pressure of other events in her life took her away from participating further in this enterprise.

177   "a gentleman of some means": "Conversation Between Miss Constance Warren, President of Sarah Lawrence College 1929 to 1945, and Dr. Henry Noble MacCracken, Chairman of Sarah Lawrence College Board of Trustees 1926 to 1936, Taped in Poughkeepsie, New York, October 13, 1961." The transcript of this interview was deposited in the archives of the Esther Raushenbush Library of Sarah Lawrence College and is liberally used with the library's generous permission.

178   "No": "Conversation."

180   "As MacCracken said": "Conversation."

181-182   Letters between William V. D. Lawrence and HNM, 1924-1925, Early History files, Esther Raushenbush Library.

181-182   "Sometime in 1924": "Conversation."

182-183   "Bradford and elsewhere": Letter, HNM to Marion Coats, Nov. 30, 1925, HNMP, box 71. (Also in Esther Raushenbush Library.)

183   "As Constance Warren later pointed out": "Miss [Constance] Warren's notes on President MacCracken," April 15, 1946, a typed memo in Esther Raushenbush Library.

183-184   Dudley B. Lawrence, "Sarah Lawrence College, Early Recollections," July 1958, HNMP, misc. box labelled "SLC etc." Mr. Lawrence wrote this recollection to set the facts straight as he remembered them. (Also in Esther Raushenbush Library.)

185   "After Constance Warren": "Miss Warren's notes on President MacCracken."

185   "MacCracken put it this way": "Conversation."

185-186   "Warren, eliciting more memories": "Conversation."

185 MacCracken must have known about the agreement. It is recorded as an agreement in the Vassar Trustee Minutes, for May 31, 1927, box 3.

186 MacCracken brought the letter into the oral history interview to jog his memory of events long past.

186 Milo P. Jewett, "Origins of Vassar College" (ms.), Special Collections, VCL.

187 "Sarah Bates Lawrence died": Letters between Coats and Lawrence in Sarah Lawrence archives.

188 The correspondence between Coats and MacCracken is in the Sarah Lawrence archives as well as in HNMP, box 71.

188 "Two days before he died": " Conversation."

188 In the conversation between Warren and MacCracken, p. 9, she explains to MacCracken that the Board of Regents and the Middles States Association of Colleges and Secondary Schools were extremely pleased that there was a college experimenting on a sound basis.

188 Dudley Lawrence statement.

188-189 Correspondence, Coats and MacCracken, HNMP, box 71.

189 HNM statement: made when Constance Warren retired, HNMP, box 91.

190 "Harold Taylor statement": *Poughkeepsie Sunday New Yorker*, June 30, 1946.

CHAPTER FIFTEEN:
HALLIE FLANAGAN'S EXPERIMENTAL THEATRE:
FILLING THE BILL EXACTLY

193 Again in this chapter, I owe a debt to Roberta Cashwell, who did much of the basic research and drafted the chapter.

195-196 Gertrude Buck, bio. folders, SC.

196-197 Information about early Vassar English department: Daniels, "History of Vassar English Department."

196 Peebles's letters are from: HFDP, box 6.

197 "acceptance had been received": HFDP, box 6.

197 Letter about playwriting: HFDP, box 6.

199 Hallie Flanagan, *Dynamo,* (New York: Duell, Sloan and Pearce, 1943), p. 17.

199   "student plays": Florence Clothier Wislocki, 1926, *She Canna Perish* (playwriting class), March 23, 1926; Margaret Y. Whitlock, 1926, *The King's Ward* (playwriting class), March 23, 1926.

200   "*New York Times*" clipping: May 20, as found in HFDP, box 41.

200   "Of the more than 100 plays": Listings entitled "Coverage of Energy Expenditure," *Dynamo*, pp. 153-166.

200-202   Interview with Mary McCarthy on Vassar campus, February, 1982.

202   Interview with Hulda Bradbury Walsh in Red Hook, N.Y. Summer, 1991.

203   Esther Porter Power, "The Vassar Experimental Theatre," *Vassar Alumnae Magazine*, April 1939, pp. 12-24

203   Sandison as found in HFDP, box 37.

204   MacCracken on MacCracken. MacCracken's address at graduation, 1939, which honored Hallie Flanagan, HNMP, box 126.

205   Lesser, *Dynamo*, p. 165.

205   Nunan quote as found in HFDP, box 46.

206   Hallie's report as found in HFDP, box 46.

207   Transcript, U.S. Congress Hearing on UnAmerican Activities, Dec. 6, 1938.

207   MacCracken speech, HNMP, box 126.

CHAPTER SIXTEEN:
FRANKLIN AND ELEANOR ROOSEVELT:
PRESIDENTIAL NEIGHBORS

209   FDR letter to MacCracken accepting position on Vassar board: HNMP, box 2.

211   "Soon after FDR joined the board": MacCracken to Roosevelt, HNMP, box 72.

212   "first assignment": HNMP, box 72.

214   "The index to Dr. Taylor's *Vassar*": HNMP, box 120.

214   "Local event": *Vassar Miscellany News*, June 10, 1931.

214-216   Roosevelt's board service: HNMP, box 3; Trustee Minutes, box 3, *passim.*

217   "study is like navigation": Roosevelt Commencement Speech, 1931, *Vassar Miscellany News*, June 10, 1931.

217 "MacCracken proudly reported to the trustees": Trustee Minutes, box 3, p. 364.

217 "course of action": MacCracken to Roosevelt, President's Personal Files, 108, Courtesy FDR Archives, Hyde Park, New York.

218 College reception for FDR: *Poughkeepsie Eagle News*, Aug. 6, 1933.

219 Letter, MacCracken to FDR on registration: PPF, 108.

219 "Harry Hopkins": As told to the author by Verne Newton, Director, FDR Library, Hyde Park, N.Y.

219 Telegram: PPF, 108 (1936).

219 "seventy-five students write FDR against war": *Vassar Miscellany News*, Dec. 11, 1937, and April 17, 1940.

219-220 Anti-war involvement, HNMP, boxes 118, 121, 122, 126.

220 C. Mildred Thompson letter to MacCracken: CMT file, FDR archives, FDR library.

221 See *"My Day"* columns: Eleanor Roosevelt archives, FDR library.

221 "Harold Ickes and housing": Vassar campus newspapers, especially *Vassar Miscellany News*, Oct. 2, 1937.

221 "Susan Ware points out": Her essay analyzes ER's causes and their effect on her political development. Ware, "ER and Democratic Politics: Women in the Postsuffrage Era" in Joan Hoff-Wilson and Marjorie Lightman, eds., *Without Precedent* (Bloomington, Ind.: Indiana University Press, 1984), p. 46.

222-223 "Dutchess Junction affair": MacCracken, HNMP, unpublished ms, pp.74-79.

223-232 "Second World Youth Congress": HNMP, box 81, *passim.*

225 Elizabeth Shield-Collins: "Second World Youth Congress," clipping, *The New York Times* [n.d.] HNMP, box 81.

225-227 Petition against MacCracken and Second World Youth Congress, HNMP, box 81.

227 MacCracken, "The Principle of Conference," *Vassar Alumnae Magazine*, 23, no. 2, p. 78.

227-229 MacCracken's greeting to World Youth Congress, Aug. 16, 1938, HNMP, box 126.

230 Vassar Peace Pact, HNMP, box 81.

230 "an alumna": HNMP, box 81.

230-231 ER's part in Second World Youth Congress, Box 3144, Folder: July-Aug. 1938, ER Papers, FDR Library.

230 "Eleanor Roosevelt's presence": in Winifred D. Wandersee, "ER and American Youth: Politics and Personality in a Bureaucratic Age," *Without Precedent*, pp. 63-87.

230 "At a banquet in New York": Wandersee, p. 77.

230 "At the Sixth American Youth Congress": Wandersee, p. 84.

232-234 ER and CMT: See CMT folders, FDR archives, *passim*. Also, CMT biographical folders, VCL, containing newspaper clippings.

232-234 Aftermath of UNESCO: interview CMT with *Vassar Miscellany News*, Nov. 9, 1944. And in CMT bio, folders (VCL) and CMT folders, FDR library. Alice Hughes (April 16, 1944) reported in her column "A Woman's New York" in the Reading, Pa. *Eagle* (as found in CMT bio. folder, VCL):

> *This new all-dame quiz show, "Listen, the Women" goes into its third verse tonight at ten o'clock. Have you heard it yet? If so, perhaps you agree with me that it is a good hunch that hasn't rung a bell so far. I went to the premier program. [The one Thompson was on]. Janet Flanner, the brilliant New Yorker correspondent, whom I knew well in Paris far too long ago, was a first-rate mistress of ceremonies and female Fadiman, but it struck me that the questions and most of the jury, swell women though they are, were too far over on the deep-dish side. Meegan and partners, Dean C. Mildred Thompson of Vassar...were handed the damnedest questions. Even Johnny Kieran, of Info Puleeze, would pick up his feet and run for his life if asked to define instantly nazism, fascism, communism, and democracy. Dean Thompson, who is very smart and also liberal, did noble—but what kind of a quiz query is that to fire?*

CHAPTER SEVENTEEN:
FROM SWORD TO PLOUGHSHARE:
MacCRACKEN'S QUEST FOR PEACE

235-236 Henry Mitchell MacCracken Papers, New York University Archives, Box 7, Folder 8, "Peace Associations and Conferences. Other Peace Conferences, 1905-07."

236   *The Hickory Limb* is our best source of information about his reforms and ethical concerns in New Haven.

238   The minutes of that meeting are in the Edward Filene Collection of the Woodrow Wilson Foundation Library as reported by Ruhl J. Bartlett in *League to Enforce Peace,* (Chapel Hill, N.C.: University of North Carolina, 1944), p. 30.

238   Century Club meeting: Bartlett, p. 38.

239   Judicial tribunal: According to Bartlett, p. 37.

239   "The day was boiling.": MacCracken erroneously recalled this date, given by Bartlett, p. 39, as July 4, 1915.

239   Reference to Taft's dinner in Washington in "My Honorable Stations," ms. MacCracken papers, VCL. Bartlett does not list MacCracken, however, as being in attendance.

240   "League's . . . views": Bartlett, p. 40.

240   Letter HNM to William Howard Taft, Jan. 17, 1916:

> *Insomuch as my time permits me I shall be at the service of the committee in bringing to the public the ideal of the League, and have so written Mr. Short. . . . We are looking forward with great pleasure to your visit on Friday.*

HNMP, box 2.

240   The information about Wilson's reception of the League's proposal in this paragraph was derived from Bartlett, pp. 48-112, *passim* as well as Theodore Marburg, *Development of the League of Nations Idea,* I, pp. 790-852. General information about the whole issue of the League to Enforce Peace came also from C.R. Ashbee, with an introduction by G. Lowes Dickinson, *The American League to Enforce Peace, An English Interpretation,* (London: G. Allen and Unwin, Ltd., 1917).

240-241   Vassar's wartime activities: I am indebted for background here to the summary in Dorothy A. Plum and George B. Dowell, *The Great Experiment, A Chronicle of Vassar,* (Poughkeepsie, N.Y.: Vassar College, 1961), pp. 38-40.

243-244   Mizwa, Kosciuszko papers, HNMP, box 95.

244   "MacCracken responded": HNMP, box 95.

244   Papers relating to National Conference of Christians and Jews, 1939-46, HNMP, box 103.

234   "O'Day": See Blanche Wiesen Cook, *Eleanor Roosevelt, Volume One, 1884-1933,* (New York: Viking/Penguin, 1992), pp. 323-324, and *passim* for discussion of the interests of O'Day. She

was a close associate of Eleanor Roosevelt's in New York State Democratic affairs as well as the Val-Kill partnership.

245   WILPF meeting, Sept. 1933, HNMP.

250-253   MacCracken's speech, "The American Way," HNMP, box 126.

CHAPTER EIGHTEEN:
WINDING DOWN DURING THE WAR

254-255   Events of Seventy-Fifth Anniversary, folders, VCL.

254-255   Roosevelt greeting, Oct.1939: Autograph Collection, VCL.

255-259   EAD interview with Elizabeth Drouilhet, Warden, January 1981 and June 1981.

CHAPTER NINETEEN :
SUMMING UP

263-264   "Buried somewhere": A free interpretation of an interview EAD with Ellen Jones 1914, and Hester Jones 1917. The story was remembered by Hester Jones.

264-265   "*First Year in English* accounts": As given by Bert Burns, *Poughkeepsie New Yorker*, April 11, 1953, after an interview with MacCracken.

266   Stevenson, as quoted in *Manual of Good English*, New York, The MacMillan Co, 1917, p. xxiii.

267-268   Macurdy-Shattuck incident, *HL*, pp. 66-67.

268   Beckwith-Monnier incident, *HL*, p. 67.

269   Jack Hennessy stories related by Christine Vassar Tall, 1947 and William Murphy; Paris story and Polk story: HNMP, uncatalogued.

270   Vernon Venable, Oral History Interview, 1981.

273   MacCracken's speech, HNMP.

"NAMED AFTER A VENERABLE PREXY"

SOLUTION
to the Double Acrostic Puzzle
by Judith Ogden Henry
(*pp. 164-165*)

■	1 C **A**	2 X **P**	3 C **E**	4 P **T**	■	5 L **M**	6 D **O**	7 B **U**	8 S **S**	9 J **E**	■	■	■
10 A **N**	11 B **A**	12 C **M**	13 J **E**	14 E **D**	■	15 N **H**	16 I **E**	17 X **N**	18 J **R**	19 C **Y**	■	20 Q **N**	21 L **I**
22 X **B**	23 R **B**	24 C **L**	25 W **E**	■	26 Q **M**	27 B **C**	28 L **R**	29 K **A**	30 I **C**	31 A **K**	32 V **E**	33 N **R**	■
34 P **F**	35 H **O**	36 E **R**	37 A **A**	38 M **G**	39 Q **E**	40 G **D**	■	41 X **I**	42 L **N**	■	43 B **A**	44 U **N**	45 K **D**
■	46 L **E**	47 X **X**	48 U **P**	49 S **L**	50 G **O**	51 K **R**	52 Q **E**	53 R **D**	■	54 T **T**	55 D **H**	56 O **E**	■
57 N **N**	58 Q **O**	59 T **O**	60 Y **K**	61 R **S**	■	62 F **A**	63 Q **N**	64 E **D**	■	65 C **C**	66 A **R**	67 Y **A**	68 E **N**
69 T **N**	70 U **I**	71 D **E**	72 J **S**	■	73 N **O**	74 E **F**	■	75 B **A**	76 C **L**	77 F **L**	■	78 N **T**	79 X **H**
80 K **E**	■	81 B **D**	82 X **O**	83 U **R**	84 F **M**	85 V **I**	86 S **T**	87 R **O**	88 T **R**	89 W **I**	90 M **E**	91 V **S**	■
92 P **A**	93 U **T**	■	94 L **V**	95 O **A**	96 F **S**	97 V **S**	98 S **A**	99 H **R**	■	100 D **C**	101 C **O**	102 J **L**	103 O **L**
104 S **E**	105 M **G**	106 W **E**	■	107 G **F**	108 R **O**	109 P **R**	■	110 K **M**	111 T **O**	112 O **R**	113 B **E**	■	114 I **T**
115 C **H**	116 E **A**	117 C **N**	■	118 V **A**	■	119 B **Q**	120 E **U**	121 X **A**	122 W **R**	123 H **T**	124 X **E**	125 R **R**	■
126 X **O**	127 E **F**	■	128 Q **A**	■	129 J **C**	130 T **E**	131 G **N**	132 H **T**	133 J **U**	134 V **R**	135 Y **Y**		

A. An informer (Br.)

N   A   R   K
10 37 66 31

B. Entertainment spectacle of swimmers

A   Q   U   A   C   D   E
11   119 7   75 27 43 81 113

C. The dearth of mirth

M   E   L   A   N   C   H   O   L   Y
12 3   76 1   117 65 115 101 24 19

D. A holler mockery

E   C   H   O
71 100 55 6

E. Small white scales trying to get a head

D   A   N   D   R   U   F   F
64 116 68 14 36 120 74 127

F. Money for the needy

A   L   M   S
62 77 84 96

G. Affectionate

F   O   N   D
107 50 131 40

H. A gait

T   R   O   T
132 99 35 123

I. A sign used to make other people believe you know more than you do

E   T   C
16 114 30

J. A hermit

R   E   C   L   U   S   E
18 9   129 102 133 72 13

K. Equipped with weapons

A   R   M   E   D
29 51 110 80 45

L. A cockroach, for instance

V   E   R   M   I   N
94 46 28 5   21 42

M. Something that grows stronger with age

E   G   G
90 105 38

N. 0°

N   O   R   T   H
57 73 33 78 15

O. Nobleman

E   A   R   L
56 95 112 103

P. Flock of ducks

R   A   F   T
109 92 34 4

Q. Marine invertebrate

A   N   E   M   O   N   E
128 20 52 26 58 63 39

R. Ponders moodily

B   R   O   O   D   S
23 125 87 108 53 61

S. Lowest in rank

L   E   A   S   T
49 104 98 8   86

T. Implant

E   N   R   O   O   T
130 69 88 111 59 54

U. An impression

P   R   I   N   T
48 83 70 44 93

V. Lifts

R   A   I   S   E   S
134 118 85 97 32 91

W. Ireland

E   I   R   E
25 89 122 106

X. Fear of strangers

X   E   N   O   P   H   O   B   I   A
47 124 17 82 2   79 126 22   41 121

Y. Long-haired bovine

Y   A   K
135 67 60

INDEX